BIRD OF TIME

BIRD OF TIME

BY
MELVIN HALL

CHARLES SCRIBNER'S SONS, NEW YORK
1949

To the Friends of my Hillside

"Come, fill the cup, and in the
fire of Spring
Your Winter-garment of Repentance
fling:
The Bird of Time has but a little
way to flutter—
And the Bird is on the Wing."

PREFACE

FORTUITY HAS NOT so shaped my ends, nor is it in my nature, to remain static for any considerable stretch of time. Recently, however, I have had the occasion to pass an interval of comparative immobility, though not infrequently broken by excursions outside, within a high-walled garden on the slope of a Burgundian hillside.

Here in a small but exceedingly quaint cottage, an ancient *gentilhommière* whose walls of solid stone are more than two and a half feet thick, its irregular roofs, with tower and dormer windows, protected against the rains and the snows and the hail by old, lichen-covered red tiles, I am surrounded with an accumulation of objects acquired during years of wandering over a changing world. All of these objects carry nostalgic recollections of episodes connected with their acquisition in many parts of the globe.

When the fire on the lounge hearth, glinting on the Renaissance iron fireback, burns in violet and gold and orange flame from the moss-covered branches of cherry trees that have lived out their time in the garden, I am transported far beyond the confines of the room, whose ceiling is supported on heavy, hand-hewn beams, and my thoughts run to a multitude of things and of experiences, some of them never likely to be repeated in similar circumstances.

There is no particular continuity to my thoughts, no sequence of years in my reminiscences, among these objects of distant provenance that recall memories of the past in the varicolored glow above the crackling outlines of the logs. And it is thus that I have written about them, as they come to my mind on a Burgundian hillside, for the memories of most recent date are no wise necessarily the sharpest.

MELVIN HALL

"La Grangeotte"
Vézelay (Yonne)

CONTENTS

I

VIEW FROM A
BURGUNDIAN HILLSIDE

MY HILLSIDE

The PRESENT TRANQUIL, even somnolent aspect of my Burgundian hillside gives but little suggestion of an agitated and often violent past.

Lovely, rolling hills of casual contour trace the horizon in all directions, their crests and upper slopes spattered with oak and elm, beech, walnut and pine woods, where wild boar roam and lilies-of-the-valley thrust their shy little faces in the spring through the carpet of dead leaves and ferns. Uneven green pastures bordered by hedges, dotted with cream-colored and red-spotted cattle, spread over the rest of the slopes and the valleys, together with patchwork quilts of vineyards and smallish fields planted in a variety of crops, their colors changing continually with the seasons but always setting one another off.

Wherever one's more distant glance may fall, in the valleys, part way up the slopes or on their crests, there nestle or cling mellow medieval villages, the spires of their Romanesque or early Gothic churches casting thin shadows over moss-grown red tiles and lichen-splotched grey stonework, whose pattern has altered but little since the decline of feudalism.

In all this, charming and changeful as is the setting, there is nothing especially extraordinary for the favored land of Burgundy.

What makes the hillside no ordinary one lies in its background rather than its aspect. It falls abruptly from the walled hilltown of Vézelay surmounted by the immense eleventh-century basilical church of La Madeleine, the sole but splendid remnant of one of Christendom's greatest abbeys. There are today fewer than five hundred people living within Vézelay's crumbling walls; perhaps six hundred if one includes the adjacent hamlets. Eight hundred years ago there were fifteen thousand. They were exceedingly prosperous in those days. The Abbaye de la Madeleine, whose fame was the cause and the basis of the town's growth and prosperity, was then the fourth most important place of pilgrimage in the Christian world. It ranked in its appeal to penitents, to sick and crippled persons seeking miraculous cures (and a multitude of others who sought profit from their passage), only after Jerusalem, Rome and Saint James of Compostella (Santiago de Compostela) in Spain. How this came about could well cause the most blatant of Hollywood press agents to suffer an inferiority complex.

There was nothing, so the records tell, shaped by the hand of man on the granite promontory of Vézelay in the year 860, or thereabouts, when the gallant and pious Count Girart de Roussillon and his wife Berthe founded an abbey for women in a Gallo-Roman settlement on the banks of the purling River Cure hard below the hill. The abbey was ravaged—and doubtless the women with it—a few years later by the Normans or the Saracens, and was shortly refounded on the greater security of the hilltop, but this time as a monastery for Benedictine monks. Count Girart may have deemed that protecting the virginity of his brides of the Church was fraught with rather too many uncertainties in those days.

Count Girart, whose legendary feats of arms and chivalric qualities were later chanted by wandering minstrels throughout the Christian world in one of the most spirited of the twelfth-century epic poems, endowed his new abbey with vast domains and placed it under the direct protection of Saints Peter and Paul. He furthermore arranged with Rome, against the modest annual payment of one pound of silver, that it should come under no other jurisdiction than the distant and nominal sway of the Pope. It was exempted from recognizing any head of any religious order, any bishop of a diocese, any prince or lord whatsoever, as having any rights or authority over it.

Such a situation, unique in feudal times and surcharged with danger in the jealousies it evoked, contributed largely to the power, the grandeur and the subsequent ruin of the abbey. But the principal contribution to Vézelay's astonishing fortune came from the brain-wave of a bright young monk. It occurred about the year 1037, after a century and a half of the abbey's existence through a confused and dispirited period. The monastic orders were then beginning to acquire widespread influence owing to the decadence of the secular clergy, and religious fervor was returning to the people.

With a fine sense of timing and of popular appeal this enterprising forerunner of Hollywoodian imagination, Baidilon by name, managed in some way that remains obscure to hijack —in 1945 one would have said "liberate"—the bones of Saint Mary Magdalene from Aix-en-Provence and bring them to Vézelay. The origin of the relics was in itself somewhat obscure, and their authenticity has variously been defended and denied by a succession of Popes. But the Abbot Geoffroy, under whose auspices and surely with whose connivance the *coup* was carried out, took full advantage of his opportunities. To all Christendom he blazoned the fact that the sanctified remnants of the gentle sinner whom Christ absolved were now ensconced in the Abbey of Vézelay. After some scores of years the abbey itself became the Abbaye de la Madeleine, adhering no more to its original patron-protectors.

Whatever their authenticity, the immediate effect of the acquisition of the saintly bones (and this continued for more than two centuries) was incredible. Pilgrims poured into Vézelay in a never-ending stream from all Christian Europe. Their pious donations and the tolls exacted from them added enormously to the wealth of the abbey; their expenditures for lodging and sustenance, for sundry purchases, the changing of money and the like, redounded to the prosperity of the community. The poor village grouped for protection under the monastic walls grew into a celebrated and an affluent town. Yet the way was far from untroubled.

The abbey's increasing wealth and influence soon excited

the envy of the powerful Abbots of Cluny (probably, after Rome, the greatest force in Christendom at that time) on the side of monastic supremacy; of the Bishops of Autun (*in* whose diocese but not *of* it the Vézelayan abbots claimed to be) on the ecclesiastic side; of the Counts of Nevers, secular lords of the area, on the side of the feudal hierarchy. The autocratic sway of the Abbots of La Madeleine was, moreover, resisted locally and with varying successes by the burghers of Vézelay, who were content to profit exceedingly from the influx of pilgrims to the abbey but sought, doubtless with some justification, a larger voice in the ultimate end of those profits in imposts and taxation. Shortly after the Abbot Artaud completed the nave of the monumental and splendid basilical church—dedicated in the presence of the Pope in 1104—which remains today the culminating glory of the hillside, the burghers, more concerned over the taxes to defray its heavy cost than appreciative of its beauty, rose in their wrath and slew him.

This was the first explosion of the communal spirit that was to manifest itself recurrently and later gain for the Vézelayans (in about 1167) the earliest charter of bourgeois rights in Burgundy. The Abbott Artaud's murderers escaped to the protection of the Count of Nevers who, for reasons that had little to do with the liberties of the burghers, was the most violent contender of the suzerainty of the abbey. Yet the abbey, its sovereign independence in the center of European feudalism oddly enough supported both by the Pope and King Louis VI, continued to prosper immensely. So also did the burghers, the while they pursued their struggles against the abbots for communal rights and liberties all but unheard-of in those days.

In 1146 Saint Bernard preached from the hillside, three hundred yards from my present walled garden, the Second Crusade in the presence of King Louis VII of France to a gathering of more than a hundred thousand seigneurs and knights in armor. They were immensely swayed by his eloquence and exhortations—those who could hear him and who passed his words on to the multitude farther away. One can visualize them, reclining in that green field against their trappings, leaning on their long swords, their caparisoned horses tethered below; and perhaps wonder (for this the records fail to relate) how far they were influenced in their zeal, as they determined to drive the infidels from the Holy Land, by the thoughts of the looting and rape that attended those manifestations of religious fervor. In any event the enthusiasm was so great, the chronicles say, that there was not enough cloth available from which to fashion crosses as insignia for the multitude of volunteers, and Saint Bernard tore his white robe into strips to augment the supply.

Forty-four years later, in 1190, Richard the Lion-Hearted of England and King Philip Augustus of France made rendezvous in the basilica of the Madeleine on their way to the Third Crusade with their respective forces. The meeting itself went off smoothly enough. Unhappily, joint winter quarters in Sicily where they duly arrived by different routes, and months of inactivity there, did not cement a beautiful friendship.

During this period the abbey reached the zenith of its prestige and power. The Madeleine, together with its possessions, was in effect a sovereign state. No other monastic establishment ever received from the religious heads of Christianity such extraordinary privileges. This does not imply that its course was unharassed.

One or another of the trio of jealous lords of the secular and religious dominance of the time—the Count of Nevers, the Bishop of Autun, and the Abbot of Cluny, who had little in common beyond their covetous will to supplant the Madeleine's independence by their own authority—was continually attacking or egging the burghers of Vézelay to bloody revolt against the monastery's despotic yoke.

The Abbot Ponce de Montboissier, perhaps the strongest character to rule the abbey and stand up against practically all the powers of the day, including the growing power of the bourgeois, was chased out by the townsfolk in 1152 (under the stimulus of the Count of Nevers) after a siege of the monastery. Despite the anathemas and excommunications he hurled at them from exile it was three years before he succeeded in returning, with, again, the support of the Pope and of the King of France (to whom, for all his backing, Ponce ceded no important concessions). Ponce took a poor view of the commune the burghers had set up in his absence, and on his triumphal return suppressed it ruthlessly. The burghers bowed their heads and bided more favorable times.

Yet the Vézelayans in the twelfth century were on the whole better off than the bourgeois and villagers of most other parts of feudal Europe. The majority of them lived in circumstances of comfort and considerable affluence. It was not until three hundred years later, in 1459, that slavery (or serfdom, which amounted to the same thing) was abolished in Burgundy by Duke Philip the Good. One may recall that it was in 1863, another four hundred years later, that this was achieved in the United States.

The thirteenth century saw the beginning of the decline of the Abbaye de la Madeleine. Its decadence was halted from time to time by the personal efforts of certain eminent abbots, but coincided with the general deterioration of the monastic orders in France. The period itself was turbulent, growing progressively worse in the fourteenth and fifteenth centuries when the Hundred Years War and its aftermath decimated the country. Swept by recurrent waves of invasion and violent conflict, of brigandage, rape and murder, visitations of the plague and widespread ruin, the fair land of Burgundy presented a sorrowful picture of human insecurity.

Under the renewed aggressions of the Counts of Nevers, after the death of the Abbot Ponce, both monks and townsfolk of Vézelay suffered in equal measure. Merchants began to desert a town so often the object of attack. Even the most credulous of Christian worshippers, noting how ineffectual were the relics of the Magdalene in protecting the place where they reposed, came to doubt their authenticity. The influx of pilgrims fell off so markedly that in 1267 the Pope caused a solemn and pompous verification of the relics to be held at Vézelay, attended by King

Louis IX (Saint Louis) of France. But the effect of this did not last long.

In 1279 the remains of a body were "discovered" in Saint-Maximin in Provence and announced to be the "unquestionable" cadaver of the Magdalene. The claim was officially accepted by Rome, and the Abbey of Vézelay thereupon lost the benefit of a belief that had been the major cause of its grandeur. It was not until six hundred years later, at the end of the nineteenth century, that other vouchedly authentic relics of the Magdalene were presented to the church at Vézelay—all that then remained of the abbey. By that time long-distance Christian pilgrimages were less in vogue. But pilgrims still come in large numbers for the Fête de la Madeleine on the 22nd of July, when the relics are carried in solemn and colorful procession around the town.

Even in the worst days of the Hundred Years War, Vézelay, with its natural strength and strong defenses, was never actually taken by enemy forces. Nearly all the towns and villages hereabout were occupied by the English, pillaged of everything they possessed and often burnt, but not Vézelay. The Vézelayan burghers were stout fellows in those days. They had to be.

From behind their ramparts on the top of their hill, in 1360, they watched Edward III, King of England, pass by with a formidable army, which had forced a humiliating treaty on the Burgundians, to take the *château-fort* of Pierre-Perthuis a few miles up the River Cure. Here Edward left a garrison that lived by pillage; looting and terrorizing the countryside far and wide. The Vézelayans laid siege to the château, broke through the defenses by a breach they made near the *donjon* (the fifteen-year-old Duke of Burgundy in the forefront with them), and chased out the English, slaughtering a goodly number on the way with right hearty spirit.

The Duke of Lancaster and the Black Prince, among others, brought untold woe to many neighboring places, but thought better of attacking Vézelay.

The incursions of the English, though they wrought misery and devastation wherever they went, differed but little in general pattern and effect from those of the French (France and Burgundy then being separate countries); of the Bretons; of the Armagnacs of Orléans; and—perhaps the worst of all—of the "Grandes Compagnies" of adventurers, disbanded mercenaries of a strange assortment of nationalities captained by knights and seigneurs of sub-human brutality, who, rejoicing in the descriptive names of *les Ecorcheurs* (the Flayers) and *les Retondeurs* (the Clippers), infested the country and sucked it dry.

There were wars as well between towns, between seigneurs, between châteaux; district contending with district, house against house, vassal against overlord. Through it all flowed an endless current of rape, murder, arson, pillage: the accompaniment and the aftermath of all wars. And as always, the simple people and the good ones were the chief sufferers.

Yet Vézelay, as a kind of theocratic island existing apart first from the Carlovingian monarchy, then from French feudalism which supplanted this, and subordinate to neither, managed to defend its integrity with reasonable, if varying, success against the vultures of avarice. It was the Christian dissensions as much as the feudal and social struggles that brought about its eventual downfall.

In the year 1280 the abbey passed, with the accord of all concerned, including the Pope, under the royal authority of the Crown of France. In thus renouncing the autonomy which had made its status unique in medieval history, a certain degree of protection from feudal violence—particularly from the Counts of Nevers—was gained, together with other benefits through the progress then being assured wherever the monarchy extended its sway. There followed for the next two and a half centuries a succession of good and bad abbots who, according to their character, built up or wasted the resources of the abbey, maintained or dissipated its prestige, kept it aloof from or embroiled it in the politics of the day, and granted concessions to the townsfolk or quarrelled violently with them.

But in 1538, as a result of some intrigue whose causes remain obscure, the abbey was secularized by Papal bull. The great foundation of Girart de Roussillon which together with the other Benedictine monasteries had, in all their admirable organization, been the schools, the archives and libraries, the workshops, hotels, hospitals and asylums of penitence of Christian society—and preserved the art of writing that but for them would have been lost in the Middle Ages—fell to the rank of a collegiate church.

A chapter of canons replaced the Benedictine monks; court favorites were rewarded with appointments as abbots, usually absentee abbots. The abbey ceased, in effect, to be a true religious institution. While still preserving a considerable part of its material wealth, it lost its political power, its moral and religious influence, its artistic and intellectual importance.

In 1569 the church was sacked by the Huguenots during the religious wars of the Reformation. These dissenters, who had suffered their full share of persecution, expressed themselves even more unamiably beside the little church known as La Cordelle which was built in the same year that Saint Bernard preached the Second Crusade and on the same place on the hillside where the illustrious monk made his eloquent appeal. The church was served by Franciscan monks whose original predecessors had been sent from Italy in 1146 by Saint Francis of Assisi.

Here the Huguenots amused themselves by playing a macabre kind of lawn bowls with the severed heads of monks against the faces of still living monks buried to their necks as markers—a game that could hardly have been very diverting for the monks. Yet the Franciscans, or Cordeliers as they were called from the white cords they wore around their robes, kept the little church going until the French Revolution in 1790. Today its twelfth-century remnants, three hundred yards away as one looks from my study, serve as a *hangar* (a storage barn) for hay.

The final and inglorious page of the decline of La Madeleine, until its revival in the nineteenth century, was written in 1790, during the Revolution. The *abbé commendataire* of the time—an abbot enjoying the perquisites of his appointment while living irreligiously in Paris—suppressed the collegiate church. His sonorous but unsympathetic name was Louis-Marie Lebascle d'Argenteuil. The revolutionaries, in their zeal for destruction of everything that was religious, old, beautiful and unrevolutionary, hacked away the heads and parts of the bodies of God, Christ, the Virgin Mary and the hierarchy of saints, carven in stone with loving skill upon the façade and sides of the church seven hundred years before.

Happily, the splendid sculptures in the interior escaped destruction through the foresight of some unremembered canon who covered them over with plaster. Shortly after this episode, but not because of it, Monsieur d'Argenteuil also was suppressed, executed by the Revolution as a close friend of the Court.

Such, in brief survey of some ten and a half centuries, is the background of my hillside.

SOME PEOPLE OF THE HILLSIDE

THE IMMEDIATE ASPECT of my hillside is one of rural somnolence. The great church of La Madeleine looks down, after its many vicissitudes, over venerable chestnut trees upon a tranquil scene. Vézelay's fourteenth-century Porte Neuve, the "New Gate" built as part of the town's defenses against the English in the Hundred Years War, is no longer closed at night. A solitary lamp illuming the steep, roughly paved road that leads through it casts a dim, medieval light.

That road, which climbs from the still more ancient village of Asquins past my walled garden and was once the main approach to Vézelay, is more than a thousand years old.

Between the massive round towers of the Porte Neuve with their crenelated tops, over the arched opening of the gate, the weather-beaten armorial bearings sculptured in stone and carrying the porcupine of the arms of Vézelay face out over the valley. Below, in the *abreuvoir*—a watering place for cattle and horses— the ducks of Madame Mandron, who sells me milk when her cows are disposed to produce it, disport themselves and quack in mild alarm when I pass by in my jeep. Young ducklings, all fuzzy and yellow, escape the querulous supervision of a foster-mother hen to splash happily in the water while the anxious guardian clucks unheeded on the bank.

For all its somnolent appearance, one should not think that the people of the hillside take life casually. During the season of the ploughing, the manuring of the fields, the planting, cultivating and harvesting they labor greatly, with few and ancient tools. They work long hours on the land, at their various trades, or in their little shops. They give scant thought to the steepness of

13

the hillside in walking distances, on matters connected with their tasks and their daily lives, that only a vigorous people—many of them are no longer young—would regard with such unconcern.

They do considerable work for one another, or in common: such as when the grapevines have to be tied up, and during the gathering and pressing of the grapes for the wine, and the threshing of the wheat. In winter they tend to some extent to hibernate, for the days are short and often foggy and there is little to be done on the land, though lumbering still goes on in the woods. Then, each Sunday and holiday and sometimes on other days as well, the enthusiasts of the chase go out with their dogs—a curious collection of canines of fortuitous breeding—after wild boar and stag and woodcock in the forests; for partridges, quail, pheasants and rabbits in the fields. The hunting varies from year to year, for though the closed season is generally observed there is little effective effort to restock the game. Two winters ago the hunters killed ten wild boar on one Sunday afternoon, cornered by the dogs below the walls of Vézelay. But that was not a normal bag.

The people of the hillside have their disagreements and their jealousies, as in most small towns and villages. Gossip is not absent; inevitably they know too much about each other's private affairs. When one walks through the town on an average day, within the walls that once sheltered fifteen thousand souls, there are not apt to be many people in evidence. But one senses more eyes than one meets openly: female eyes, mostly, observing all movement with keen interest through the partly closed shutters. I have had something of the same sensation in the jungle where the paired eyes of its animal denizens regarded one's every move, seeing but unseen, through the tangled foliage.

Some of the younger men of the hillside spent long months in German prison camps: the lost years show in their faces. Some families were thoroughly pillaged by the invaders, though rather those who fled or left their properties unguarded during the occupation than the ones who remained to face it. Several did stout work in the Underground—the Resistance. A few in the neighborhood, though I believe not on the hillside, managed in ways they do not generally discuss to improve their financial status materially during the occupation and the operations of the Resistance.

There are gaps, of course, among the younger men. Quite a number disappeared; killed in action, died in prison camp, or unaccounted for. Some came back from prison camp too shattered to face the heavy labor in the fields, the lack of amenities in the villages and hamlets, and departed to seek opportunity elsewhere.

The people of the hillside are a fair cross-section of post-war rural France, though they have their own special characteristics.

Burgundians as a race (some inhabitants of the town are not native Burgundians and do not have the Burgundian temperament) are friendly, jolly, self-assured, resourceful both in their daily lives and in adversity. They have a good sense of humor, a natural gift of eloquence with a rather New England type of wit, a keen appreciation of good foods and wines. They are neither dour and suspicious as are some French from the north, nor as volatile as those of the south. Like rural New Englanders they have a strong sense of personal independence and a love of the land. They are essentially Gallic in their ability to drive a hard bargain one moment, to face death for an ideal the next. They have courage, energy, and remarkable powers of recuperation. They are, in a word, a substantial people.

Some of the residents of my hillside rejoice in quaintly inappropriate names. Mr. Butterfly (Papillon) is the mason. He cements up the basin in my lower garden which freezes and cracks in very cold winters even though emptied, and repairs the ancient lichen-spotted red tiles of my roof, when some of them get broken in the tremendous hail-storms. Mr. Butterfly is a very good mason, if one can ever get him to the task. He has more than a sufficiency of work to do in the summer season, being the only mason in the village, and his sense of timing is negligible. When he promises to come in three days he very likely believes it himself at the moment of saying, but the only thing one knows is that he will in no event show up in three days. He may come in three weeks, he may come in three months, but he will *not* be on hand in three days.

Mr. Butterfly is also the town crier. He beats a little drum and makes the announcements of local interest or annoyance, such as the enforced vaccination of children or of cows. He is a good crier, to my personal knowledge, for he announced one morning the loss of a wool scarf of mine and within half an hour the missing item was brought to me by the lad who had found it.

Mr. Night Club (Cabaret) is the plumber. He is an excellent plumber, hard working, capable and always cheerful. He, too—for he has more work than he can readily handle during most of the year, cannot find an apprentice-assistant, and has the greatest difficulty in obtaining materials—shows a tendency to be erratic in keeping promised engagements. He is yet more elusive in presenting his bills.

I tried without success to get a bill from him on various occasions in August and September a year back for a considerable amount of work he had done for me in May and June—my house having had little internal care for almost seven years, during which the German visitation had not improved it. Mr. Night Club replied that he had been much too busy since April to make out any bills. I managed to get it out of him with threats and cajolling in December, a day or two before my departure for an absence of several months. It was surprisingly modest. In this as in a number of other ways Mr. Night Club differs notably —and to my point of view, most happily—from the run-of-the-mill plumber in the U.S.A. and certain other enlightened areas.

Mr. Pastry-cook (Patissier) is the garagist. (The principal pastry-cook of the village is Madame Jojot, who turns out beautiful *pains-briochés, croissants* and pastries if one supplies the white flour she is now unable to procure.) Mr. Pastry-cook was a local leader of the Resistance during the German occupation, and did very well. He is assisted by Félix Olart, the forty-year-old son of my gardener, who also served in the Resistance. Both are keen hunters of the wild boar and stag in the wintertime—on Sundays and holidays—and work incredibly long hours on their jobs on all other occasions.

The garage is rather like some I have seen in back-country villages in Virginia or Tennessee. Its limited earthen floor-space is almost completely occupied by the mournful carcasses of two unrecognizable vehicles that have not budged for years, nor are likely to do so soon again. In the dim and oil-laden atmosphere of the small, incredibly cluttered adjoining workroom the more delicate operations of machining and rehabilitation of worn parts are carried out.

Much of the work is done in the open air in front of the entrance, there being no feasible way of getting anything larger than a motorcycle inside under the existing arrangements. By the side of the road a Rube Goldberg kind of contraption can, with considerable manual effort, raise one end or the other of motorcars in need of adjustment or repair, and Félix can usually be found lying on his back under some decrepit vehicle in a posture reminiscent of the early days of motoring.

Beside the garage, and also across the road, are the gutted remains of the walls of two houses burnt by the Germans in the "Battle of Vézelay" on the 24th of August 1944, when a retreating German mechanized column fleeing from the U.S. Seventh Army was ambushed by the Resistance just outside Vézelay, and a bitter five-hour fight ensued. There were a good many casualties on both sides, considering the size of the forces involved. Both Mr. Pastry-cook and Félix Olart took part in that fight.

When I first returned to Vézelay after the "liberation," having been wounded in the invasion of Normandy and unable to get back until the winter of 1945-46, I came in a borrowed military jeep which had, in theory, been "checked" by an Army sergeant. I arrived well after dark, in a cold, driving rain. The windshield wiper did not function; the accelerator pedal came off; the generator did not charge; three hours' use of the headlights had exhausted the battery, and there was no starting crank or any other tool that could conceivably have served a useful purpose.

The next day was a Sunday, and I had a moribund jeep located about a kilometer from the "garage" down a steep and rocky road that for all its ten centuries of history had received remarkably little maintenance in recent years. I sent for Félix, who walked down the hill to confirm my own conviction that there was no reasonably feasible way of getting that dispirited piece of mechanism started in the soggy field where it stood chained under a walnut tree. The two of us were unable to push it.

Félix went back and dug out Mr. Pastry-cook from his house. Together they got Mr. Pastry-cook's wood-burning jallopy going, which involves a certain amount of time and effort. It is to be remembered that this was a Sunday, a day sacred to relaxation in France; though happily for me the boar-hunting season had closed.

Mr. Pastry-cook and Félix drove down together, gravely risking the jallopy's worn-out tires (which could not then be replaced in France) on my rugged hillside road. With considerable difficulty they dragged the jeep out of the field and towed it up the hill. They repaired the broken accelerator pedal, fixed the windshield wiper, adjusted the generator and charged the battery for twenty hours. The next morning I started off down the main road. Two miles away the engine cut out dead: a battery terminal had broken, and for good measure the distributor points were all fouled up. Through the intermediary of an ancient greybeard slowly pushing a bicycle up the hill—the only traffic on the road that morning—I relayed a signal of distress back to Mr. Pastry-cook in his Rube Goldberg garage in Vézelay.

In due time he and Félix arrived, having got the wood-burning breakdown jallopy going. They repaired my troubles and set me happily, if tardily, on my way to Paris; whereafter they returned to their interrupted work in the garage. For all this the charge was a hundred and fifty francs—one dollar and twenty-five cents—and that was before I gave Mr. Pastry-cook any cigarettes. Yet some say that all the French are grasping?

Another of our local lights whose name has a quaint flavor is Madame Can (Bidon). She is a somewhat garrulous lady of indeterminate age who serves my friend Rhodes Robertson when he comes to Vézelay. (The Germans pillaged his house of bed linen, shirts and other clothing, but Madame Can managed to save most of his effects from their grasp.) Madame Can is a river of background information on all the denizens of the town. Just as any can held at the proper angle with its lid off will empty its contents, so Madame Can, given an appropriate opportunity, spills freely the gossip of Vézelay.

The oddest character of the hillside, though without benefit of humor either in her name or in her mentality, is the Widow Vincent. While she hails from St. Père-sous-Vézelay, a village hard below the hillside that dates back to Roman times, she is not at all a typical Burgundian in temperament. Madame Vincent is a pinch-penny of extraordinary intensity. She is not a bad soul at heart; but she has devoted her entire life, and that of her husband while he lasted, to *not* spending money: a far more definite attack on the problem of existence than merely saving.

Madame Vincent is a doleful old lady of eighty-five, completely self-contained and thoroughly disillusioned. She does her own marketing, in minute quantity; raises her own vegetables and fruit on her terraced garden patch atop the fourteenth-century walls of Vézelay; and keeps her closely shuttered house, her red-tiled floors and her copper pots—few of which, I suspect, she ever uses—spotlessly clean. The balance of her time she spends sitting on a hard wooden chair with her stockinged feet on a hot brick when the weather is cold, or without the brick when it is warm. The wooden shoes that she puts on to go to the door, when I occasionally call to see her, stand beside the neatly polished stove.

It is a peculiarly depressing experience to visit Madame Vincent. She moans incessantly over the devolution of the world and of France in particular since the days before 1914; the relativity of values; the excessive cost of basic commodities; the

calamitous decrease in the purchasing power of the franc. Everything to which she has devoted her life has collapsed. Her husband died twenty-odd years ago, starved, worked and frozen to
death: like the husband of Mrs. Hetty Green, American and the
world's richest woman, whom my father knew well. "Old Green,"
as Mrs. Hetty called him, died of undernourishment, underheat-
ing and lack of proper care in a cold, grey-stone house in Bellows
Falls, Vermont, at a time when Hetty could add up the income
of some sixty-four million dollars of investments; and in those
days there was no income tax.

The Widow Vincent's only son was crippled in the war in
1915. He lived on for twenty years, and her sole interest in life,
besides not spending money, ended with his death. Yet when his
inclinations seemed to be veering in the direction of matrimony,
and having discovered him kissing the girl of his favor from the
relatively innocuous position of his motorized wheel-chair, Madame Vincent chased her potential daughter-in-law down the
main street of Vézelay with a broom. The son died celibate in
1935. His mechanical go-cart, which I believe was a present from
the French government or some veterans' organization, reposes
in cleanly state in the entry passage of Madame Vincent's house.
Any suggestion to Madame Vincent that it could serve a more
useful purpose in some hospital for cripples falls on deaf ears.

Madame Vincent has property of value, though her income is restricted in terms of the purchasing power of the franc.
She plans to divide her property equally between her three neph-
ews, who live elsewhere—two of them at considerable distances
from the hillside. It would never enter her head to spend more
than the bare minimum for existence to ease her declining years.

When she was an active young thing of around sixty-five,
twenty or so years ago and before her husband passed away, she
kept a shop on the hill where she sold postcards and souvenirs
to the pilgrims and summer visitors who came to Vézelay. Once
a week she went to Avallon to replenish her stock of the more
rapidly moving items.

To Avallon and back, from Vézelay, is nineteen miles. Madame Vincent always did the trip on foot, rather than spend the few *sous*—pennies—that it cost to travel by bus. Furthermore, she went barefoot in order to save shoe-leather. And she returned with thirty-five pounds of postcards and other items on her back.

One day, when it was raining heavily, she took her umbrella. In Avallon the rain ceased. At Pontaubert, three miles on her homeward way with her thirty-five-pound pack, she sat for a moment to rest at a roadside café. Naturally, she did not indulge in a beer or any other unnecessary expenditure. While resting there she suddenly recalled that she had left her umbrella in Avallon.

She got up at once and started back to Avallon. The proprietor of the café, an amiable gentleman who knew Madame Vincent and her eccentricities quite well, suggested that she leave her pack under his care while she made the six-mile trip there and back. Did she do it? Not Madame Vincent. She took the thirty-five-pound load with her on the six-mile barefooted walk that her momentary forgetfulness had added to her normal nineteen miles. Her mind was not unaware of the possible pitfalls in the proprietor's well-meant suggestion. He, or someone else, might have sneaked a postcard from her sack when her back was turned.

For some reason beyond my power to explain, Madame Vincent was persuaded to lend her sister, a good many years ago, a thousand francs (then the equivalent of $200). The sister was in momentary stress which involved hospitalization and attendant charges that had "unbuckled her budget."

It appears there was some delay in the repayment of the loan, and that Madame Vincent made her disapproval of this only too evident. People, who have long memories in these parts, tell of her standing outside her sister's window daily, on the main street of Vézelay, shrieking imprecations for all and sundry to hear. In course of time—very overdue course in Madame Vincent's view—the money was repaid. Madame Vincent's husband showed up at his work one morning looking weary and wan.

"You are ill?" he was asked.

"I am worn out," responded Monsieur Vincent dispiritedly. "I have had no sleep. I sat up the whole of the night counting the money my wife's sister sent in repayment of the loan. She sent it all in pieces of one sou, and my wife made me count them all three times." The sister, it seems, had gone to considerable pains to collect the money in one-sou pieces—1000 francs; 20,000 sous. Counted three times, sixty thousand counts during the night; lest there might be one sou short.

The sisters lived across the street from one another for many years after that, without exchanging a word.

Of all the characters on my hillside, the closest to me, and by no means the least quaint, is the Père Olart. He is my gardener, the guardian of my property and some part of the things I have acquired across the years in a good many parts of the world. His title of Père is purely honorific, as the oldest living member of his family. He is in no wise to be confused with a religious Father.

Once by slip of the tongue I referred to the Père Bernard, the senior Benedictine monk and curé of the revived monastic church of La Madeleine, as the Père Olart.

"There is a certain difference in those Fathers, you know," remarked the person to whom I had made the slip, with a twinkle of the eye. There is a distinct difference. The Père Olart is a naughty old boy of seventy-five. He is a gardener of understanding and patient effort, a teller of curious and well-flavored tales (in a strong northern dialect, though he has been twenty-eight years in Burgundy), a faithful guardian of my property and possessions—save for anything alcoholic or sweet: but he is no monk.

Among all the people of the hillside he is the one who carries my thoughts beyond the horizon—he and the various objects from distant corners of the earth that surround me on walls and floors. He is a primitive, with little knowledge of the written word. Yet Père Olart has travelled (as far as Salonika in the war of 1914–18) and appreciates the sentiment, if not the relative worth, that attaches to objects of decoration or utility which take one's memory back, especially when the dry wood of dead cherry trees burns blue in the fireplace, to the places where they were acquired. Many of these objects would not be around me now had it not been for Père Olart. The German cohorts occupied Vézelay during several years and left little behind them in a number of other houses.

Père Olart is not outwardly impressive. He is small of stature and unkempt in appearance, with a straggly "Old Bill" moustache and very scant equipment in the way of teeth. Usually, though not so regularly as to be a fixed habit, he shaves on Sundays; and always on days of local funerals in which he serves as grave-digger and pall-bearer. But his keen hazel eyes, with an inquisitive and naughty glint like squirrels' eyes, miss little; and he has the understanding of the land, along with a fund of information on a remarkable variety of topics.

During his solitary labors in the garden, some two acres of which he turns by spade, plants in orderly rows of vegetables, cultivates and harvests, all by hand (and tends the espalier fruit trees and the grapevines on the walls), he talks on and off to himself in guttural mutterings into the stubble of his beard. From time to time he stands, leaning on his spade or hoe, in silent contemplation of the property which I have no doubt, at least in so far as the fruit trees, the vegetable garden and the vines go, he regards as his own. Now and then he whiffs the weather, and rarely is he far wrong in his predictions. But he relies on the *girouette*—the weather-cock—that surmounts the little tower of my house to give him the wind. It is an ancient iron girouette in the form of a mounted knight in armor galloping across a field above a rusted ball. In feudal times none but the seigneurs—the lords of the fiefs—might sport girouettes.

"It is much the best girouette in Vézelay," Père Olart says proudly. He means this, of course, in terms of its accuracy in indicating the wind, not for its design or antiquity.

Many of the objects that take my thoughts over the horizon, along with such useful items as mattresses, linen and blankets,

Père Olart saved from the grasping hands of the German invaders by transporting them in a wheelbarrow to his own cottage up on the hill. The hill is steep and rough. Père Olart avers that he made two hundred trips with his *brouette*—his wheelbarrow—carrying these things to the security of his domicile which resembles a witch's nest, whose appearance was made the more odd under the influx of various *objets d'art* from far provenance into that incongruous setting. Most of the bulkier items he hid in his attic; but others of more modest proportions were installed in the one room below, except for the kitchen; which was already littered with the accumulations of a peasant's lifetime. Here for nearly five years "M'sieur" Buddha reposed beneath festoons of cobwebs, along with Persian brass trays, Chinese bronzes and other objects of decorative purpose, flanked by hutches filled with large, edible rabbits.

M'sieur Buddha is a bronze Siamese Buddha, about fifteen inches tall, with an expression of slightly amused serenity. Père Olart has the greatest respect for M'sieur Buddha. He never refers to the little image without the prefix of Monsieur, pronounced with the usual slurring of the two syllables into one. Père Olart appreciates M'sieur Buddha's liking to have flowers always in front of him, and of his own initiative, when I am away, will refill the small Persian bowl which M'sieur Buddha has come to regard as his own special receptacle for the floral offerings placed below his crossed feet.

On the first of the old man's two hundred wheelbarrow trips to save my belongings from the invaders' hands, M'sieur Buddha was moved in solemn state as an honored refugee up to Père Olart's cottage. Ensconced there under the festoons of cobwebs, the fattening rabbits munching their greens around him, he was kept contented and reasonably happy with the fragrance of the flowers that the old man spread before him. On the day of "liberation" M'sieur Buddha was wounded, but he kept his slightly amused look of serenity, inhaling the perfume of a double bank of blossoms which Père Olart offered in lieu of an anaesthetic.

It was on the 24th of August, 1944, that a retreating German mechanized column—the last, sorry appearance in this area of the once arrogant invader—was attacked by a force of the Resistance on the outskirts of Vézelay. In the fight that ensued, in which Mr. Pastry-cook and Félix Olart took part, Père Olart's cottage was machine-gunned and M'sieur Buddha received a bullet-graze through the arm. (I, at this time, was hospitalized in England with a bullet through the knee.) Père Olart describes the action with dramatic gestures when sometimes I give him a cognac or a *marc* on my terrace after the day's work. This I avoid doing too frequently, for the old boy needs little encouragement as far as alcoholic drink is concerned—the one thing, barring sweets, that I feel it better not to leave around unguarded.

"I was standing right here," Père Olart recounts, pointing westwardly with a forefinger whose nail has never been trimmed save by toil, "when those types of toads"—his descriptive adjectives, nouns and verbs are not always politely translatable—"came down the road from Clamecy, just over there. Our men attacked them from the woods. They were surprised, and there was heavy fighting. I watched for a time, then went up to my house. The battle lasted five hours. A dozen bullets went through the room in which I live. One of these hit M'sieur Buddha in the right arm; but he was not badly hurt. I fixed his arm—it hardly shows—and I put more flowers in front of him."

The "Battle of Vézelay" was not a great battle in the annals of the war, if indeed it is recorded at all. But there was a moment when the Germans, who were in far stronger force than the attackers and much more heavily equipped, were, in their rage, on the point of burning down this ancient and historic town. In all probability they would have done so had it not been for Madame Danguy, a lady of well over sixty, who owns the principal hotel which the invaders had occupied for several years as an administrative rest center. A strong character, clear-headed, and determined, she argued with the officer commanding the column. There was a dead woman by her side as she argued, a refugee who had been shot by the Germans after having been driven out of the hotel cellar; and several houses were burning fiercely around Mr. Pastry-cook's garage a little below on the right.

Madame Danguy persuaded the enraged and highly excited German that the Americans were right on the tail of his column, and that any delay in the column's moving on could well prove fatal to its escape. A reconnaissance party had gone up the main —to all intents and purposes the only—street of the town, and had returned in haste after finding that this ended on the terrace behind the church, above the escarpment that falls sheer to the little River Cure. The remnants of the column then took off hell-for-leather down the road to Avallon, along which Madame Vincent used to patter in her bare feet carrying her thirty-five pounds of postcards. In such a manner was Vézelay saved. The column was harassed by the Resistance on its way, and reputedly was destroyed by American dive-bombers before it left Avallon far behind.

M'sieur Buddha sat cross-legged on his lotus flower in Père Olart's cottage under the festoons of cobwebs, nursing his wounded arm. Surrounded by munching rabbits, he looked out at the "liberation" with his slightly enigmatic smile of serenity over the double bank of flowers that Père Olart had arranged at his feet.

II

REORIENTATIONS

"For to admire and for to see,
For to be'old this world so wide—"

M'SIEUR BUDDHA AND THE
SPITTING FISH

M'SIEUR BUDDHA, as already mentioned, came from Siam. He accompanied my wife and me from Bangkok to Paris in 1929. After that he occupied a prominent place in my Paris apartment. Yet, though flowers were kept constantly in front of him and he was treated with great respect, he did not seem to be happy. Nor was the Wheel of Life then turning for me quite as smoothly as I would have wished.

One evening the Siamese Minister, Phya Vijitavongs, a friend with one of the most aesthetic heads of anyone I have ever met, came to dine in our apartment on the Rue Chernoviz. We talked a good deal about Siam, and in the course of the conversation mention was made of the fact that M'sieur Buddha did not appear completely happy. This was imaginative, to be sure, and doubtless reflected something of my own feeling at the time. In those days the little image was not called *M'sieur* Buddha. It was Père Olart, several years later, who gave him that prefix.

"He may be lonely and feel a bit *dépaysé*"—out of his element: a 'displaced person' in today's parlance—said Phya Vijit, whose name had been colloquially shortened for convenience when he was Siamese Minister in Washington. "He is perhaps not as yet wholly acclimated to the foreign scene and misses his Siamese friends." Before the Minister departed he made a suggestion.

"If you permit," he said in his gentle way, "I will take the Buddha with me to the Siamese Legation tonight. There he will be installed in a place of honor in a room where there are many other Buddhas. He will be among friends of his own persuasion. There is a servant who places fresh blossoms—you know we have our own greenhouse—in front of each Buddha every day. He will not be lonely, and I believe a sojourn amongst his *confrères* will restore his spirit and that he will be happy then under your friendly roof."

Phya Vijit is a highly cultured and much travelled gentleman who is no worshipper of idols: yet this was all said in perfectly serious vein, though there may have been a slight twinkle behind it. I agreed to his suggestion with thanks. M'sieur Buddha was borne off that night—some twelve pounds of him on his stylized lotus-flower base—under the arm of the Siamese Minister. The Rue Chernoviz apartment was on the fifth floor, and though there was an elevator it was not possible, as is the system in most Paris apartments, to summon the thing up in order to descend. Phya Vijit refused to let me walk down to bring it up. He also refused to let me carry M'sieur Buddha. In his evening clothes he descended the five flights bearing the bronze image on his arm like a baby, stepped into his waiting car and was driven to the Siamese Legation in the Rue Greuze.

A week or so later we dined there. After dinner Phya Vijit took us to the room where many solemn Buddhas, some of bronze and some of stone, in various sizes and postures, stared contemplatively out from behind their banks of flowers. M'sieur Buddha was in a central position, highly placed. His slightly enigmatic smile through half-closed lids was on us when we came in.

"You see?" said Phya Vijit gently. "I think he already feels more contented."

I left the following day for Finland and Estonia. Three months later, shortly after my return to Paris, Phya Vijit again came to dine with us. He arrived carrying the bronze image under his arm. Very gently he placed M'sieur Buddha on the table reserved for him, and put some special Siamese blooms, grown in the Legation greenhouse, in front of his folded feet.

"I think he is all right now," said Phya Vijit. And from that time I have never felt M'sieur Buddha to be discontented.

M'sieur Buddha had no direct connection with the spitting fish, other than for the fact that I first met these oddities in his country at the time when I made his acquaintance. Siamese waters are remarkable in the variety of fishes that inhabit them, many of curious conformation, of peculiar habits, and of vivid coloring: some combining all three. The spitting fish is by no means the only one notable for a rugged individualism.

The first fish of eccentric behavior that I encountered was a piscine character that walks about in the open air, crossing considerable distances of dry ground and the raised causeways of Siamese roads in proceeding overland from one canal to another. It clambers easily over rocks, and has been reported to climb trees. It is the "walking fish" or climbing perch, *Anabas testudineus* (Bloch), and there was rarely a day in Siam when I did not see up to a half a dozen or so on their cross-country peregrinations.

It is a small, brownish-grey fish some six to nine inches in length, with accessory respiratory organs by which it takes oxygen directly from the atmosphere. It walks nearly upright, supported on spread-out paired fins like a performing seal on its flippers, and propels itself over the ground at a surprising speed by lateral wagglings of its tail. Though I had come across this quaint animal some years before in Ceylon, I never quite got over a slight feeling of improbability on seeing a fish determinedly walking across the road in front of me, upright and wagging its tail.

The spitting fish I had not met before. I had never even heard of it when a jolly young Siamese prince took me one afternoon by launch a short way down the river—the Menam Chao Phya which is the main channel of communication of central Siam—for tea and drinks at a small wooden pavilion on the left bank some ten miles below Bangkok.

We sat on a platform perched on stilts over the water, and watched the rafts of teak logs and barges full of rice floating downstream in the swirls of the silty current reflecting the afternoon sun. I was seated close to the outer railing, smoking a cigarette in a long ivory holder. From time to time I rested my elbow on the rail, with my forearm and hand, the cigarette-holder between my fingers, dangling perhaps four feet above the turbid water.

We were talking about certain, at that time, recent developments in aeronautics, when I heard a sound like a drop of water on a hot stove—*psst!* I did not give this any particular thought, but a moment later I took a puff on my cigarette and found it was out. As I relighted it I noticed that the end was moist.

The conversation continued, and my arm rested on the rail with the burning cigarette in the holder extending out over the river. There was another *psst!* and once more my cigarette was doused. I looked up into the air. It was not raining, nor did I see any birds flying overhead. I looked at my Siamese friend: his expression was a complete blank.

Very deliberately I lighted a fresh cigarette, inserted it in the holder and held it out over the water, more than forty-four inches below. Within two seconds, while I watched as intently as a physicist about to split his first atom, the head of a smallish fish emerged from the surface of the river, there was a *psst!* and my cigarette was out again, extinguished by the fish spitting a single drop of water so fast that I could not see it. Once more I looked at my Siamese friend. His face was now wreathed in smiles.

"Just *what* is this anti-nicotine submarine patrol?" I asked.

"Oh," he said, "you don't know our spitting fish? They shoot at insects—what you call bugs in America—and knock them down into the water where the fish eat them. This one make good joke for me; ho, ho! He thought your cigarette end was some kind of firefly. These fish very good shots, never miss."

The "spitting fish" of Siam, known also as the archer or

shooting fish, *Toxotes jaculatrix* (Pallas), subsists principally on insects that it spits or shoots out of the air on the wing, or off vegetation growing in or overhanging the water. Its aim is amazingly accurate and it has very keen aerial as well as underwater vision, enabling it to spot its prey at considerable distances and to estimate effective range and deflection. It is a most intelligent and purposeful fish. The average adult runs to about seven or eight inches in length, with a grey body strikingly banded in black, some of its fins black and some white. It is much esteemed as a food fish.

The spitting fish shoots down its prey by expelling a drop of water, or several drops in quick succession, through a small groove in the roof of the mouth which becomes a tube when the fish presses its tongue against its palate. Water is forced into the tube by compression of the gill covers, and the shots, or drops, are controlled by the tip of the tongue acting as a valve. The shots are of uniform size; the force with which they are ejected—often knocking the insect shot at high into the air— and the percentage of direct hits, are astonishing.

Were some imaginative inventor to devise a water-pistol modeled on the inner workings of the spitting fish, how many a lad could find enchantment in a new weapon! But none would ever be likely to attain a hundredth part of the deadly accuracy of *Toxotes jaculatrix.*

Among the quainter fishes of Siam are two tiny ones cultivated for their pugnacious qualities. Fighting them is one of the national sports, and the contests, often involving large wagers, are curious and picturesque. Of the two types, one fights with the teeth; the other wrestles its adversary.

The true fighting fish is about two and half inches long, with crapy fins like diminutive Japanese goldfishes. *Betta splendens* (Regan) is its name. Only the male fish is used for fighting. When in repose it is greyish-brown or green, but under the stimulus of anger it undergoes a remarkable color transformation.

And the male *Betta* always becomes violently enraged on viewing another male *Betta*, or even its own image in a mirror.

I attended several fighting-fish contests in Bangkok. The two contestants were carried into the room in separate glass bowls which were placed side by side. As soon as the drab-colored little fish saw each other through the glass walls they turned the most vivid iridescent blue, red, green and lavender hues, spread their fins, and their gill membranes projected outwards like the hackles of fighting cocks. After this display the owners or attendants poured them carefully into a third, rectangular glass container, which was the arena for the fight.

The fish straightway faced each other head-on, their fins and gill membranes extended, waves of brilliant color sweeping over their bodies as if they were on fire. Then they swung cautiously into sparring position, side by side, pointing in the same direction, one a trifle behind the other. This attitude they held for perhaps a minute until suddenly, quicker than I could follow with the eye, they attacked.

With diminutive, sharp-pointed teeth they tore off chunks of each other's fins, and scales from the sides of their tiny bodies. The attacks were repeated in rapid succession, the water becoming flecked with detached bits of fin. Now and then there was a lull during which they resumed the sparring position; and frequently a breathing spell when the fish rose to the surface to take additional oxygen from the air, since they are so constructed as to be unable to obtain a sufficient supply through their gills even when in repose.

These breathing spells were evidently by mutual agreement, somewhat like the intermissions between rounds in a boxing match. During them no attacks were permitted under the rules of the contest (as known to the fish), nor did either fish attempt to infringe upon the rules. After the intermissions the attacks were renewed with undiminished vigor. Occasionally the two contestants hit head-on and locked jaws. Then they would roll over and over, sideways, but this grip always resulted in a stalemate. After a short time the two fish would sink to the bottom of the jar hanging on stolidly to each other's jaws, remain there immobile for fifteen seconds or so, then relax their grip and rise to the surface for a gulp of air.

The fights I watched lasted from two and a half to three hours. Some contests endure much longer than that. Each ended when one of the combatants, exhausted by the struggle, turned tail and swam away from his still bellicose opponent in sign of having had enough. The two fish, more or less denuded of fins and lacking some of their scales but otherwise intact, were taken from the arena, the bets paid off, the owners of the contestants carrying away their fighters in little glass vessels. There is nothing brutal in these spectacles. The fish are keen on fighting and recuperate rapidly from the wear and tear of the contests, growing new fins and scales in short order to replace those lost.

The *Betta* prefer mosquito larvae to all other food. Owners of any considerable number of fighting-fish often employ coolies whose principal duty is the locating of mosquito breeding places and the collection of larvae to feed the hungry little fish. Quite a number of people in Bangkok earn their living in breeding mosquitoes for their larvae, to sell to the amateur fanciers and those who deal professionally in fighting-fish.

The other popular type of fighting-fish, or in this case more accurately wrestling-fish, to use the descriptive name given it by Dr. H. M. Smith, former Adviser in Fisheries to the Siamese Government, is *Dermogenys Pusillus* (van Hasselt). This remarkably pugnacious little fish, about an inch and a half in length, is a half-beak, its lower jaw projecting far out beyond the upper. It exists in quiet waters throughout Siam, but all contestants of the wrestling matches are cultivated fish, selectively bred for stamina. It is called "needle fish" by the Siamese.

The wrestling-fish have to be kept in earthenware vessels as they cannot judge the distance of transparent material and are apt to break their lower jaw against the side of a glass container. For the same reason, the contests are held in large, widemouthed terra cotta water jars about three-quarters full.

Two male fish are placed together in the jar for a wrestling match and instantly attack. There is no preliminary sparring, as between the fighting-fish. With remarkable dexterity each seeks an effective hold on the other's jaw, though not a split-second is wasted in coming to grips. The usual hold is with inter-locked jaws. But one fish may get the other by the tip of the beak, or at the base of the jaws, or across the gill openings. Some strive for an oblique grip that turns and keeps the adversary on its back or side.

They struggle and heave like two human wrestlers, sometimes for several hours on end, during which time their owners and other Siamese friends who have placed bets on the outcome keenly follow every movement. From time to time one of the fish breaks out of an unfavorable grip; the other instantly seeks to regain it. The match terminates with the complete exhaustion of one or both contestants. In the latter case the winner is decided on a basis of points as in a boxing match when there is no knockout. The fish rarely suffer any permanent injury.

The Siamese take these contests very seriously. Selective breeding over many generations has developed in some wrestling-fish an uncanny knack of getting a disabling hold on its adversary. The value placed on such fish is absurdly out of proportion to their diminutive size, but so is their pugnacity.

Though I have other memories of Siam, my recollections are interspersed with animals of curious behavior or quaint appearance, from spitting fish to white elephants. While I was in Bangkok a white elephant captured in the northern jungles was presented to the city. The whole Siamese population made a tremendous to-do about this when the ungainly beast was brought ceremoniously into town, since white elephants are endowed by the Siamese with an aura of demi-sanctity. Everything was decorated with flowers and banners and ornamental trappings—the city, the honorary attendants of the elephant and the elephant itself.

The show was picturesque and colorful, but I admit having

been considerably disappointed in the elephant. It was not a very large elephant and it certainly was not white. On either side it had an inch of tusk for each of its twelve years of age. It looked ill at ease and gloomy in spite of its flowery decorations, with little of the serenity one expected from a revered Buddhist vehicle of the animal kingdom. To my eye, it was a dingy light grey in color. But to the Siamese it was a white elephant, and would doubtless bring good fortune to the city.

We stayed some while under the hospitable roof of Hermann and Mable Schultz. They had a pair of Siamese cats, or what passed for cats. In effect these were miniature tigers. They spent most of the night hunting in the garden and the surrounding countryside. Each morning, when we went onto the screened veranda for early breakfast, their night's bag of game would be laid out on the floor in an orderly row for our inspection. The bag usually comprised snakes, unappetizing before breakfast but better dead than crawling around the garden alive; rats and other rodents, also a good riddance; and unhappily a bird or so. The two cats stalked back and forth on either side of the line of their kill, switching their tails and uttering low, rumbling growls.

When we came onto the veranda they would look up at us to make certain that we were appreciating the results of their prowess. When the female made too much of a show of eliciting our approval, thereby drawing attention to herself, her mate would cuff her on the side of the head and knock her clear over into a corner. She took this reproof demurely, as befitted an Oriental wife. After the inspection had been completed and the hunters' skill duly recognized, the cats removed their kill outside and started their own breakfast on the choicer items.

There was a European resident of Bangkok to whose house we went for tea. The house, as was usual in Siam, was a single-storied wooden structure built high upon stilts above the damp of the ground and the snakes that infest the gardens. The open space between the floor and the ground was filled in with a wooden trellis over which grew flowering vines.

Our host had a particularly fine specimen of Siamese cat

which he had promised to show us. The cat was not present at tea, and after we had been served he sent one of his servants to fetch it. There was a considerable lapse of time, and neither cat nor servant appeared.

"What the devil is that boy doing?" muttered our host. He went out onto the verandah and bellowed for the servant. There came a response from somewhere below.

"Sir, have found cat!" This was in the rather high-pitched voice of the 'boy,' who had long since passed his fortieth birthday.

"Well, then, bring him up here as I told you!" cried the master of the house.

"Sir, no can bring up cat! Please come see!" the boy replied.

"Idiot!" snapped our host, and in an aside to us: "That cat never hides in trees!"

We followed our host down the veranda steps to see why the cat could not be brought up to meet us. The cat was not in a tree. The servant was standing near the foot of the steps pointing to something under the house. The something was a fourteen-foot python, tranquil at the moment, though its tail was gently waving. There was a hole in the trellis where some of the lattices had been broken.

The python had tried to crawl through this hole. It had stuck halfway along its own length in the broken ends of the lattices, because there was a bulge in the middle of the python. The bulge was the Siamese cat which our host had wanted to show us.

The Menam Chao Phya, the great central waterway on which Bangkok is situated, is, so to speak, the Nile of Siam. It serves as the country's most important line of inland communication, and in its annual flood brings down the rich silt that fertilizes the rice fields. It is connected by canals with other streams, and with a series of lakes that vary in extent between the wet and dry seasons.

On the canals in the vicinity of Bangkok, along the edges of tributary streams and up the dead-end backwaters of the river, are located numerous villages of fisherfolk, rice cultivators and river boatmen. In some of these villages one or the other of the two British banks, or both, had established local branch offices for the convenience of their customers and of their own business. These sub-branches were served from the head offices by launch; and as there was a continual transfer to and fro of silver currency and banknotes, each launch was equipped with a safe firmly bolted to the deck.

The manager of one of the banks decided that the ancient safe aboard his launch no longer offered sufficient security for the often considerable sums transferred back and forth along the river. With the approval of the home office he ordered to be sent out from London one of Messrs. X's latest models of burglar-proof safes, built to exact specifications. Among other things, as additional security, the safe was to be provided with both a combination and a key operated lock. For the latter there were to be five keys.

After a considerable delay the new safe arrived in Bangkok and duly replaced its outmoded predecessor. The bank manager thereupon gave a sort of christening party aboard the launch to celebrate its installation. Sandwiches and drinks were served while they ran down the river, passing between rafts of teakwood logs, barges filled with rice, and the small boats of fishermen.

The bank, the manager and the safe having been suitably toasted, the party was invited to inspect the last of these. The safe stood open, all shiny and impressive. To show its smooth operation, one of the bank staff shut the heavy double door. He did not know, or had forgotten, that all five keys were on a ring inside the safe and that the lock had been set for automatic operation on the closing of the door. The door, of course, would not reopen. A blank look came over the manager's face as he realized what had happened. There was not another key nearer than the basic model deposited with the makers in London, and in that day there was no air service between England and Siam.

"Good God!" he said, very deliberately, and poured himself a drink. The members of the bank's staff held a hasty consultation. They headed the launch back to Bangkok. There one of the staff went ashore. He returned about half an hour later accompanied by a Chinese locksmith, the latter carrying a small bag of tools like a barber's kit. Messrs. X's latest burglar-proof safe was pointed out to him, its heavy, hinged door firmly locked.

The Chinese stared at it for a moment. Then, expressionless as an owl, he said: "Ten tics"—ten ticals, the equivalent of five dollars. The amount was paid over to him. He took out his tools: a few split razor blades of different widths, some wire hairpins, a child's magnet, a stick of wax, some odd keys, a couple of files, and a handful of instruments that might have belonged to a dentist. In just over twenty minutes the door of Messrs. X's most recent contribution to foiling the artful burglar swung open.

The poker-faced locksmith packed up his gear and departed without a word. The five keys were extracted from the safe and swiftly handed over to the three staff members who were authorized to have access to it, with two to be kept in reserve in the vaults of the bank. The manager heaved a sigh, but whether of relief or not it would have been hard to tell.

"Well, that's that!" he muttered ruminatively. "Damn clever, these Chinese, as the saying goes. We've got our safe so that at least it will open and shut, but for heaven's sake don't let's lose the combination. I'll wager that our Chink savior would work it out in half an hour. Burglar-proof safe—*ha!* Not while there's a Chinese locksmith around!"

One of the most interesting places in Bangkok was the Pasteur Institute and snake farm, established by Prince Damrong after the death of one of his daughters from mad dog bite while on her way to Saigon for treatment. This occurred some years before I went to Bangkok, but I knew the cultured and charming Prince, and at his house met many dainty little Princesses, other daughters or nieces of his, who gave the ethereal impression that they could dance on one's outstretched hand and one would feel no sensation of weight.

Siam is the happy breeding ground of several varieties of highly poisonous snakes. We never went out after dark without a servant proceeding us with a lantern to show up the snakes that might be lurking in our path. The deadliest of these are cobra, Russell's viper and krait. Before the establishment of the Pasteur Institute the annual death toll from snake bite ran very high, as did that from rabies.

The individual serums developed by the Pasteur Institute, if injected fairly promptly, were said to have a record of better than ninety-five per cent effectiveness as a cure for snake bite, providing you knew the snake that bit you. A combined serum for all snake bites was less sure but still very effective. The rabies serum, I believe, was ninety-eight per cent certain when taken in time.

Within the ground of the institute, in addition to the main medical buildings and infirmary, were three large pits labelled POISONOUS SERPENTS, followed by the type contained in each: *Cobra, Krait, Russell's Viper*. Not far from these a number of sorry looking horses grazed listlessly in a green field, having been injected with snake venom to produce the serum to combat the deadly poison of the snake bites.

Off in the other direction, in a luxuriant garden, there was a black and white gibbon with very long arms and tail, attached by a length of wire leash to a ring that ran free on a much longer, horizontal wire, allowing the monkey considerable latitude in gallivanting through the low trees by his arms. When the leash got entangled in the branches, the gibbon showed real ingenuity in disengaging it. The gibbon had nothing to do with snake serum. He was a well-known cinema actor, having been much the best actor in the film called *Chang*. Success had spoiled him, as so often happens. He had grown bad tempered. So his activities were now restricted to the length of a run on a wire, swinging arm over arm through the trees in the pleasant grounds of the Pasteur Institute.

In the snake pit marked *Russell's Viper* there was a basket-ful of tiny, squirming little vipers just hatched from the eggs. Though they were but a few hours old their bite had the same deadliness as that of a fully grown adult.

The cobras were housed in bee-hive shaped shelters on a concrete island at the base of the pit, surrounded by water. With the head keeper I descended into the pit to take moving pictures. The keeper turned over several of the bee-hives, which were hinged in the back, exposing a tangled mass of sluggish and sleeping cobras. These he stirred with a forked stick, until some of them stood up angrily and spread their hoods.

The cobra is a gentleman (or a lady, as the case may be) compared to krait and Russell's viper, which will bite you with-out warning from sheer malevolence. The cobra only strikes in self defense, or when angered or frightened, and gives notice by rising to about a third of its length and spreading its hood. It strikes downward from the height to which it has risen, and be-cause its envenomed fangs curve backwards they cannot make an abrasion—lacking which the venom has no effect—other than in a downward strike. A Tamil servant of mine, rather a timorous character in most respects, once pulled a cobra with his bare hands out from under a low-bottomed chest of drawers in my room in an Indian dâk bungalow. I would have been extremely reluctant to try this myself; but he knew that the cobra could not strike effectively from its position under the chest.

As the cobras rose in sleepy anger from the base of their bee-hives, the head keeper shovelled them out with his forked stick into the water. This cooled them down somewhat. When they attempted to crawl back onto the platform he shovelled them off again until they gave up and swam aimlessly about.

In one of the bee-hives there was a twelve-foot hamadryad or king cobra, which the keeper unceremoniously forked into the water with the others. The hamadryad did not try to return to the platform but swam rapidly and smoothly round and round the island, slipping between the angry-eyed cobras milling about the surface, Some years before I had run over a hamadryad with a motorcar on a jungle road in Malaya and finished it off with a 20-gauge shotgun. This proved something of a test both of my nerve and my aim, as I had to approach pretty close to hit it in its lunging head and the great serpent kept on lashing out violently long after I had practically blown its whole fore-part off.

The head keeper did not shovel into the water all the cobras that stood up and spread their hoods angrily when he stirred them with his stick. Several, in a motion as quick as the movement of a serpent's tongue, he pinned down with the forked stick, then with his bare hand seized the cobra back of its head and held it aloft. While the then thoroughly enraged serpent thrashed about with its tail he "milked" it, holding a small, flat disk of glass in his other bare hand under the venom ducts behind the cobra's fangs.

Still holding the lashing serpent by the neck he placed the glass, smeared with venom, on the ground by his foot, fed the cobra two raw eggs through a funnel, and threw it into the water. This he repeated four times with different cobras, and in the end carried the four glass disks with the deadly virus on them over to the medical building to be injected into sorrowful horses.

His was not, it occurred to me, an occupation that I particularly envied. One gets used to such things in time, but I would rather milk some other animal than a cobra. And even in this, familiarity bred contempt.

"He is the most complete vindication of the efficacy of our serum," the chief nurse told me, referring to the head keeper of the cobras. "He gets bitten every so often, simply walks across to the clinic, bares his arm and says: 'Snake bite me; please, want a shot!' He does this exactly as someone with a small cut might ask for a few drops of iodine. But his confidence in the serum has made him really too careless. So now we charge him the regular fee for his injections, and he doesn't come in quite so often to ask for a 'shot.'"

EX ORIENTE LUX

FLANKING M'SIEUR BUDDHA on either side, beyond the bookcases which afford him a calm, literary atmosphere, are two Japanese prints. There are three others in the dining room, and several more in the rooms upstairs. Père Olart does not appreciate them. I think he feels that I would not place anything inappropriate so close to M'sieur Buddha, and therefore has a certain obscure respect for the two prints that hang on the lounge walls facing the little bronze image. I doubt if he has ever even noticed the others.

Père Olart is not alone in his failure to appreciate their charm of line and color. Perhaps Japanese prints are an acquired taste, like oysters or champagne. A French friend of mine, by no means lacking in artistic sense, once asked me what there was to appreciate about them. Coming from him, it was a question I was hard put to understand, for I acquired the taste at an early age.

Probably no people in their *ensemble* have ever been so naturally and consciously artistic as the Japanese. The golden age of Japanese art carried through to the end of the eighteenth century, yet continued to be medieval in spirit since Japan remained medieval until the latter half of the nineteenth century. The revolution of 1868 which brought an end to Japanese feudalism, together with the impact of Westernization that followed, also brought an end to the really creative art of Japan. But the people retain a deep, emotional love of beauty, particularly for the beauties of their beloved landscapes.

I have seen Japanese in springtime by the hundreds, both townsfolk and villagers, with their women and children and nested bowls of provisions, close up their little shops, leave their fields, and go many miles to sit at the edge of some river and watch the blossoming cherry trees reflected in the current. The first time, I asked what was the holiday.

"But it's not a holiday," I was told. "The cherry blossoms are at their prime, and there is no other place anywhere hereabouts where their reflection in the rippling water is quite so lovely. Wherefore the people come to sit on the banks and regard the beauty of the springtime."

The Japanese artists of the seventeenth and eighteenth centuries were marvellous technicians who depicted every phase of the Japanese scene with intense curiosity, with humor—often ironical but usually sympathetic—and infinite skill in catching the characteristics of objects in motion. They found an inexhaustible reservoir to draw from in nature, in the forms and the harmonies of their deeply indented, conifer-forested islands, in all the life of woods and grasses, of skies and flowing water, even to the smallest of insects. They stylized nature, but they did so with skilled hands and an immensity of knowledge behind them.

They pulled back the *shoji*, the paper-covered inner shutters of Japanese houses, and portrayed young Japanese women at their toilets, washing their breasts or combing their hair. They stressed the power of the forces of nature: a beating rain shown so realistically that one can feel the sting of the wind-driven drops; or as in Hokusai's "Wave," an enormous, foaming comber with a small sampan engulfed under it and a diminutive Mount Fujiyama in the distant background.

They had a sinuous conception of form, with linear precision and economy of line, which has rarely been equalled and perhaps never surpassed; and their use of color, in any case by the great masters, is delicate and extremely effective in tonal relation.

There is a story of Okyo, leader of the naturalistic school in the latter half of the eighteenth century and best known for his portrayal of animal life—fat puppies rolling around in play; wild geese gliding down to water at the edge of a reed-bed in the moonlight; carp slipping lazily between the stems of bulrushes. The story is characteristic of the meticulousness of Japanese drawing.

Okyo was the son of a farmer living near Kyoto, who wished the boy to become a carpenter. But Okyo junior made a very poor apprentice. When planing a board out in the open—most carpentry was done in the open—he spent his time gazing at the swallows and other birds in flight around him. He made sketches of them with sticks of charcoal on the wood he was supposed to be planing. Whenever he found a dead bird or other small beast he cut it up and studied how it was constructed.

"He'll never be any good," said the carpenter to whom Okyo was apprenticed. "He just isn't interested in his work. He keeps looking at birds all the time, or anything else that's alive. He never gets a piece of wood planed!"

Okyo's father was upset over this. But the boy persisted with his sketching and his impromptu anatomical research, in which he was assisted by a gentleman from Yedo who assured Okyo's father that in the city good artists were not badly regarded and some of them made a reasonable living.

As his competence grew, Okyo went to unusual lengths to improve his knowledge and technique. To such end he managed to get himself accepted as an apprentice by the boar hunters of the Hokkaido, men of certain villages in the northernmost of the main group of islands who fished in summer and hunted the wild boar in the snows of winter. Okyo put in three winter seasons on the Hokkaido. He tracked the boar and assisted the hunters in the chase, in the meanwhile studying boar in motion and at rest, examining their structure, drawing sketches of them in various attitudes, and also of the huntsmen who were after them.

At the end of the season the hunters sat around a camp fire, smoking the long-stemmed Japanese pipes whose bowls hold only a few puff-fulls, spitting in the fire and cracking jokes about the hunt. Each huntsman was called upon in turn to tell a story, and each told one, dramatically but with an underlying current of humor. The hunters guffawed and made quips at one another's tales.

When the turn came to Okyo he said that as a humble apprentice he had no story to tell, but he would offer them something else. From the sleeve of his kimono he pulled a drawing done up in protective covering of cloth, unwrapped it and without further comment passed it around the circle.

In the light of the camp fire the men looked at the drawing, grunted and passed it on. "Good picture of a dead boar," they said. When the drawing came back to him Okyo silently rolled it up and put it back in his kimono sleeve.

The following year he was more familiar with the procedure of the hunt, more useful to the hunters and more knowledgeable about the boar. He continued making drawings of boar and amused the huntsmen with sketches of themselves. The season passed off much as before, the last evening being spent around the camp fire telling tall tales.

"How about a story this year, Okyo?" they asked when it came to his turn. "Have you one to tell?" Yes, he said, he had, but after his fashion it was a drawn one, not a verbal one. He again unrolled a drawing and passed it about the circle.

"H'm," they said, "that boar has been freshly killed!" Okyo once more rolled up his drawing without remark.

He returned for the third season, now a full-fledged boar hunter. The pattern was the same, through Okyo had gained self-confidence both vis-à-vis his co-hunters and in his understanding of the boar. At the end of the season he was, when it came his turn, as usual called on for a story.

"Come on, Okyo," they said. "Surely this year you have one to tell!"

"No," said Okyo, "I'll let you tell it for me." And he passed another drawing around the camp fire, as always without comment. The hunters looked up.

"But Okyo, you've done it differently this time," they said. "This boar's not dead, he's asleep!" And then Okyo was satisfied that he had mastered the technique of drawing wild boar.

For with a few brush strokes on rice paper from which no line once put down can be erased, without any "modern" aids such as breath coming from the animal's nostrils, he had succeeded in showing by sheer sinuosity of line, to illiterate boar hunters with no knowledge of drawing, that the boar he portrayed was asleep, not even freshly killed.

My Japanese prints were acquired fortuitously some thirty-five years ago in the course of a walking trip around Fujiyama. I was accompanied on this tour by a man named Arnell, Oriental Secretary of the American Embassy—an American who was considered to speak Japanese better than perhaps any other person not born Japanese—and for a short time by a Lieutenant Campanole of the United States Army, then assigned to the Embassy as a language student.

We stopped overnight at village "tea houses," which are inns, after pushing our way each time through a horde of children attracted by Arnell's bright red hair and narrow, pointed face. The children would stare at him, crying loudly: "He looks like the Fox!"—the hero of a sort of Hans Christian Andersen fable that every Japanese child knows. Arnell would respond: "I *am* the Fox!" and in the first person recount some of the legendary tales of the Fox's adventures while the children shrieked with excitement.

When we eventually broke through the importunate crowd of young fry and entered the inn, the landlord would be waiting for us, bowing very low and sucking in his breath. We would take off our shoes and be conducted up a steep flight of wooden steps, usually of cryptomeria wood, to a room on the floor above which was always spotlessly clean and entirely empty save for the thick, neatly fitted mats of rice straw. There were no doors. The walls could be opened anywhere by sliding back in their grooves one or more sections of the wood-and-paper shutters that formed them.

The first thing then was the bath. Japanese are the cleanest people on earth. There are few indeed who do not take a hot bath every day, though this may be in a barrel outside the house shared in descending succession of age by the whole family from grandfather to the youngest child. In the inns, the little *mousemés* or *nésan*, the serving maids, would bring clean bathing kimonos to our room and stand by while we undressed, giggling over the queer clothes we took off and the whiteness of our skins. Then they would help us into the kimonos and lead us down the narrow stairs to the bath.

There we would remove our kimonos, soap ourselves over until the mousemés handed us buckets of warm water with which to sluice off the soap; and quite clean, slip into the rectangular wooden bath, all together, to parboil quietly for a few minutes. If anyone else happened to reach the inn at about the same time that we did, he—or she—would be almost sure to arrive in the bath with us. It was all very *intime*, in its way.

After crawling slowly out of the bath so as not to stir up any waves to scald our skins, and being dried off by the mousmés with steaming cotton towels dipped in very hot water and then wrung out—surprisingly effective for the purpose—we put our kimonos on again and returned up the steep stairs to our room. Three little tables about fourteen inches high would be placed in a row, and after a few cups of warm *saké*, the Japanese rice wine, we would take our evening meal cross-legged or squatting on our heels upon the mats. There would always be rice, beautifully done; sometimes broiled trout; often raw or pickled fish which one got used to; and usually a sort of seaweed and other strange appearing messes that turned out to be not unappetizing when one tried them. I had already become fairly handy with chop-sticks.

Arnell was an interesting character who knew Japan probably as well as any non-Japanese. He was something of a Lafcadio Hearn, though without the latter's genius for painting pictures in the written word. He appreciated Japanese virtues, of which there were many; and while recognizing the faults which they also possessed, he ascribed these in large part to the sudden transition from feudalism less than fifty years before to a confused and uncertain attempt at Westernization. In this attempt the Western powers and their nationals had not been particularly helpful preceptors, and the Japanese absorbed many of the less estimable features of our so-called civilization while seeking a substitute for the Oriental feudalism that was all they had ever known.

"Also," said Arnell, "the Japanese are naïve. Take their mixed bathing, for instance. They're quite accustomed to bathing together naked. They see nothing wrong or immoral in this. Nor do I. Morality very often runs in the inverse ratio to the amount of clothes worn—the fewer clothes (I do not mean when they are peeled off for effect) the greater the morality. That is, along with certain other things, where I disagree with the missionaries."

On a small island southwest of Sumatra, known as the "Island of the Naked" because the natives wore nothing except a few decorative strings of beads, I had been told that sexual morality was higher than perhaps anywhere else on the globe.

"In Tokyo," Arnell continued, "there are many bathing establishments that cater to both sexes, at the same hours, in the same large baths. They are very popular. As far as I have heard, there has never been an unpleasant incident in any of them. But lately the missionaries reproached the Tokyo municipal authorities for permitting such an unseemly practice as joint bathing of ungarbed males and females in public bathing establishments.

" 'It is wrong, bad and dangerous, and is *not* done in the West,' they said." (Those missionaries obviously had never been to Finland.) "The Tokyo Municipality did not understand any of this except that bathing together by both sexes without clothes was not done in the West. They don't understand what advantage is obtained from taking a bath with clothes on rather than without, but they are keenly desirous of following Western manners. So they recently passed an edict that mixed bathing in public bath houses is forbidden, unless the bath is separated into two parts—one part for men and one for women—or if not separated, then the bathers must wear costumes.

"Meticulously," continued Arnell, "and with no thought of evading the spirit or the letter of the edict which they do not comprehend, the owners of the bathing establishments now follow one of two courses. Some of them place a slim bamboo pole midway across the large communal bath, on one side of which the naked men bathe, on the other side the naked women. No one tries to pass over or dive under the pole because that sort of thought is not in their minds.

"Other owners have maintained their baths as they were, undivided, but the bathers have to wear costumes which the management provides. The management also provides a large dressing room in which their clients of both sexes meet, disrobe, bow solemnly to one another, put on the unaccustomed and inconvenient bathing togs that the West has ordained, and enter the bath furtively, feeling that there is something a bit immoral about the whole procedure. Then they come out, take off their bathing garments in the communal dressing room, dry themselves off and chat for a while before putting on their clothes to go home. They don't feel really well bathed, but if that is part of Westernization, they say, so be it."

One night we spent in an inn which was different from the ordinary run of "tea houses" in that our room was not completely devoid of furnishings. At one end stood a large Western object, a plain, rectangular chest with three drawers. It gave an odd effect in that otherwise purely Japanese room. Arnell called for the proprietor of the inn after we had finished our evening meal and the mousmés were bringing in our bedding to spread on the mats.

"How," he asked the proprietor, indicating the chest of drawers, "did you happen to come by that?" The proprietor looked puzzled. It had always been there, he said, as long as he could remember. He thought that his father had received it, a long time ago, from some foreign ship captain in Kobe as part payment for certain commodities he had furnished. His father had been dead these many years.

"And for what do you use it now?" Arnell inquired. It was not used, the proprietor said; it just stood there. Arnell examined the chest. "Do you permit that we look inside?" he asked.

"Honorable opening deign," said the proprietor, sucking in his breath. We pulled on the drawers which had not been opened for years; after a struggle they yielded to our efforts: They were full of Japanese prints.

"What are these things?" Arnell asked, knowing quite well what they were. The proprietor said that they were pictures, that his father used to like such things, but that since his father's death they had all been put away. With the proprietor's consent we went over them. Mostly they were crude, but amongst the lot were some splendid prints by several of the best known eighteenth- and early nineteenth-century masters: Utamaro, Hokusai, Hiroshige, Okyo, Harunobu and others.

Arnell asked the proprietor whether, since he did not appear to care for the pictures and they rather amused us, he would sell us a few we particularly liked. We would pay him a yen a piece for them, said Arnell. (A yen was then the equivalent of fifty cents.) The proprietor diffidently expressed his opinion that the pictures were not worth such an amount, but if we insisted he would be glad to make the exchange at our price. We made two piles: a big one of discards, a smaller one of very worthwhile prints. The latter pile, at the end of the division, contained thirty-six. We matched coins to see who would have first, second and third choice to start with, and in the same order went through the small pile three at a time.

That was how I acquired my Japanese prints.

It was in the course of another trip the same year that I first went to Gifu, driving a four-cylinder Packard with my mother and a Chinese "boy." Since then much water has poured down the Nagaragawa river, and many pink-fleshed trout have passed into the capacious gullets of the cormorants that fish its limpid waters for the masters who disgorge their catch onto the bottoms of sampans lighted by red-flaring torches.

In those days the Japanese—in any event the ones who lived in the interior and had not been corrupted by the less amiable features of Western manners—were gentle, friendly and courteous to foreigners such as myself, who spoke their language only in the parrot-patter extracted from a phrase-book. They also were greatly intrigued by the strange automotive contraption I drove over their meandering roads, across their flimsy bridges and narrow, hump-backed granite culverts which made progress around the innumerable right-angle turns a fanciful problem of engineering.

To reach Gifu then by motorcar was a test of one's ingenuity, patience and luck. Following the winding Nakasendo, the "Central Mountain Road" into Mino Province, involved processes that even in those days were unusual in motoring over one of the main highways of a populous country: such, for instance, as hauling the car out of numerous deep gullies on the chainfalls (an essential item of equipment at that time for motoring in Japan) after the rotting bridges across the chasms had collapsed under our weight.

The road wandered in aimless fashion over paddy fields, perpetually turned away from its course in 90° angles, played hide-and-seek amongst the houses of the drawn-out towns. At each town we came to there was a strong doubt of being able to get through without taking the automobile or some of the houses apart. The streets were scarcely wider than the car, which scraped on both sides between tiny booths jutting out beyond their neighbors, while the windshield had frequently to be folded to avoid the low, overhanging eaves.

In every town the streets were alive with babies, sprawling at various games, who tried to pat the car as it passed or were content to sit and gurgle in its path until my Chinese boy clambered out and pulled them aside. Innumerable others, slightly larger, came dashing full speed from the houses, with frantic mothers following in hot pursuit to drag their offspring distractedly from one side of the road to the other.

There were not only babies athwart our path. Wooden tubs, boards with washed clothing spread out to dry, small stands displaying pinwheels, pushcarts full of odd, indigestible foods, *shoji* (paper shutters) being repapered, straw pans spread with drying rice, and countless other obstructions blocked our way and had to be removed. But the ubiquitous Japanese telegraph poles were unyielding, and in combination with the low roofs of dumpy little houses sometimes stymied all my efforts to get around the narrow corners. Then it would be necessary to make a scouting expedition afoot to map a possible course through the congested town or village.

During these surveying jaunts I sometimes wandered far. As we never stopped for as much as two minutes without the whole town becoming aware of our advent and seething out to look us over, I found that to follow the crowd was the simplest way of getting back to where I had left the car. On one occasion this expedient failed to work. There was an even greater attraction than ourselves in the town that day. I eventually found myself in the midst of a huge fête in the grounds of a Buddhist temple.

Seated on a low chair outside the main building, surrounded by great numbers of devotees, was a wooden statue of Binzuru with a red cloth cap and a white bib around his neck. Although dismissed from among the sixteen Rakan, Buddha's disciples, for breaking his vow of chastity in speaking of the beauty of a certain woman, Buddha conferred upon him the power of curing all human ills, wherefore he is a very popular deity. Each pilgrim in passing the squat figure rubbed his hand over some part of the statue and then upon the corresponding part of his own person. Sore eyes seemed to be the prevalent disease in that locality, for all traces of the eyes of the statue had been completely worn away. One might suspect that the dumpy wooden image may have had something to do with preserving the popular complaint, since there are few surer methods of spreading a disease than this way of seeking a cure.

My map showed only about half the roads, and that half inaccurately. After crossing a mountain range to a broad plain we were confronted by the characteristic moss-covered tile roofs of a large inland town. In my parrot-Japanese I accosted a one-eyed man who was the first to come up and gape at the unusual vehicle.

"Here as for, what say place is?"

"Here as for, Ogaki is," he replied. I feared that would be the answer, having hoped to avoid Ogaki which was some miles off our course.

"Gifu to, goes road as for, which by is?"

"Gifu?" he repeated. "Gifu?" He turned his head to one side and with his single eye gazed into the air in the comical, bird-like expression which a Japanese assumes when he cannot answer a question but is unwilling to admit it.

"Gifu-Gifu!" cried Chang Siu, my Chinese boy, whose name, though transliterated thus was pronounced Ching Say. But evidently the man had never heard of it, nor had any of the other dozen or so persons whom I asked. We had stopped at a crossing, blocking all traffic, and by now the streets in every direction were a solid mass of people squirming for closer views. I stood up and interrogated in phrase-book questions on one side while Chang Siu, whose Japanese was very feeble, stammered ineffectually on the other.

"No talkee samee here like Nagasaki side!" Chang Siu burst out, and subsided into perplexed silence.

"Next town as for, what that say place is?" I tried, pointing up one street after the other. But pointing merely confused them, for such sign language meant nothing to a Japanese; and the town names I did glean from my questioning meant nothing to me, since they were not on my map. In the end I laboriously wrung a spark of recognition from one of the crowd after endless repetition of the word "Gifu."

"Straight-in honorable exit deign," said he, and bowed, with a hiss of indrawn breath.

"*Arigato!*"—thank you—I replied, and we started off. The clatter of *geta*, wooden clogs built up on stilts above the mud, and shouts of laughter did not die way as rapidly as they should have on leaving the crowd behind.

"Chang Siu!" I cried to the back seat, slowing up, "chase off children from luggage!" Chang Siu leaned over the rear of the car, armed with a folded paper parasol.

"Plenty child!" he exclaimed, grinning, and pried off numerous small fry who clung to all parts of the trunk or dashed breathlessly along behind hanging onto the loosened strap ends.

The "honorable exit" was straight for a few blocks only, then bore abruptly to the left, flanked by low houses with wide overhanging roofs. In the center of the corner a sharply arched, heavy granite culvert, just five feet wide, bridged a deep gutter and, together with a clump of telegraph poles planted thickly alongside, challenged our passage. There was no other way to turn. After a prolonged interval of backing and filling, a few inches at a time, I accomplished the feat before a rapidly increasing audience which obviously failed to comprehend why we wanted to perform such maneuvers. Was the foolish *jidosha*—go-wagon—afraid to cross, that it kept jumping ahead and jumping back? The interested spectators had never found any difficulty in taking their two-wheeled carts over that bridge; why should we make such a task of it? The drawbacks of a 125-inch wheelbase did not enter into their calculations.

In the next mile or so this performance was repeated some seven times and began to grow tedious. After every few turns I had to stop and again go through the involved process of asking directions. When I did succeed in obtaining any light on the way to proceed, which was infrequent, it invariably required turning again; and no street that we were on ran more than a few hundred yards without ending at some house-front and starting off afresh at a right-angle.

I finally escaped from the long-protracted town and there was momentary relief, but it did not last. The road, which was almost exactly the width of the car, strayed purposelessly across

the flat rice fields, changed its direction squarely a dozen times
to the mile, and seemingly was laid out to cover as much distance as possible in getting to no obvious destination. In a few
miles of level plain we encountered thirty-seven right-angle turns,
with irrigation ditches on each side, stone culverts at the corners,
and barely the width of the car to reverse in. But we reached
Gifu, after having gone several miles on the opposite compass
bearing, presumably—from my inarticulate map—to cross a large
river, where the road played a last joke by bringing us directly
back again.

Darkness had fallen, and small lights sprang out as we
entered the town, passing between the rows of tiny houses, each
in the same style as its neighbor though no two were identical.
Lines of upright wooden bars guarded their ground floors; while
their *shoji*, the oiled paper shutters, formed glowing squares of
dull yellow light in the dark, upon which the shadows of figures
inside, kneeling or flitting silently across the rooms, made entertaining silhouettes. Other figures scarcely less shadowy clumped
past along the edge of the street and turned in at different houses,
leaving behind their wooden clogs as they slid back the *amado*,
the heavier wooden shutters, and disappeared within. Slowly
through the streets we passed, catching brief glimpses into open
interiors, where shopkeepers knelt amongst their wares on thick
mats of rice straw and chatted over shallow, diminutive cups of
tea; or smoked long-stemmed pipes with tiny bowls beside the
hibachi, the charcoal braziers, with their customers.

The Tsunokuni-ya inn at Gifu had a narrow court between
it and the street, enclosed by a high wooden wall with a covered
gate. I left the car outside while I made arrangements for rooms,
but the crowd which gathered was so large and so intensely curious that I dared not leave it within their reach unguarded over
night. The inn-keeper proposed that I drive it into the courtyard. I measured the width of the opening and found it identical
to that of the car. It also was evident that the gates could not

be closed after the car was inside, but there seemed nothing to do but try it. As I drove through, the hub caps scraped along both sides and I had to duck my head—the windshield being lowered—to avoid bashing it on the fixed cross-bar of the gate.

As the front wheels came up against the inn's raised floor, the acetylene headlights glaring into the rooms beyond startled several nésan, the little serving maids, into precipitate flight. The rear end of the car with the trunk upon the rack still projected some three feet beyond the gate. This blocked the foot-path, while the long rear hub-caps touching on each side effectively closed the courtyard opening. Chang Siu and the proprietor were holding a staccato conversation as I stopped the engine and got out. Then Chang Siu came up and announced: "He say now turn round!"

I explained as clearly as I was able that I would be glad to do so, but it would first be necessary to take down the inn and rebuild it differently. The proprietor was not satisfied.

"He say, yes can do!" said Chang Siu, who always spoke very fast. I did not argue but merely shook my head. The inn-keeper drew attention to the gates which could not be shut, and to the obvious fact that no one could get in or out without crawling under the car. I was unmoved. I could not very well turn the car around in a court ten feet by fifteen, when it was touching in front and against projections on both sides. Making the best of the situation which he still failed to comprehend, the proprietor chased out several children who had wedged themselves inside, and rigged up a barricade of bamboo ladders, ropes and poles around the end of the car. This kept back the crowd, a precaution that was becoming necessary though they were mainly small fry, for already they had acquired two grease-cups and several cotter-pins and their appetite was whetted for more loot.

We removed our shoes and went inside the inn, while Chang Siu carried the small luggage upstairs. The trunk on the rear rack could not be brought inside except over the ten-foot wall. It remained sticking out into the street during the night, and was found undisturbed in the morning. Japanese in those days, at least in the parts away from the so-called Treaty Ports, were not addicted to thievery, though their young were in no wise averse to acquiring souvenirs.

By the inn stairs there hung a card with the announcement:

"Tsunokuni-ya—Only hotel in Gifu accomodates for forgien guest. Electric lightning. Agent met at station in receipt notice.

What is that one which tourists in Japan, shall not forget to see once? Ukai the world-wide known Ayu fishing by cormorants on river Nagara. Fishing commences on ehe 11th of May yearly and ends on 15th October from 6 P.M. to 12 P.M. every evening. Unless the full moon night and the river water swells to prevent. Celebrate sights and scenes."

Gifu was famous for this nightly fishing, which doubtless is still carried on though I have not been there of recent years to participate in it. I attempted to gather some information from the inn-keeper but he spoke no English, and as cormorant fishing was rather too complicated either for my Japanese or that of Chang Siu, we did not make much progress. Many Japanese who have studied English in their schools can read and write the language to some extent without being able to speak it at all. The inn-keeper was one of these. He was the author of the enlightening sign on the stairs. When our conversation had died a natural death, he bowed himself over to a six-inch-high desk in the corner and set to work with a large blue pencil. After twenty minutes of arduous labor he produced the following communication which told me just what I wanted to know:

"We have receive a report, the fishing become early. please take a supper on with heast. (You must go to the river by in Rikisha on 7.20 o'clock). I have much obliged for you. ayhow it is fishing I can't tell you exact time."

So we "heastily" took on a supper of broiled *ayu* (fine pink-fleshed trout caught by the cormorants) and afterwards clambered by a back way out of the inn, through another house, and were whirled in rikisha down to the Nagaragawa.

Out upon the river many red torches were moving slowly through the darkness, and thick columns of crimson smoke mounted lazily in the still air. Beneath the glowing flares shadowy sampans gradually took shape, with queer, dimly outlined tackle and mysterious straw-coated figures. Below us, in a backwater of the river, floated a tiny oblong boat whose waving paper lantern signalled us to come down.

The steep bank dropped behind as we were poled into midstream, sitting cross-legged on the boat's flat bottom under a woven rattan awning that barely cleared our heads, the distorted image of the paper lantern dancing fantastically in the ripples at our side. Above the scraping of the bamboo pole a raucous cackling drifted over the water, and as our little craft drew into one of the torchlit circles the droll faces of twelve bright-eyed birds, seated in line on the gunwale of a sampan, peered solemnly down upon us from out of the crimsoned gloom.

The oldest bird, a grizzled veteran of many seasons, occupied the head position near the bow, and each of the others had his own rank and place according to his years and experience. Woe to the unfortunate fisher-fowl that accidentally or otherwise usurps a seat above his station, or whom the master lowers into or raises from the water out of turn! The clever *ukai*—the cormorants—are great sticklers for precedence and express their disapproval in no uncertain terms, nor is the offender gently treated by his comrades.

Attached to a harness about the body of each bird a strong cord was held by the master in the bow. As an expert driver tools his four-in-hand, so he, with marvellous skill, directed his birds, both in and out of the water. While we watched he dropped them one by one into the river, lowering "Ichi"—the privileged "Number One" *ukai*—last, all the while keeping perfect order with their dozen reins.

There were three men in the sampan besides the master. One assisted him with the birds; one did the steering and sculling of the sampan with a large oar astern; the third stoked the fire of charcoal fagots in a wire basket swung on a rod out over the gunwale. The blaze of the charcoal flare, together with much shouting and beating on the side of the boat, attracted the fish in swarms. In the semicircle of light from the beacon flame the cormorants ducked and dived in hilarious, though methodical, fashion.

Hot ashes dropping from the torch sizzled as they struck the water, but the birds worked steadily on. Frequently all would be under water at one time, surfacing only to let their captures slip endwise down into their gullets. In the clear, shallow river we could see them darting about under the red glow of the flare, zigzagging back and forth at lightning speed as they ran down and caught their dodging prey close to the river's bottom. A small ring—never removed—encircled each long neck and prevented the catch from passing into the bird's stomach, though large enough to admit smaller, unmarketable fish for food.

From six to ten good-sized *ayu*, or river trout, fill up a cormorant's gullet. The gorged bird then lurches helplessly about with its swollen neck held rigid in the air. But the master in the bow, watching intently as he controls his flock with long, stiff reins, is quick to note the signs. Without disturbing or entangling the other birds, each gorged one is dragged into the sampan, with one movement of the hand made to deliver its catch, and dropped back into the water for another raid.

The work of the cormorants is astonishing, though hardly more so than the marvellous skill of the master. (In olden days in England the Master of the Cormorants was one of the officers of the royal household.) With what rapidity the birds—and the master—work is evidenced by the fact that while each trip nets only six to ten fish to each bird, a cormorant working under good conditions will average from one hundred to one-hundred-fifty trout an hour, and a top-notch bird can catch five hundred fish in a night.

Other crimson patches in the darkness told where the rest of the fleet was operating. In amongst them drifted numerous flat-bottomed boats similar to the one we were in, all gay with fat pink lanterns and filled with Japanese men and women as interested as we. Soft strains of *samisen* (guitars) and fragments of Oriental songs floated over the water as we followed along with the fleet, while the eddying surface twinkled with reflected torches and paper lanterns. The sampans worked gradually across the river. When the opposite shore was reached the birds were taken in, made—despite vigorous protests—to disgorge the last of their catch, and placed in loquacious rows back upon the gunwales.

In lifting each bird the master could tell by its weight whether or not it had caught enough small fish for its own supper. Some of the *ukai* were found a bit light, so a few of the poorer fish were cut into pieces and snapped up by them voraciously. To show how the catching was done the master of one of the boats threw eight or nine squirming *ayu* on the floor of his craft and set a cormorant amidst them. With hardly more than a single sweep of the bird's long bill the fish all disappeared into the *ukai's* capacious gullet. Then the master passed one hand up the cormorant's neck in the reverse process of milking a cow, forcing open its bill with the other, and the fish shot out again with equal rapidity although the bird protested with loud indignation.

Presently the sampans were poled downstream to their respective beaching places. As they passed, row after row of wise, solemn cormorant faces gazed at us from the gunwales. They disappeared in the darkness, but the fading chatter of *ukai* voices continued to drift back as we crossed over to the other side of the river. Then silence fell once more, and there remained only the red spots of the dying flares, flickering distantly. Soon they, too, vanished into the night.

MORE LIGHT FROM THE EAST

I HAVE A LITTLE Tibetan gadget that represents the acme of painless religious observance or, in any event, of prayer. It is a prayer-wheel, in the form of a three-inch cylinder of ornamented bronze mounted on a stick which is held in the hand and whirled with a slight rotary movement. The devout can keep this up almost indefinitely, while carrying on their normal occupations. A short chain with a small, octagonal bronze weight at its end revolves the cylinder under the activation of a gently moving wrist.

The devotee writes out his prayer and inserts it in the cylinder. With each revolution a prayer is said. Almost effortlessly, a comparatively untrained utterer of prayers can keep up an average of five revolutions a second, three hundred a minute, eighteen thousand an hour. That amounts to a respectable lot of praying.

Père Olart is amused by this devotional mechanization. I doubt if he ever has prayed, though he is one of the official pall-bearers at Vézelay and quite frequently informs me in the morning that he has to leave early: he must go back to his cottage and shave, there is to be an interment at eleven o'clock. Occasionally this is of some young Vézelayan who was killed in the Resistance or died in a German prison camp, and whose body has been brought back to repose in the chestnut-shaded cemetery on a terrace just below the basilica, overlooking the now peaceful valley of Asquins.

But Père Olart feels that, should one really wish to pray, to be able to do so with a mere twist of the wrist at the rate of eighteen thousand prayers an hour is undoubtedly a labor-saving device on which he would not frown. As a general thing he is unreceptive to innovations. With the innate conservatism of the French peasant he inclines to regard with disfavor most of my suggestions in such way for the garden—I admit that few have been advanced—but that is primarily because he is old and accustomed to maintaining the garden in his own fashion. His memory is excellent, and memory *au fond* is hostile to innovation.

I acquired the Tibetan prayer-wheel many years ago in Darjeeling, the Indian hill station close to the southern border of Sikkim. The scenery around Darjeeling, with its background of "the world's great white roof-tree"—the highest range of mountains on our planet—is indescribably grand: formation piled upon formation, with the valleys carved sheer to depths little above sea-level. Through one of the more distant chasms, though not visible from Darjeeling, runs the holiest of all rivers. In its setting of massive pine forests, at 7100 feet altitude, Darjeeling's climate is remarkably even and salubrious throughout the year.

The local residents and those who come in to trade are a curious assortment of Himalayan, Tibetan, Chinese and Indian types. Lepchas, the aboriginal inhabitants of the hilly district of Darjeeling, mingle with incomers from Nepal, Mechs, Bhutanese, Sikkimese and Tibetans, for many of whom a seven-thousand-foot altitude represents a considerable descent from their accustomed habitations. Mostly they are hillmen, and the "hills" of the Himalayas, where people live and thrive in a rarefied atmosphere, are not quite like the highlands of Western experience. Darjeeling means "place of the thunderbolt."

I recall an evening at Singapore, perhaps fifteen feet above sea-level, with a group of men of different ages forgathered as was their wont around a table in the Club for a few rounds of drinks before dinner. As elsewhere in the East they rolled dice for each round, an excellent custom in that a late arrival feels no hesitation in joining a group at a table or bar, takes his chance of paying for a round or perhaps more, has a drink or so with his friends and, in the improbable event of not wanting another, can leave without embarrassment or any sense of obligation to buy

a round before he goes. It works out pretty evenly over the course
of time.

That evening there was at the table a young man of about
my age who had been brought by one of the regular members, as
I had been. He had just arrived from Europe on his way around
the world and was rather full of himself for having climbed
Mont Blanc during his tour. With the third round of pink gins
and *stingahs* (half-sized whisky-and-sodas) he began to expatiate
on the beauties of mountain-climbing in general.

"You fellows down here in this steaming heat," he said, "I'd
think you'd all want to get up into the Himalayas and climb
mountains during your holidays. It would do you no end of
good, and mountain-climbing is the greatest sport on earth. It
gives you a sense of superiority over Nature, if you understand
what I mean. When I reached the top of Mont Blanc I felt that
I'd really conquered something. Highest mountain in Europe,
you know."

Mont Blanc has an altitude of 15,780 feet. There is a well-
marked trail all the way to the top, with aids for the climber im-
planted along the rougher passages. One is not permitted to make
the ascent unless accompanied by a licensed guide who knows
the trail by heart. While it is a stiff pull requiring good legs and
lungs and there is the chance that one may be caught in a blizzard part way up, with consequent unpleasantnesses, it is not
really a difficult climb in itself.

"But how many of you go up to the Himalayas and climb
mountains?" pursued the young man. "They're not too far away
from here, if you take a fast boat to Calcutta. Quite easy, in fact,
with a month's holiday. But do you do it?" He became a bit
challenging. There was a moment of silence. "I'm inclined to
bet you don't. It's a pity. Mountaineering makes you all intimate
with Nature, and above her, so to speak."

A moderately sized man of perhaps thirty-four with a deeply
tanned face, sitting on the opposite side of the table from the
young Alpine climber, slowly refilled and relighted his pipe.
When the tobacco took the flame he looked up.

"I've just come down from India for my holiday," he said, speaking very quietly but perhaps with some intent for the non-mountain climbing group at the Club table, in reply to the young man who had conquered the Alps. "I don't have much time to do any mountain climbing, as such, though I've knocked around a good bit at fairly useful altitudes. I belong to the Survey of India, you know. I spent most of last summer up in the Himalayas, surveying some of the ridges." He struck another match and held it to his pipe while he puffed.

"We don't call them mountains up there," he continued, "except for a few really high peaks. We call them hills. My camp was usually at about 19,000 feet. I had to send porters down to 17,000 feet for my drinking water, where they could chop their way through to a spring. The doctors say that snow water, over a period of time, is bad for one—I don't quite know why. Gives you goiter, or something. I was up in the hills for about three months, so I followed their precautions."

Our glasses were empty. Someone at the table reached for the dice. We heard no more about conquering Nature from Mont Blanc.

Many of the types one saw milling about Darjeeling's open markets bore the unmistakable stamp of hillfolk. Their faces were deeply tanned by the sun; their eyes had a look that comes from gazing over vast distances. Their clothing was heavy against the cold and the winds of high altitudes.

Most of the men wore long, padded coats belted at the waist, and upward-flaring, round hats. The women were more picturesquely garbed than the men. Their dark hair, parted in the middle, was drawn down tightly and roped in a heavy pigtail or twin side braids. Large, elaborately wrought silver ornaments dangled from their ears, and long strings of ornamental beads hung around their necks over embroidered waistcoats.

Their skirts or long overgarments were fashioned of coarsely woven striped material, tied around the waist. Some had jackets

with fur cuffs. In the way of foot-gear they wore leather mocca-
sins turned up at the toes, over heavy wool socks. Many carried
large, Swiss-type baskets on their backs (one saw no men so
equipped), supported by a broad, embroidered tump-line over
their foreheads.

The women porters of Darjeeling were stout carriers in those
days. I presume they have not lost their prowess. I watched them
tramping stolidly up the steep road with three five-gallon tins
of kerosene on their backs, a good hundred pounds of weight
including the wooden pack, which I was informed was considered a moderate load. One woman toted a piano without as-
sistance up the nearly seven-thousand-foot ascent from the foot
of the hill. I did not see her do this, but she was not unduly
weary, I was told, when she delivered the item to its destination.

The Tibetans and Sikkimese in Darjeeling gathered nightly
to watch a kind of pantomime performed by Tibetan actors in
the open, under the light of torches. This was extremely well
done, with humor and imagination, rhythm, and a marvellous
sense of mimicry. I have never seen anything of its kind presented with quite such verve. The Tibetans and Sikkimese loved
it and applauded loudly, especially when the performers, all men,
dressed up as dragons and did a sinuous dance which would have
had a terrific success in Paris, London or New York.

Though the view of the Himalayan *massif* from Darjeeling
was splendid, one could see the great range and the glory of the
sunrise on its peaks far more effectively from an adjacent summit called Tiger Hill, about fifteen hundred feet higher as I recall it, where there was a government rest house. I rode up there
one afternoon on a small but sturdy Himalayan pony, followed
by my Indian servant Anthony on another pony, carrying my
gear.

The trail was steep and narrow, now on the edge of an
abrupt declivity, now overarched by towering conifers. The
ponies took it easily, with a shuffling mountain stride. About
halfway to the summit I caught up and passed another rider

heading toward the same destination. He was a tall, long-legged man on a very small pony, with his feet stuck out so as not to drag on the sides, as if he were on a sled. He evidently was a European. I made a salutation of sorts as I passed him, and he raised his hat in response.

Late in the afternoon, having started after lunch, I reached the rest house on Tiger Hill. The mountains were shrouded in cloud. I went to the edge of the narrow, flat summit and looked down into the valley well more than a mile below. There were tea plantations down there, but I could not see them in the purple shadows of afternoon. When I returned to the rest house the tall man on the small pony whom I had passed part way up the trail had arrived.

His servant was carrying his gear into the bungalow, and I noticed the marking, "Count Hermann Keyserling." He was the German metaphysician, who later wrote *The Travel Diary of a Philosopher* about the world tour he was then making, in which he described certain of the sensations produced in him by the Himalayas. Among his less abstruse impressions he wrote: "I have never faced such overwhelming substance. Never have I, the stranger, felt such wings given to my soul. In the Himalayas man is marvellously near to God. This nature widens the limits of consciousness more than any other on earth." And further: "While I am looking out upon the snow-covered peaks . . . a nameless longing burns within me to get altogether beyond the limits of personal existence."

We were the only occupants of the rest house. The mountains were invisible; so we dined together on the food we both had brought, prepared by the rest house keeper and our two Indian servants. As the mists failed to lift we talked into the evening. I was some years the younger, at an age when the difference counted more than it would have later, and I was no metaphysician; but I had several stories of experiences in India that interested him. When he turned to philosophy, though I was an intent listener, he soon progressed well beyond my conceptions of a subject in which my knowledge was confined to what I had acquired from an undergraduate course at Princeton University.

In studying nations, he said, he sought to view things from the mental outlook and inner spirit of the peoples whom he was among, to share their method of life as far as possible. This seemed an excellent approach, and one which I could follow appreciatively; but he went away beyond it. My mind began to reel. I felt that I was an uninstructed and unimaginative realist, or else that he had seized a metaphysical dragon by the tail.

I cannot recall, precisely, much of what he said, for my brain was too bewildered and my thoughts kept swinging to the mountains that I had come to view. But as he warmed to his theme his discussion was not very different in substance from certain passages I now quote from his *Travel Diary*.

"No, essentially I am not a human being; my humanity is accidental . . . or necessary, just as one happens to take it, but certainly no more. In the air of the Himalayas, which gives wings to the mind as no other, the singular tragedy of my existence becomes painfully plain to me." And again: " 'Essentially' I am no more Hermann Keyserling than an animal or a tree or any other human being, and if it seems different it is not my fault. Never, throughout the whole of my life, have I felt myself to be identical with my person, nor regarded what is personal as essential; never felt myself affected by what I was and did, what I suffered and what happened to me."

Now this sort of thing was pretty strong mental meat for a full-blooded youth intent on getting such sensations as life had to offer, but in my own person. Keyserling felt himself to be so little identical with 'himself' that he thought he should be able to change his bodily substance, like Proteus; though he admits that he had later to disavow the Protean goal. I, too, would occasionally like to manifest myself as a tree or an animal or perhaps another human being, for a limited period, and return to myself to evaluate such experience as I may have gained. But to disassociate myself completely from my personality, to feel that "my person is not identical with myself," is beyond the grasp of my mind, nor can I conceive of this as an ultimate goal.

I am not a philosopher, or should perchance I have developed to any modest degree in such respect, my philosophy differs from that of Count Hermann Keyserling—if indeed I approach an understanding of his. I, too, agree that the air of the Himalayas gives wings to the mind as perhaps no other air. But what I felt in that environment was the singular fortune of being alive and able to appreciate it, even if not to the whole range of its implications. I had neither the ability nor the wish to divorce myself from my personality, though feeling no particular self-satisfaction in that personality.

Perhaps, again quoting Keyserling, I am one of those "inward natures of small intelligence" who "do not need to understand before that which is alive in their soul becomes real in their consciousness." But whether or not I understood, something became clear in my consciousness under the immensity of the Himalayan upheaval. And it was this: how vastly more soul-filling an effect the infinite silence and mystery of that upheaval had upon me than any metaphysical dissertation on the matter of being.

When it was evident that the mists enveloping the mountains were unlikely to break that night, we said adieu to each other and repaired to our separate cubicles. Very early in the morning I was awakened from a sound sleep on my camp cot by my servant Anthony. He woke me in his own fashion: I have never been so awakened by anyone but Anthony. It was at once the quietest and one of the most effective awakenings of any that I have experienced. He gently encircled one of my wrists with his hand, very gradually increasing the pressure on it. I opened my eyes, to see him standing there bare-footed with a glass-shaded candle in his other hand. There was no shock, I was fully awake, and had not even twitched.

"Master, *mountains!*" he whispered. I rolled off the cot and put on a dressing gown, a pair of fleece-lined boots, a short fleece-lined overcoat and a fur cap. Led by Anthony I went outside the rest house into an opaque darkness, walking slowly with my head down for I wanted to get the full effect of the first rays of the sun on the eternal snows, to the edge of the flat-topped peak of Tiger Hill that fell sheer nearly seven thousand feet to the Ranjit valley below.

My first look was downward into the valley, which had the texture of black basalt. Where I stood, the darkness was of nightshade. There was no moon. I did not know whether there were any stars in the sky for I had not yet looked up.

Very slowly I raised my eyes, more than a perpendicular mile upwards over darkly toned steep slopes; up, far up beyond this, now searching for the mountains until my tense gaze came to a pale bank of cloud, well above where I thought the peaks should have shown themselves at a distance of a hundred miles away.

I felt a sharp sense of disappointment. The clouds, or mists, had evidently covered the mountains: I would not see the sunrise on them, this morning in any event. I had been too slow in looking up, now they were invisible. The mists must have risen to enshroud them in the short space of time since Anthony had awakened me so gently with his report: "Master, mountains!"

Damning myself inwardly for my slowness in trying to get the full effect of the sunrise on the most formidable heights on this earth, I started to turn back, resolved to stay on Tiger Hill until the mountains should reveal themselves in the early sunlight, if it took a month. I glanced into the sky, wondering vaguely whether the stars were out. And then I saw the Titans of the Himalayan range, protruding far above the bank of clouds, all pink and roseate and mauve in the rays of the invisible sun.

At first I thought it was an illusion, an effect of cloud formations playing on my imagination. It seemed incredible that mountains could be that high, a hundred miles away. But the contours of Kanchanjanga, the world's second highest peak stabbing 28,000 feet into the heavens, were unmistakable, with the deep purple streaks down its center where the granite formation is too steep for snow or ice to cling to. Around this purple gash the rays of the unseen sun turned the slightly less precipitous slopes and the crevasses into a glowing marvel, so high above the clouds that it seemed to have no connection with our earthly sphere.

Mount Everest, whose Tibetan name of "Mother-Goddess of the Snows" is so much more appropriate than its more common English designation, glowed like a pear-shaped opal from its altitude of 29,000 feet; mysterious, secretive, unconquered by man; somewhat farther away to the west of Kanchanjanga. Tibetan superstition has it that the winds around its summit wail like the black hounds of hell. But where I stood, I have never sensed silence so complete. It has been said that silence is golden. To me, because of that unimaginable silence beneath the Himalayan snows, silence is silver.

The "Mother-Goddess of the Snows" was somewhat less effective than Kanchanjanga in the aspect from Tiger Hill, because her rose-pink summit lacked the great streak of contrasting purple of Kanchanjanga's uncovered rock. But the world's two highest mountains with their galaxy of slightly lesser satellites of the Great Himalayan range projecting far above the clouds, dimming the astral bodies in the first rays of the sun still hidden behind a blacked-out world, had an effect on me that no other manifestation of Nature has ever approached. No small part of the effect came from the mystic beauty of the silence beneath that glittering opalescent wall of perpetual snow.

The mists that hung around eighteen to twenty thousand feet crept upwards. After perhaps forty-five minutes they gradually veiled the mountains. I turned, and almost bumped into Count Keyserling standing close to my left shoulder. I had not been aware that he was there. We walked back to the rest house in the dark of night. The mountains had disappeared. We said nothing. Though he may have approached closer to the infinite than I, yet I think our feelings at that moment were not dissimilar.

We lay on our camp cots for an hour or so, then had breakfast while our servants packed our gear and saddled our ponies for the return to Darjeeling. We spoke little, and never mentioned the mountains. The intensity of thc impression of those forty-five minutes in the magic of the silence under the star-stabbing peaks was too close and too overwhelming to profane with any comment.

I have in my lounge upon the hillside, within the purview of M'sieur Buddha, a few Chinese bronzes. M'sieur Buddha, I feel, approves of these, because though he is from Siam the bronzes reflect a distinct buddhistic influence. Some of them I picked up in Pekin when that walled city, then capital of the Middle Kingdom, was perhaps the most agreeable and interesting spot in all Asia for Westerners to reside in, and one of the more highly prized diplomatic posts of the world.

Other of the bronzes I acquired in Canton and Shanghai. There was a very good antiquary in Shanghai in those days, just after the Sun Yat-Sen revolution, whose name I have now forgotten. He was a splendid type of the old regime, an intellectual with a thin and straggly beard, kindly eyes behind a pair of horn-rimmed spectacles which he always took off in greeting me and in bidding me farewell, and an ineffable politeness of manner. He wore beautifully embroidered silk garments in the classic Chinese style.

I spent many pleasant hours in his shop, drinking tea and smoking cigarettes with him, talking about a wide variety of subjects—he spoke quaint but adequate English—and now and then haggling in a friendly manner over the prices of *objets d'art*. From him I gained some insight into the character of a cultured Chinese and a deep appreciation of Chinese courtesy, as it was then.

In his shop, filled with the treasures of past ages, chatting and laughing with that gentle old man who showed the greatest tolerance for my youthful views and lack of proficiency in the Chinese code of etiquette, I felt that I was in China. This I have rarely sensed, despite the multitude of Chinese, in the former

International Concession of Shanghai. I liked and respected the old gentleman very much—more than anyone I met in Shanghai —and I think he liked me not merely as a potential customer but because I wholly lacked the feeling of superiority that so many of the Western "barbarians" exhibited towards Chinese irrespective of their mental attainment or background, and because in spite of the difference in our ages, nationality and languages, we could laugh together.

Shanghai has always impressed me as a somewhat crude though pretentious and expensive picture of modern materialistic civilization, if one can call it civilization. It is like an abstract painting in Western style with most of the faults and few of the virtues of East and West portrayed with calculated smugness. It has the bigness-complex of the new world, mostly unsupported by beauty, and the idolatry of the large bank account. It has scant regard for culture as such; and in the International Concession it used to be considered *infra dig* to associate with Chinese of any class, no matter what might be their urbanity, except in matters of trade.

Among other evidences of the bigness-complex, Shanghai boasted the longest bar in the world. (It still does, as far as I know.) I was informed of this quite often, with considerable pride. It was in the Shanghai Club, and most of the city's foremost business tycoons met there daily before lunch to down a few pink gins or Martinis while discussing matters of potential profit.

I used to visit that bar occasionally at the noon hour with friends, and they would find difficulty in forcing their way through three lines of cocktail drinkers to get a drink for me and for themselves. The bar was a hundred and four feet long, or thereabouts, in those days as I recall it. Later it was increased in length to a hundred and forty feet or so—I am not sure of the figure—and was still insufficient to take care of the noontime customers.

I did not return to Shanghai for some years. In 1929 I spent a short time there when it was the headquarters of an American financial mission striving earnestly though with but modest success to prop up the failing finances of China. Professor Kemmerer from Princeton, sometimes known as the "doctor of sick currencies," headed the mission.

The United States was then in the throes of prohibition. Professor Kemmerer, who was not much of a drinking man, deemed that Americans stationed abroad should maintain the precepts of their country, a sort of remote control so to speak. He gave a series of official dinners, all dry, in Shanghai of all places on this globe. They were held in the Hotel Majestic.

The first of them went off without undue incident other than the horrified astonishment of the guests when the waiters served a kind of pink lemonade, and nothing else but water. The second came a week or ten days later. Most of the people invited had been forewarned by stories of the first party, and took measures against the drought in advance.

Among these was an Englishman who had fortified himself with several cocktails beforehand. When the guests were seated at a large, oval table, Chinese boys circled round with glasses of pink fruit-juice on trays. One of the boys came to the Englishman.

"Master likee dlink?" he inquired.

"Yes," said the Englishman, looking the boy firmly in the eye. "Master likee one bottle whisky." The boy passed on. A little later he appeared with a bottle of Haig & Haig.

"Now pullee cork," said the Englishman, "and catchee one bottle fizz-water." The boy did as he was bid. The Englishman calmly poured himself a whisky-soda, placed the bottle in front of him and from time to time replenished his glass. He thoroughly enjoyed his dinner, ignoring a sharp personal unpopularity among certain of the other guests suffering from the pangs of thirst and of furious jealousy over his success.

"Well," said the Englishman afterwards, "I was asked if I would like a drink, was I not? I merely made it simpler for all concerned by saying what kind of drink I would like. My country hasn't yet been hit by prohibition, thank God!"

In Shanghai, the first time I went there, I heard a story of coastwise travel on the China Sea that stuck in my memory. It was not a particularly sympathetic story. It was recounted over sundown drinks by a man I met who had just returned after a trip from Hang-chow to Saigon on one of the vessels of the China Steam Navigation Company which plied up and down the coast, and on some voyages proceeded as far as Singapore. His name, not that it matters now, was Spotwell. He was an Englishman, as will be apparent from the fact that he dressed every night for dinner aboard that dingy little steamer.

The China Steam Navigation Company was a British-owned line operating British-built steamships of modest size under the China flag. Their crews were Chinese, their officers British. As usual throughout that part of the world, the chief engineers were nearly all Scottish, the captains and first mates Englishmen or Welsh, the ship's doctors also English. Many of them were very capable officers.

Most of them had some reason for navigating the China Seas which they did not talk about. It may have been trouble at home: financial, marital, perhaps a spot of bigamy, an upped check, or accidental death in circumstances that a cold-hearted judge might be disinclined to consider mitigating.

The Scottish engineers often had Chinese wives, or their equivalent, whom they were reluctant to leave. A few of the captains had lost previous ships and their master's certificates along with them, and could no longer operate as masters under the British flag, though it may have been a malevolent Fate rather than any dereliction of duty or lack of ability that brought their downfall.

The doctors were usually well qualified by training and experience, but not infrequently had some blot on their escutcheons which they wished to forget in the China Seas, or perhaps certain tastes that they found more readily gratified around those waters than on the conventional runs. It should not be inferred that all the officers had spotty pasts: simply that a number of them were too good in professional ability to spend their best years on little coastwise steamers plying the China Seas, had there not been some slip behind them.

Spotwell had taken passage on one of these steamers from Hang-chow to the south. He was, he said, the only first class passenger. There were no second or third class passengers; but there were eight hundred and eighteen fourth class passengers. These were Chinese coolies going to Singapore to work on the rubber plantations or in the tin mines of Malaya.

They slept all over the ship, but mostly on the open deck under awnings, stretched out in rows like a fine-tooth comb on such bedding as they had brought with them. Throughout the day and most of the night they chattered in sing-song intonations, smoked tobacco and opium, combed the lice from their hair, and slept noisily on and off.

Twice a day they were aroused by a bell and filed in a long line past two immense cauldrons astern from one of which the insides of ducks and of fish and other unappetizing offal were ladled, along with rice from the other, by a sweating, half-naked Chinese cook who from time to time stirred the offal with a broken oar. The coolies bore the food on rarely washed tin plates back to their stations on the deck, or below, and there ate it with their fingers to an accompaniment of sonorous regurgitations.

Spotwell, as the only first class passenger, dined at the officers' table, dressing each evening in dinner clothes for the occasion. The captain, he said, was a very dour character who never spoke a word. The Scottish engineer was a loquacious man with oily hands, to whose long-winded stories no one paid the slightest attention. The doctor, who had first seen the light of day in Surrey, was reserved at the table. He was the only one with whom Spotwell struck up a spark of congeniality.

"He was a good sort," Spotwell said, "and though I never really saw him tried out, I imagine he's a damn good doctor. The first afternoon out of Foo-chow we got talking together, and he asked me up to his cabin to have a drink with him. He dug out a bottle of Johnny Walker Black Label. I sensed from that, as well as from his conversation, that he was a man of discernment and taste.

"We talked about many things, until the time came for me to dress for dinner. He said that it wasn't necessary, but I rather think he appreciated my insistence. I noticed, when he came down, that he had changed into somewhat more formal attire than he had been wearing. It was a bit grim, that first dinner aboard, with the captain saying nary a word and the Scottish engineer telling his endless tales to which no one listened. The food was nondescript and tasted as if it had been flavored with insecticide.

"After that ordeal was over I went up on deck and walked about a bit in the open, trying not to trip over the outstretched coolies. The doctor had invited me to come back to his cabin for a liqueur. I did; and we sat half through the night drinking his cognac and whisky and talking of a multitude of things. He was an intelligent and an interesting man. I told him that I had brought a few bottles with me and asked if he would join me the next evening in my cabin, such as it was.

"He declined amiably, saying that he had to be on call, and adding that he had enough bottles in stock to quench our thirst. He urged that I make it my evening practice to visit his cabin before and after dinner. 'Don't often have people aboard whom I can talk to on an even footing,' he said. 'You've seen the ship's officers.'

"I followed his invitation, bringing along a couple of my bottles, but he would not permit me to open them. Among other things, we talked of the complications of transporting shiploads of coolies down the coast from ports where a wide variety of diseases, often including cholera, were endemic. 'There's no proper check on our deck passengers before they come aboard,' the doctor said. 'Quarantine is pretty much of a farce and the health authorities, where there's no British control, are generally venal as well as unqualified. Most anyone, with the judicious expenditure of a certain amount of money, can get a thousand coolies cleared for export to Malaya in half an afternoon. And we have to take 'em on just as they are.'

" 'If one of 'em happens to develop cholera on the voyage,' he continued, 'and the others catch onto the fact . . . well, you can probably imagine the panic that may quite easily result. People think that ship's doctors on the China coast have a pretty easy life, but they don't realize what can happen when things go wrong.'

"One evening," Spotwell said, "I went up to the doctor's cabin a bit earlier than usual. The doctor was not there. I had not seen him since the night before. Taking advantage of the opportunity, I uncorked one of my own bottles that were still standing unopened in the wardrobe and poured myself a drink, leaving the bottle temptingly on the table alongside the doctor's glass.

"After a few minutes the doctor came in, looking very grim. He thumbed a push-button bell that was supposed to communicate with the boatswain. Without a word he poured out a stiff drink from my bottle and drank it in a few large gulps. Then he turned to me. He was obviously not in a very happy frame of mind.

"He looked at me for a moment as though I were a complete stranger, and then suddenly he spoke. His voice was harsh and throaty, as if he had smoked too much. 'Do you remember what we were talking about the other night—cholera amongst the deck passengers, and a resulting panic and that sort of thing?' he asked. 'You're not a panicky type, so I may tell you that's just about what I've been up against today . . . Where the *hell* is that bloody boatswain?' and he punched viciously on the push-button of the bell.

" 'Some of these ruddy coolies, you know, get themselves into a proper stupor with opium, eaten or smoked. At one time we tried to control 'em, but we just didn't have enough hands and they'll do it anyway, despite hell and high water. The Chinese crew are no use at all in stopping them. When they get well doped and the grub bell rings, they just lie there on the deck in a coma. We've given up trying to herd 'em: it's no use. If they don't want their grub, why that's that. You just don't get anywhere trying to force-feed a drugged man.'

"He poured himself another drink and again punched the bell for the boatswain. 'I go around the deck twice a day, just after the calls for grub,' he continued, 'and have a look at those still stretched out, who haven't responded to the call. God knows the gong is loud enough to wake the dead. Some of 'em look pretty dead; but they're not, they're just damn well drugged.

" 'But this morning I saw one who looked suspiciously as if he *were* dead. I examined him: he was dead right enough— and it was cholera. No question of it. I won't go into the un-pleasant details.

" 'I thought fast,' the doctor said, with a worn look in his eyes. 'God Almighty, I thought, if the rest of them realize this, we're for it. I've got to keep the others from knowing it. I went to the boatswain, and led him off to a corner where no one could hear what we were saying.

" 'There's a dead Chinese, I told him, just abaft the num-ber four stanchion on the starboard side. I want him got rid of before the line-up come back with their grub. I want you to go at once and throw him overboard, quietly; you understand? Don't let anyone see you do it. There are a few others stretched out asleep there, near him, but that doesn't matter; they're well drugged. You can't miss him.

" ' "Aye, aye, sir," the boatswain said, and went off. I had some abdominal cases to attend to and one premature birth— we have women on board as well, you know—and it was late in the afternoon when I finally was free. I walked around the deck, and saw that the coolie who had died of cholera was still lying there.'

"There was a knock on the cabin door," Spotwell said, "and the boatswain entered. He was a fortuitous mixture of nationali-ties who chose to consider himself English. He touched his cap to the doctor. The doctor glared at him with the look of an un-derfed tiger.

" 'I told you,' the doctor said, articulating very slowly, 'to get rid of a dead Chinese coolie who was lying on the starboard deck. I told you that it was important and to do this quickly and quietly while the other coolies were off getting their food— and you are experienced enough to know what I meant. *Why didn't you do it?*' The question was put in the voice of an impassioned prosecuting attorney demanding of an accused: " 'Why did you kill that man?' "

"The boatswain touched his cap. 'Beg pardon, sir, I did, sir,' he said.

"The doctor glowered at him. 'In addition to being a bloody bad boatswain,' he said with venom in his voice, 'you are also an eternally damned liar. I have just walked around the deck, and that same dead Chinese is lying just where he was.'

"The boatswain again touched his cap. 'Beg pardon, sir,' he said, 'but I threw some Chink overboard.'

That was the end of the unsympathetic story. They never knew whether it was another dead coolie or just a heavy sleeper whom the boatswain had heaved over the rail to feed the sharks of the China Sea. The cholera victim was dropped overside during the course of the night. There were no repercussions of any kind. The ship plied its way down the coast with a clean bill of health.

"Life hasn't the same value out here," said Spotwell, "as we seem to feel that it has with us."

III

THE WINE WAS RED

"Waste not your Hour, nor in the vain pursuit
Of This and That endeavor and dispute;
*   Better be jocund with the fruitful Grape*
Than sadden after none, or bitter, Fruit."

THE GRAPES ARE RIPE

"I wonder often what the Vintners buy
One half so precious as the stuff they sell."

I T IS EARLY AUTUMN on the hillside. Heavy
ground mists often fill the valleys in the beginning of the morn-
ings, slowly lifting as the sun climbs up above them. The walnut
trees stand in dark green pools of their own leaves, not yet turned
to autumn colors, where men and boys have beaten them with
long poles to shake down the ripened nuts.

The shooting season for rabbits and partridges has opened.
Occasional groups of men in threes and fours, with shotguns and
a dog, or it may be two dogs, stalk slowly across the harvested
fields below my terrace. Now and then a dog gives tongue, I
hear a shot, and perhaps there will be a rabbit in the pot tonight; or I may see a covey of partridges take wing from the
stubble of the fields and glide swiftly in easy curves down into
the valley beyond.

Père Olart sometimes goes shooting on Sundays, accompanied by Civa, his venerable hound. One may see him moving
very deliberately through the fields, smoking his pipe, his well-
worn tweed cap pulled down over his eyes. But often he stands
in silent contemplation, looking reminiscently out across the
valley and beyond the horizon, leaning with folded hands on
his shotgun as he does in my garden on his spade, puffing at
his pipe.

Owls have taken the place of the nightingales that filled
the springtime with burbling song. They hoot mournfully as the
blue-grey of evening turns into the deep blue of night. Yet their
hooting is not unsympathetic. It is rather a friendly sound, an-
nouncing as it were that the fraternity of owls is on the job,

guarding my property against the inroads of field-mice and other noxious rodents.

A curious thing is that quite a lot of Madame Mandron's spring chickens, now fully fledged, have faces very much like owls. I have suggested to Madame Mandron that certain of her hens may have had illicit affairs with male owls, probably by night. This slur on her chickens' parentage she stoutly denies, averring the owl-faced chickens are a special type of *poulet* that has by inheritance a round, fat face with a lot of feathers sticking out sideways from under its oval chin. But the fact remains that a good many, though not all, of her chickens look, from the neck up, remarkably like owls.

Up in the town a *batteuse*—a threshing-machine—has been set up in one of the two through streets to thresh the grain, the oats and barley and precious little wheat, of Monsieur Small-joist (Soliveau). It blocks the street effectively and, when running, fills the narrow, steep passage with dust and chaff. Its running is far from continuous for it is an ancient and temperamental batteuse of a design that might have been evolved by Rube Goldberg's grandfather, and it breaks down with persistence and marked regularity. At each break the pieces have to be welded, there being no spare parts obtainable anywhere. By now it must be practically one complete weld.

A goodly proportion of the town's manpower is there for the one day of its operation in front of Monsieur Small-joist's ancient stone barn; a day which will certainly stretch into two and perhaps three because of the frequent breakdowns. Monsieur Jojot, the Mayor, is there, as is his assistant. So is Monsieur Butterfly, the mason and town crier; and Maurice Gauthé, the *cantonnier*, with his long-handled broom for sweeping the streets; and Monsieur Lelac, who drives two cream-colored oxen hitched to a long cart (and always wears gloves when he drives them), raises pigs, has blue eyes, a close-cropped white moustache brushed fiercely upwards, and looks like an English county squire. So is Père Olart, smoking his pipe and relaxing when the batteuse is inoperative. They all swop jokes and banter during the periods of inactivity, and by the end of the afternoon Père Olart has managed in some not too obscure fashion to get himself fairly well oiled with red wine of last year's vintage.

"It is the dust, you know," says Père Olart with a naughty twinkle in his grey-green eyes, "that gets in one's lungs and one's throat, and creates a formidable thirst!"

After Monsieur Small-joist's grain has been threshed the batteuse will move on to other jobs on the outskirts of the town and Père Olart will follow it. Then it will depart to work in the surrounding villages, and I will doubtless see Père Olart back in my garden again.

The *vendange*, the harvesting of the wine-grape, has commenced; two or three weeks earlier than usual owing to the extraordinary heat and dryness of the summer. This year (1947) will be long remembered as a year of magnificent vintage. Many other products of the soil have failed and there will be grave shortages in foodstuffs. The winter wheat was nearly all frozen by the exceptional cold and lack of snow, and the less important spring planting was largely dried up in the summer drought. Most of the late vegetables—the beans and peas and cabbages and beets, the succulent leaves of lettuces and other greens for salads that the French know better than any other people how to prepare—were grilled on the ground; and the potatoes, which along with the bread that is in catastrophically short supply, constitute the basic diet of the villagers and peasants, are puny in size and scant in quantity. But the wine-grape yield is good and its product throughout the whole of Burgundy, and in most of the vineyards of France, will be superb.

"One has not to complain," say the cultivators of the vine. "There was no rain at all and many of the grapes dried up. But the crop is not bad in extent, and the grapes are sweet and fruity. Taste them!" And they hand me a bunch of white or black grapes that are full-flavored and delicious.

Burgundy, or those sections of it where the cultivation of the vine, and the ancillary services which have to do with this, are the primary concern of a large part of the population that lives on and from the soil, produces some of the finest wines in the world. The best *crus*—the wine-producing slopes—are to the eastward of my hillside, along a narrow strip running from Dijon to a little south of Beaune, on the "Golden Slope" of the Côte-d'Or. From there come the great wines known generically as burgundy: Chambertin, Clos de Bèze, Musigny, Clos de Vougeot, Grands Echézeaux, Romanée-Conti, Richebourg, St-Georges, Corton, Hospices de Beaune, Pommard, Volnay; the splendid white wines of Meursault and Montrachet; and many others.

The vineyards around my hillside bear no famous names. The nearest of wide renown are those of Chablis, some forty miles to the north. Yet the local grapes produce good wine, both white and red, and if the *vendange*—the harvesting and processing—is somewhat less pontifical than at certain of the more noted *crus* of the Côte-d'Or, it is nevertheless a jolly occasion when the crop, as in this year, is well favored.

In every village round about, preparations have been going on for the past fortnight. Large barrels that have held the grapes of many seasons have been brought out, repaired where needed, washed and left to dry in the autumn sun beside the entrances of cellars and lichen-covered stone barns. Long carts or wagons, some two-wheeled with very high wheels, some four-wheeled, are arranged in readiness alongside the barrels. A spirit of gaiety, of *comaraderie*, pervades the villages as at no other time of the year. This is the culmination of long and arduous effort, for the cultivation of the vine entails many processes that must be carried out by hand, as well as a continuous gamble against the calamities of season which ends only with the picking of the grapes.

This year, as already noted, the season has been remarkably kind to the viniculturists, though most unkind to other cultivators. So the grape-gatherers set forth in the morning, gay of mind, in little groups of three or four to a dozen or more men and women and youths, after a solid breakfast of bacon soup, sausage, sandwiches of bread and jam with strong cheese that has been heated under the cinders in an aroma of fermented garlic, washed down with a jugful of the previous year's wine. The last gulps of the wine are taken standing so that it will descend straighter, and the men may perhaps end up with a small glass of modestly aged *eau-de-vie de Marc*—a fiery spirit distilled from the residue of the grapes after the pressing—before they start out. Each one takes a basket of wicker or of wood, a pair of short, stout shears or a curved knife to cut the bunches of grapes from the vines; and one of the youths carries a large V-shaped pannier on his back to transfer the culled bunches from the pickers' baskets to the barrels, which will be placed at the nearest point of the roadside to the vineyard.

The men load the empty barrels onto the carts and hitch their animals to the vehicles: heavy-bodied Auxois horses or cream-colored Charollais oxen, or sometimes a horse and a donkey in tandem. If the vineyard where they are to pick is far they all clamber aboard the carts, sitting or standing amongst the barrels, cracking jokes as they wend slowly over the country roads. Otherwise they walk, save for the drivers of the carts.

The better vineyards are located on the limestone slopes facing the southwestern sun, neither so high up that they get insufficient moisture, nor so far down that they receive too much or are blanketed in the ground mists that sometimes fill the valleys in early autumn. The slopes assure proper drainage; but it is the sun and the soil that are all-important.

The cultivation of the wine-grape in Burgundy dates back at least seventeen centuries. It was an important production in the Middle Ages, when the lords of feudalism and of the church received their payment in kind from the vine-slopes cultivated by their tenants and their serfs, and drank robustly of the product of the grape. The areas so cultivated in the years before 1875 or thereabouts used to be far greater than at present. Then came from America the fearful scourge of the phylloxera, which by the mid-eighties had all but destroyed the vineyards of the whole of France. The direct loss to the country from this was estimated at two billion dollars, or double the indemnity France had to pay Germany in 1871.

Some well-intentioned growers had imported from the United States a small quantity of vinestocks to try out on the soil of Europe. These vines were themselves immune to the depredations of the pernicious insect, but they brought the insect with them. The phylloxera spread with astonishing rapidity, ruining the indigenous vinestocks. The only way found to combat its ravages was the complete reconstitution of the vineyards with American plants, or by graftings of the higher grade old French stocks onto American roots immune to the scourge their fellow vines had imported. And this still continues, for the immunity fails with increasing age and the vineyards must be refreshed with new American roots after a certain number of years, lest the vines again fall victim to the disease.

During the war years this was not possible, and for various reasons that have to do with dollar exchange and priorities and transportation it is still extremely difficult. So the vineyards of France are greatly depleted; and the production in this favorable year of 1947, estimated at forty-five million hectoliters (approximately one billion two hundred million gallons), is well below the average of fifty-eight million hectoliters in the years 1930–39, and far less than in the pre-phylloxera days some seventy or so years ago. But the 1947 product will be remembered by connoisseurs until long after the last drop of it has been consumed. This has been the greatest vintage year, as to quality, certainly since 1865, and perhaps in the history of France.

My friend Jean-Marie Defert of Fontette village is a vine-grower whose vineyards face the southwest over the pleasant valley of the River Cure. Monsieur Defert himself is a product of the Burgundian countryside with many generations of self-respecting and substantial cultivators of the soil behind him. He speaks seventeenth-century Burgundian French in the manner of Bossuet, a noted cleric, orator and writer of that century who was likewise a Burgundian, and whose literary style reflects the influence of Isocrates, Demosthenes and Plato.

Monsieur Defert is a genial and hospitable gentleman who would be surprised if he were told that his manner of expression traced back to the writings of three ancient Greek philosophers. It is highly improbable that he has ever heard of Bossuet. Yet Monsieur Defert is a philosopher in his own right. His philosophy is that of the soil and of the grape, of a friendly but never-ending struggle with Nature who is sometimes benign and often ill-disposed; and it is based on tolerance and respect for the rules of the game.

On my arrival at Monsieur Defert's substantially built farmhouse in Fontette to go with him to the vendange—for this is the merry season for the viniculturists and I like to follow them —I find him organizing his party to set forth to the vineyards and cull the grapes. There are perhaps twelve or fourteen in the party, each with a basket and a pair of shears or a curved knife. Some are members of the family, some are neighbors who exchange different sorts of toil with one another; a few are paid in cash for their efforts. Madame Defert remains behind to cook the lunch that they will consume heartily when they return in the middle of the day, for the vineyards are not far distant.

They are backing the stout, even-tempered Auxois mare in between the shafts of the long cart, hammering the hoops of barrels whose insides are dyed a rich wine-color from the grapes of previous years, lifting the empty barrels onto the cart and tying the donkey behind: a mournful and patient beast that will be hitched in front of the horse for the return trip with the barrels full of grapes. They all chat to one another, to the horse and the donkey, on equal terms, exchanging quips which the beasts seem to appreciate along with the humans. All are part of a team going out to the vendange.

But before they start, Monsieur Defert insists that I step inside for a nip of eau-de-vie de Marc. In a spacious room with a large fireplace, substantial Burgundian peasant furniture and stout beams from which sometimes may be suspended hams and long sausages and strings of onions, he places me at the table and serves a shot of Marc that would stir the blood of a sluggard. He himself takes a thimbleful, to clink glasses and wish me health. Then we go out to the vineyards; perhaps on foot, or in the cart, or in my jeep, depending on where the pickers are to work. The atmosphere is perfumed with the odor of ripened grape, and there is the smell of new wine in the air.

The vineyards run up the slopes in orderly rows of vines, now heavy with grapes. The party starts off, one to each row, working upwards, clipping the bunches and dropping these into the individual baskets that each carries. They all munch grapes continually as they proceed, gossip with Rabelaisian indelicacy and chaff one another without cease in their progress. Some of the men wear long aprons; the women have kerchiefs or bonnets on their heads. Monsieur Defert, in wooden shoes, moves steadily onward, but being more interested in the state of the vines—which are *his* vines—than many of the others, he may drop a little behind in the progress up the slope. Then some of the workers are sure to call out in genial banter.

"Isn't the *patron*"—the proprietor—"supposed to lead the way? One would think that he should set the pace we have to follow. But look at him—he's behind all the rest! Should we slow down?" Monsieur Defert grins and continues on his course, lovingly and critically regarding his vines, shearing off the bunches of grapes with his short, curved knife. But he points out from time to time some partly concealed bunch within the range of his view that one of the other pickers has missed, and though he is no longer as young as he used to be, he very seldom misses one himself.

As each basket is filled, the young man with the V-shaped pannier on his back stands beside the picker, who dumps the basketful of cut bunches into the pannier. When the pannier is full the youth takes it up or down the slope to where the barrels have been placed along the edge of the nearest side-hill road, beside the empty cart, and dumps its contents into one of the barrels. Then he returns to the pickers for another load. Some cultivators leave the barrels on the cart, and the pannier carrier clambers up a short length of ladder to turn his collection into the barrels. But Monsieur Defert does not do it that way. The manner of carrying out the vendange varies from location to location, as do the baskets and other equipment; and each viniculturist has his own pet habits acquired from his ancestors and from long practice.

When the barrels are full, the party returns to the farm to lunch copiously on Madame Defert's good Burgundian country cooking, bringing the loaded barrels back on the cart. Just enough barrels are taken out in the morning for the party to fill, though it may be anywhere from twelve-thirty to two o'clock before the pickers return. In the afternoon they go out again with more empty barrels, perhaps to the same vineyard, perhaps to another; to return as the sun slips down behind the hills.

When the barrels full of grapes are deposited at the farm, three of the men remain there to empty them: the morning's collection in the afternoon, the afternoon's collection in the evening or perhaps the following morning. The red-wine grapes (which the French call black, though the wine they produce is known as red) are passed through a *broyeur*—a small hand-operated mangler—which partially mashes them, and the marc or mash is poured down a chute into one of two enormous *cuves*, great vats, in Monsieur Defert's cellar. In these the mash immediately starts to "work" or ferment and remains there from eight to ten days. The wine is then drawn off and placed in casks for the secondary fermentation. That makes the prime quality of the red vintage.

Following this the mash is taken out and put through a *pressoir*—a large hand-operated press—which squeeezes out a further yield of wine, but of second quality. Finally the mash is placed in a still, usually a portable affair on wheels; steam is passed through it, and the potent, colorless liquor called eau-de-vie de Marc is distilled. That is the ultimate product of the grape, and if taken in sufficient quantity will induce normally well-controlled human beings to act in curious ways. But a good Marc, reasonably aged and consumed with caution, is an estimable drink, though it does not possess the flavor of a good cognac.

The white grapes are treated differently. The juice must not ferment in the mash or the wine will not be clear and will have a sharp taste from the seeds and stems. So the white grapes, after being mangled in the broyeur, go directly into the big pressoir, down below one of Monsieur Defert's barns, and there they are crushed until the golden juice runs into a cement trough. From this it is carried in a *broc*, a wooden jug holding twelve liters, and is poured directly into wooden casks to mature. The marc or mash is subsequently distilled into eau-de-vie in the same manner as the mash of the black grapes.

Much of the pressing is done today by portable presses on wheels, which are dragged about from place to place where the barrels of grapes to be pressed have been collected. But Monsieur Defert, as a viniculturist of substance, has his own press. This is a large round affair of vertical wooden slats held together by three circular brass bands, mounted on a heavy rectangular base of iron with four short iron feet, and is actuated by a rack and worm gear above. It fills a considerable part of a large room under the barn where Monsieur Defert's cows munch their fodder. The barn is built on the slope of the hill, so there is access to the cow stable from the front on the upper level, and to the wine press from behind on the level below. The press is a cumbrous and solid piece of equipment, yet it is a child's toy—the toy of a very stout child, it may be said—compared with the ancient type of Burgundian wine press of which a fair number of examples are still extant.

In a village some sixteen miles away there were eight of these ancient presses in 1940. The Germans came; and now there is one. They simply destroyed the others, using the venerable beams as firewood, for these were not objects that could be transported easily to the Aryan homeland. They were all generically similar in design; six gigantic oak beams bound together in a sixty-foot-long shaft, one end of which was raised by a wooden worm gear actuated by a dozen men and women with interlaced arms turning a great wooden wheel. The sole remaining example in the village of Accolay—nobody knows why the

Germans failed to burn this—is identical to the four that remain at the Clos de Vougeot, one of the great vineyards of the world. It is said to weigh eight tons.

As I follow the various processes, sometimes lending a hand, I am urged from time to time to sample the product. There is the *vin doux*—the sweet wine—as it trickles from the pressoir: cloudy, hardly fermented, but headier than one might think. There is the new red wine that is drawn from the vats after the preliminary fermentation, a week or ten days old but with more power than it shows outwardly. There is the partially fermented but still immature wine after it has remained for a short while in the casks. And in the cellars where the casks are stored there are always other casks full of the robust wine of previous years, which is to be savored with much rolling around the tongue, a suggestion of gargling, and a final appreciative smacking as it passes by one's palate.

Then, later, there is the eau-de-vie de Marc, sampled as it comes warm from the mobile still that moves around the villages and usually is set up on the main street, or in the Place in front of the church when there is one. As to the fiery potency of this product there is no illusion in the very first sip when it is but a few seconds old.

The sampling of the young wine used always to be done in a little shallow, fluted silver cup with a handle for fore-finger and thumb, which every substantial viniculturist carried in his waistcoat or hip pocket. This is called a *tasse à vin*—a wine-cup —or in and around Beaune a *tastevin*, pronounced ta'te-vin. It is so designed that one can readily remark the color and quality of the wine, and even the degree of alcoholic content indicated by the clinging of the alcohol, as one swirls the little cup, in certain angular incisions on the inside of the bowl. It is still used by some of the older viniculturists and vintners; and at the public auction of the Hospices de Beaune, among the Chevaliers de Tastevin—the Knights of the Wine-cup—its use is a ritual. These little old cups are of pleasant line and charming in their varied designs. But today they are hard to find.

Cheery though he is during the season of the vendange, and more mellow, generally, than other cultivators of the land at all times, the viniculturist in Burgundy leads a far from easy existence. His is a rugged occupation, fraught with the multiple perils of a Nature that often turns ungenerous. The wines of Burgundy, great and simple alike, are the product of human toil as much as of the earth. Perhaps no branch of agriculture requires more minute attention than the cultivation of the vine.

The very soil itself is harsh, made by the erosion of the mountains, rose-colored with the salts of iron, and with the annual wastage of the vines themselves adding an important vegetable debris of decomposing stumps and roots to the debris of the rocks. The vines like this rubbly soil of chalk and gravel, which is not too rich, has good drainage and holds in winter the heat it has acquired from the summer sun. But it is no infant's play to cultivate those tough slopes.

The vineyards, some of which produce perhaps the finest wines on earth, have to fear the winds of the north, the late frost of spring, the hail-storms of late summer, as well as many other inclemencies of season. Partial or total failures of the crop occur only too often; whereas the wine producer of the south, though his product varies according to the year, hardly ever has a seriously deficient yield. Yet for elegance of bouquet and flavor, however much the vine loves the sun, the wines produced in a temperate climate such as that of Burgundy—when the vintage is successful—are far superior to those of hot or semi-tropical regions.

The two months of full winter are the easy days for the *vigneron*—the viniculturist. He has work to do in preparation for the next season, but this is not pressing. It can wait on his convenience; there is no immediate dead-line, so to speak.

He repairs and washes his empty casks and barrels; racks the maturing wine of the past vintage, drawing it off from the casks in which the sediment has gathered, into clean casks to separate it from the deposit, at the same time replenishing the lowered level; and from time to time he tastes it. He helps set up the still to make the eau-de-vie from the wine-expended marc. And he forgathers now and then with his cronies of the vineyards to do a little clinking of glasses.

Then comes the spring. After the frosts of winter the tough soil must be loosened with a special plough, and worked frequently with a pick and a heavy-toothed iron rake around the base of the plants to keep it light and "running." The vines need bracing and earthing up; the supporting wires must be looked over, perhaps realigned or replaced, and the young shoots trained to follow them. For the latter, the gentler female touch comes in, to give the vines their spring toilet, to trim them and attach the tender new sap-filled shoots, yet not bruise them, with wisps of straw to the wires. Then, also, comes the grafting of old and proven stock on new and hardy roots.

June and July bring a constant struggle against the *oïdium* (mildew)—the deadliest disease of the vine after the phylloxera —and black rot, and a host of other fungoid infections which attack the plant and ruin the grape. This involves frequent spraying with copper sulphate from a little tank carried on the sprayer's back, and the sprayer returns from his work all pale blue and with his garments disintegrating from the effect of the spray.

Throughout the season the ploughing and weeding has regularly to be repeated in the fight with the weeds for the sustenance that makes the grapes rich and fruity.

And so, with labor superposed on labor, one comes to the vendange, which if Mother Nature has been in a kindly mood is a happy and genial period: even though the final toil of gathering the grapes is tiring and back-breaking work and the gatherers return in the evening, after having been bent over all day, with their "spines like hoops" as they say. But even this they say jovially.

It is an extraordinary thing how a real connoisseur can trace the provenance of different wines by taste and aroma alone. In this I do not only mean wines from different areas: I mean wines of slightly different savor and bouquet from the same area.

Take, for instance, the vineyards along the River Mosel, or Moselle, which are close to the northern limit of viniculture in Europe. The river flows in a northeasterly direction, winding between the steep slopes of eroded hills. The geological features of the hills are much the same throughout the vine-growing district; the vineyards of greatest repute, and others of lesser fame, face the same sun in the same southerly or southwesterly direction. The vines are basically the same, and the care given those of the more reputed slopes, and shown in the preparation of the wine, varies little in skill and devotion.

Yet an expert will tell you, with only an unlabeled glass of wine in his hand, from just which slope the grapes that produced it were culled, and in all probability the year of its production. The slight difference in composition of the soil of neighboring slopes, all of them geologically akin, distinguishes the product. The same vine, exposed to practically identical conditions of climate, will produce markedly different wines if planted in even moderately differing soils. But the ability of the connoisseur to trace this distinction to its source on a particular slope, with no other aid than his eye, his nose and his palate, is a highly developed gift of long experience.

I do not lack an appreciation of good wines, yet it is probably just as well that I never carried it to such an extent. For today it would be a highly costly and often discouraging talent. I like my good burgundy, bordeaux, Côtes-du-Rhone and Alsatian wines, not to mention many others, well aged and of splendid bouquet; but I drink simpler vintages than the *grands crus*, hearty wines of the countryside, with pleasure, especially when consuming them with my genial Burgundian friends during the vendange.

It was in 1915—an exceptionally good year for burgundy, though I did not then know it—that I received my first serious instruction in the quality of wines. The instruction came from Eugene Kuhlmann, then French *adjutant*-interpreter with British 6th Division in the Ypres salient, and a member of my mess at Poperinghe. Kuhlmann, who was a good bit older than the rest of us, had a number of special attainments. His appreciation of Gothic architecture, sculpture and painting was highly developed; he had a broad knowledge of medieval literature and of the location of practically all existing copies of the more important manuscripts of the Middle Ages; and he was deeply versed in heraldry.

While these particular attributes were of questionable value to the conduct of the war, he possessed another which considerably intrigued the Poperinghe mess and formed the basis of a lasting curiosity on my part in sampling the products of the grape. Kuhlmann was a remarkable connoisseur of wines. And it happened that the Poperinghe mess, through fortuitous circumstances abetted by certain efforts of mine, was well provided with wines that ranged from good to excellent.

I had been making a reconnaissance of the cellars of Ypres for British Second Army. This unhappy town had been completely evacuated on the night of the 22nd of April 1915, during the first gas attack on the salient. It was under constant shell-fire from all manner of guns, and was burning in a score of places. It was not a pleasant spot to operate in.

Some of the cellars themselves were not very pleasant, because of what one found in them—decomposition, an unlovely assortment of stenches, and singularly unalluring animal life—though the strong vaulting of those under the older buildings stood up against anything but direct hits from the heaviest shells. Most of them had been pillaged of everything of value that the looters could lay their hands on.

But Belgians have a habit of storing their maturing wines in niches or indentations in the cellar walls, which they then often brick up, cover the bricks over with whitewash, and paste a label on the outside with the name of the wine mellowing therein and the year for its exhumation. Most of the labels had been removed during the early days of the war, though I found one inscribed *"Pommerol pour Maria, à sortir 1915"*—to be brought out in 1915—which seemed particularly opportune. Maria, whoever she may have been, had decamped to parts unknown and the houses on either side were burning. So the Poperinghe mess became the beneficiary. To the credit of the mess let it be remarked that we always toasted the health of Maria as a solemn ritual, whenever consuming her Pommerol.

The Poperinghe mess became the beneficiary of a very useful stock of well-matured wine as I learned—and I learned without undue sluggishness—to combine a certain amount of excavation with my reconnaissance of the Ypres cellars. The bottles I brought back, except for the Pommerol for Maria, had no indication of what they contained. But Kuhlmann, after regarding, sniffing and tasting a very little of the contents, would tell us exactly where the wine had been produced and in what year. As time passed, some of us became a little suspicious of Kuhlmann's proficiency in tracing unmarked wines back to their source by eye, nose and palate. He seemed too good, too certain. But in the end he showed how good he was.

Belgium produces no wine, being north of the line where vines are successfully grown in Europe. But the Belgians, in any event before the wars of the first half of the twentieth century, maintained and served at their tables French wines of better average quality and condition than the French themselves.

The reasons for this were, and I hope still hold true, that the Belgian has a cultivated appreciation for good wine; that a Belgian who leaves a well-stocked cellar to his inheritors leaves something far more precious than mere bonds or money; and because a considerable section of Belgium has a chalky subsoil. This area lies south and west of a line that runs roughly through Brussels and Liège, and the cellars in the chalky soil, where the temperature does not vary more than 10° centigrade (18° Fahrenheit) throughout the year, are ideal for the storage and maturing of wine.

The Belgians have three national sports. There are others with considerable popular appeal, such as association football, but these three are characteristically Belgian, though two are shared with other nations. One is bicycle racing, in which stout-limbed young men pedal their way over the paved routes of the country and sometimes well beyond its borders. One, for older sportsmen, is shooting little wooden birds with bows and arrows off the upper branches of simulated trees. The third, which appeals to all ages, is pigeon racing. This last they combine with the replenishment of their cellars.

Georges Bloch, a young Belgian messmate who was killed shortly afterwards when the mess was hit by a large shell, explained to me how that was done.

"It is quite simple," he said, "and is a matter of timing and economics, as well as of sport. My Uncle Joseph is a passionate pigeon racer. He also possesses a famous cellar. To give you an example of how he combines the two I will start out in the spring of the year. My Uncle Joseph, when he goes on a Sunday to dine with Aunt Mathilde, about fifteen miles away, takes with him from the cote a young pigeon that he has named Henri. From Aunt Mathilde's he releases Henri to fly home—the pigeon's first homing effort over any distance.

"A week or so later he goes to Uncle Maurice's for dinner, and takes Henri with him. That's a good forty miles. Henri flies back, and his time is roughly clocked because Aunt Louise—she's bed-ridden, but can note the time the pigeon returns—is waiting at home. And so on, during the summer, my Uncle Joseph takes Henri farther and farther afield to practice homing.

"As autumn comes, my Uncle Joseph makes his annual trip to France. During this he combines a number of things. He takes Henri with him and releases the bird from Paris to make its first long-distance training flight back home. Henri has shown promise and will be a hopeful racing bird next year. Uncle Joseph also takes three or four of his most experienced racing pigeons with him. He transacts his business in Paris and goes on to Bordeaux, carrying very little baggage besides his pigeons, among whom Alphonse is the hope of the family, but more particularly of my Uncle Joseph.

"My uncle times his arrival at Bordeaux so as to be there

just after the vendange and a little before the big pigeon races
from the south. He samples the young wine, and when it is good
he buys it in considerable quantity and has it shipped back to
Belgium in casks, where he will let it age for six months or so
and then will put it in bottles to mature for the requisite number of years. The bottles will be walled up in his cellar and will
not be touched for from five to ten years, depending on the wine.
My Uncle Joseph knows his wines.

"Then he goes on to Pau, and to San Sebastian in Spain, to
enter his pigeons in the big races. There are many pigeon fanciers
from Belgium doing the same thing and they take it all very seriously." I came upon a confirmation of this after the war, in 1919,
when I saw a large two-engined Farman airplane in Brussels
specially fitted out to carry fifteen hundred racing pigeons to the
races, complete with a steward to minister to their needs en
route.

"Uncle Joseph waits," continued Georges Bloch, "for the
telegrams to tell him how his pigeons fared in the races. He bets
quite substantial sums on his racers, and orders corks from Spain
for the bottling of his wines. If it has been a year of good vintage,
and Alphonse wins his race, my uncle's happiness is complete.
Then he returns through Burgundy, to attend the wine auction
at the Hospices de Beaune, where he will buy beautiful wines
from the delicate *pineau* grapes of the Côte-d'Or. He will probably visit Nuits St-Georges and one or two other wine centers
in Burgundy. My uncle buys some moderate bordeaux for ordinary use, but he only goes in for the best burgundy.

"Then he returns to Paris to complete his business there,
and heads back to Belgium well satisfied with his trip—if it has
been a good wine year and his pigeons performed creditably.
And that," concluded Georges Bloch, "is how we combine
pigeon racing with the replenishment of our cellars."

When we became a bit suspicious of Kuhlmann's extraordinary faculty for identifying the wines I retrieved from the cellars

of Ypres, I concocted a plan with Bernard Blanchy to trap our expert. Bernard Blanchy, a French Lieutenant liaison officer, was the son of a prominent vintner of Bordeaux. He knew wines well, particularly bordeaux of course, and he was one of those who felt that Kuhlmann just could not be as sure in his knowledge as he seemed.

So Blanchy wrote his father to send him up a bottle of not too easily identified bordeaux, unlabeled, and to write separately in a letter exactly what it was. The letter arrived, and in due course the wine. I took the bottle to Ypres and placed it in a cellar in the Street of Butter. It remained there during the day and I brought it back with me that evening, after carefully smearing it with the dust of underground Ypres. I allowed it to stand for a couple of days to let the sediment settle after its voyage, and then produced the bottle at dinner.

"What is this wine?" Kuhlmann asked, as I placed it in front of him.

"I don't really know," I said. "It's a new lot we haven't tried before. I brought it back from Ypres day before yesterday. You can tell us what it is." Kuhlmann decanted half a glassful quite slowly, stared through it, smelt it, tasted it. Then he looked at me coldly.

"You didn't get that wine in Ypres!" he snapped.

"I tell you that I did!" I said. "I brought it back two days ago from a cellar in the Rue au Beurre." Kuhlmann looked at his glass again, his eyes narrowing, and once more he smelt it. He put the glass down.

"Then someone—a North African private, perhaps—left it there. Belgians don't stock that kind of wine!" He glared at me with suspicion in his cold grey-blue eyes.

"What do you think it is?" I asked innocently. "You've told us where all the other wines I've found in Ypres came from. Where would you say this was produced?"

"Well," said Kuhlmann, sampling a few more drops of the contested beverage, "I don't often drink wine of this sort. But I would risk a guess that the base of it came from the Entre-deux-Mers district, between the Garonne and the Dordogne, east of Bordeaux, from one of the *palus* or low-land vineyards which produce a red wine that is only fit for blending. It is probably three years old, and has been fortified with about a third by volume of Algerian wine of the same year. If *that's* what you're going to bring us, you had better give up going into Ypres!"

Bernard Blanchy and I looked at one another. "My God!" said Blanchy quietly. He produced his father's letter from his pocket. I had seen it, of course. He read slowly his father's description of the wine that had been sent to trap Kuhlmann. It corresponded exactly with Kuhlmann's identification of the small sampling he had made from the unmarked bottle which he had seen for the first time five minutes before.

"You win!" I said to Kuhlmann. "Let's break out another and a better bottle and we'll never question your knowledge again!"

"You should be reprimanded," said Kuhlmann acidly, "for introducing such a wine into the Poperinghe mess. My confidence in you as a wine retriever has been rudely shaken."

DEATH OF A CITY

ACH MORNING Père Olart comes down from his cottage on the hill, smoking his pipe, bringing the milk, and to light the kitchen stove. On the kitchen table in a metal plate are the *mégots*—the butts—of the cigarettes consumed in the house during the previous day, from which he supplements his ration of pipe-tobacco. He takes rather a dim view of the fact that I smoke my cigarettes in a holder, and so my mégots are extremely short. When there are week-end guests they usually leave more and longer mégots, and Père Olart is gratified.

On the kitchen table he also finds, done up in a paper, the tops of carrots, uneaten leaves of lettuce, pea-pods, stale crusts of bread and occasionally a bone or the remnants of meat, to feed to his rabbits and his ancient hound.

Across the kitchen, over the sink and serving as a faucet for the pumped-up cistern water, is a bronze swan's head. When it faces outwardly the water flows from its beak; when it looks sideways the flow is cut. Mr. Night Club, our genial plumber, put this in for me. It dates from the early sixteen hundreds, well over three centuries old. Père Olart is fascinated by it, not for its antiquity or graceful lines, but because he finds it a most practical piece of mechanism. He is amused by its likeness to a barnyard fowl—a goose or a duck: I doubt that he is very knowledgeable about swans, though he claims to know what they are. He turns the head and the water flows; he turns it back, the flow ceases. His keen eyes gleam.

"That is good," he says. "You did well to put that in!" Père Olart is also interested in its provenance, for he fought in northern France and Flanders in the 1914–18 affair.

I acquired the swan's-head faucet in Ypres in 1915, and for thirty-one years—Powers of Darkness, was it that long ago?—never used it. Now it is in daily use, and many times a day. I rescued it—one would say "liberated" in modern parlance—from a burning house in the Rue de Lille, along with a pregnant part-griffon bitch who later presented me with four puppies as a token of her appreciation. Ypres was then surrounded by an unamiable horde of Germans on three sides, enfiladed and being pounded incessantly by heavy fire. It was at that moment probably the most uncongenial spot on earth.

The ancient and charming town, with its Flemish Gothic houses and splendid Cloth Hall, was disintegrating rapidly under the impact of the bombardment and the fires burning fiercely in many quarters. Day by day it changed, disappeared under the vicious bursts of heavy shells and the flames. On a clear afternoon at the end of May, I clambered up the tower of the Church of St. Jacques, just before the upper half of it collapsed. The church itself was burnt out. The tower appeared to have been bitten by enormous prehistoric animals, drilled full of holes by slightly lesser ones like pterodactyls. Its battery of bells had dropped from the belfry, carrying with them successive wooden floors and the stone vaulting of the vestibule. There were large gaps in the spiral stone stairs; the top half was entirely gone.

It was a tricky and an unpleasant climb, hauling a length of ladder by a rope which I looped around unsupported bits of broken ledge or projecting stones overhead; raising it, and then myself, from one hold to another yet more unsubstantial, none much over five inches wide. But though I had not come for the view, what I saw from the top repaid the effort.

The ragged outlines of empty, roofless houses lay spread out in fantastic pattern, dead, deserted and silent; like another Pompeii, like the excavations of an Inca or a Chaldean city. A lifeless maze: broken by the empty space of the Grand' Place, made larger and emptier by the disappearance of the buildings along its edges. The shells of the Cloth Hall and the Cathedral wore the gaunt dignity of ancient ruins, every detail acid sharp in the clear air, casting distorted shadows under the afternoon sun.

Lesser empty spaces with black and gaping centers showed where the 420-mm shells had done their work. Leprous cavities, these were, like craters on the moon. Dead as the moon, the whole uncanny warren lay exposed at one's feet, sliced open as by a giant scythe. Cold and monotone it lay: a Satanic picture etched in narrow, precise shadows, framed behind in splashes of contrasting color.

On one side the semicircles of the trenches—ours and the Germans'—were picked out by white puffs of shrapnel beneath the deep blue sky. Lazily peaceful it seemed out there, at the moment. On the other, in a narrower segment of black and red, dark columns of smoke mounted to the heavens from angry crimson bases that were the flames consuming the remnants of Ypres. The two segments joined where the lines of the canals led north and south, thin lines of mercury aglint in the sunlight. These stretched out from the horseshoe of the moat that glowed in turbid crimson under the red glow of the fires.

The claret-colored smoke-columns rose straight upwards to a great height, for the wind was weak. There they flattened out above the angle of the afternoon sun, joining each other in a curious pall that seemed to take vaguely the shape of the heraldic arms of the once proud city. It glowed with a weird, unnatural light, that pall; luminous under the inverted bowl of the sky. One wondered if it was really a pall. Was it not, rather, the disembodied spirit of Ypres, the ghost of the murdered town hovering there above its own skeleton?

I thought that Ypres should have remained as it was then, for posterity, forever a fantastic, crumbled monument to human destructiveness. Yet how many other ancient cities have since followed in that same pattern!

It was before this, in the late afternoon of the 22nd of April 1915, that 2nd Lieutenant Ivor McClure and I—then also

a 2nd Lieutenant in the British Army—were having a drink together in our billet at number 16 Rue de Carton. We had been
shelled out of the top of that house a day or two before. Now
we were reinstalled on the floor below. It was a pleasant billet,
even though it lacked a part of its roof.

The day had been calm. Tranquillity, of a comparative sort,
reigned over the salient. There were three Divisional headquarters then located in Ypres. The sleepy old Flemish town was almost gay under the influx of so many officers and other ranks,
with nearly half of its civilian population of nine thousand souls
still about.

We were leisurely sipping our whisky-and-water when there
came a sound of onrushing doom. It was such a sound as one
might hear if hanging by the arms from a high railway trestle
while an express train passed at full speed overhead, its emergency
brakes set and all wheels locked. It signalled the approaching
death of a city which had stood up under repeated assault for more
than a thousand years. The sound we heard was the first 420-mm.
shell hurled on the town, the starting-gun of the "Battle of
Ypres, 1915."

The shell burst a little more than half a block from our
billet. It left a great void where there had been a number of
ancient, well-built houses. The sky-flung debris crashed interminably through black and acrid smoke, while Ivor and I looked
quizzically at one another over our drinks.

"And *that*, old boy, doesn't mean perhaps!" said Ivor, a
trifle over-deliberately. "Cheeri-o! Might be our last, you know!"
We drained our whisky. It was about 4:40 P.M.

Of the rest of that day and night I have confused recollections; in which certain semi-detached pictures with little or no
sequence stand out acid-sharp, etched for all time on the retina of
memory. One was when a British limbered artillery wagon came
down the Rue de Dixmude at full gallop, the six horses covered
with foam, their drivers beating them with short-handled whips.
They took a right-angled corner in a great shower of sparks from
the iron tires and shoes as the empty limber skidded wildly over

the paving blocks, side-swiping the fronts of three or four houses with its brass-tipped hub. Clinging to the caisson were five African spectres whose faces should have been black as coal, but were not. They were greenish-grey, with enormous blood-stained eyeballs that looked like something erupted from the bottom of the sea.

One of them kept screaming in bastard French: "*Allemong vienn-n-e! Allemong vienn-n-e! Allemong vienn-n-e!*" over and over again in an hysterical shriek. Two rolled off at the corner. They were dead when I went over to look at them, ghastly distorted faces the color of cold ashes, greenish vomit down their fronts. Those blanched and gruesome Negro faces were my first sight of the effects of chlorine gas, used that day for the first time in the history of warfare. I did not then know what the effects were from. The limber disappeared into the thick black spume of a big shell burst, with the parrot-screeches of the frenzied African still carrying above the terrific din. Never before or since have I heard any human utterance so fraught with terror.

The French 45th Division had fallen back on the canal, their trenches and lungs full of chlorine gas. This left a wide-open gap between them and the Canadians. I was ordered to round up men to shove into the gap: all stragglers, and every man not on combat duty with his unit, that I could collect. I do not recall how the order came to me. All our headquarters in Ypres were then burning.

At the railway crossing on the west side of Ypres, the only practicable exit from the town towards the rear, another Lieutenant and I collected the nucleus of a force that was as mixed in its composition as could very well have been formed. The casuals and men who had lost their units included cooks and officers' batmen (servants), dismounted cavalrymen, spare truck drivers or those separated from their vehicles, military police and a dismounted bicycle patrol, and battle stragglers from some twenty different battalions—the British infantry field unit being a battalion rather than a regiment. Many of them were without rifles or ammunition.

A 420-mm. shell that burst near the intersection where we were forming killed fourteen men outright. A slightly smaller one mopped up eight more a few minutes later. That intersection became a perfect inferno. For a time it was a seething, confused mass of humanity, of wagons, artillery, ammunition limbers and ambulances rushing in both directions, cavalry columns moving up, long lines of walking wounded, and five thousand panic-stricken civilian inhabitants of Ypres fleeing to the rear. Smashed vehicles, dead animals, dead and dying men, were shoved to the sides in a desperate attempt to keep a passage clear, which was blocked over and over again by direct hits, the craters hurriedly filled with debris, with bits of wagons, with dead horses. Anything to keep the road open: that road whose eastern end had turned into a bloody shambles. All of this was under a cloud of dust and smoke, stained blood-red by the flames of Ypres.

There seemed to be no future in waiting there longer, when I was losing more men than I was collecting. The officer with me—I never knew his name—had been killed. So I marched my odd company, some hundred and forty strong though I could not keep apace with its fluctuations, to the abandoned 28th Divisional Stores close by the Cloître Saint-Martin, which were then burning in half a dozen places. There I equipped them with rifles, ammunition, and one machine-gun which we came upon by chance, and then rushed them out through the Dixmude Gate where a Major I never saw before nor again took over command and led them towards the gap.

In the frightful confusion, decimated by heavy shell-fire, without the leaven of their own accustomed organizations, one could have expected some show of reluctance on the part of those men to follow unknown officers to an unknown end. But that irregular mosaic from different units and different arms obeyed without hesitation to form under violent shelling, to advance into an indeterminate breach—a breach with the terror of poison vapors all about them and annihilation in unpleasant ways only too likely to be their lot. It was an impressive example of the result of training and discipline on men of good spirit.

Not all of them knew into what they were going. Many of

the battle stragglers did—men who had lost their units and their locations in the mêlée of the fighting. Some may have felt that nothing could be very much worse than the concentrated fury of heavy shells falling on Ypres. But out along the Langemarck road I had seen men running, foaming at the mouth as they ran, writhing as they fell. In the hollows floated wisps of greenish-yellow cloud. There was a faint sweetness to the air, a sweetness of fearful death, down in the hollows where the vapors hung thick. One had no protection against those vapors. We did not have gas masks.

The chlorine clouds were localized. Gradually they dispersed, but in the dark only the glint of star-shells, reflected on the low-lying mists, gave warning of their presence. They were noxious even when partially dissipated. The grim fear of renewed discharges had a strong effect on morale. But the German Command fortunately had not appreciated the full potentialities of their new weapon, along with the element of surprise. They tried it out on a limited scale. Otherwise Ypres, and in all probability the whole of Flanders, would have been lost that night.

All that was saved was the reconstituted line, of questionable strength, and the blasted, gutted skeleton of a town. Ypres was now but a flaming shell-trap; deserted save for a few Royal Engineer and other details who crawled over the debris of the streets, where fragments of walls kept collapsing with dull rumbles in clouds of black smoke and reddened dust. Among these details I was one, on occasions the only one.

Ivor McClure and I, after having been separated under the impact of the battle, were proceeding on the afternoon of the 29th of April up the Street of Butter on our way to the Street of the Dogs, ducking each eight minutes into some sort of cover that could serve as protection against fragments and concussion. For the Germans were lobbing over their 420's on a precise eight-minute schedule, garnished with 4- or 6-inch shrapnel and high-explosives, two to the minute, in between. These lesser evils we had grown used to, but the 420's were something else. One never reached the point of disregarding them. As to direct or near-direct hits from any of them, one's only defense was a fatalistic attitude.

A 420 had just burst near the Cloth Hall. It threw large chunks of town all over the place. We emerged from a momentary retreat while it was still raining pieces of Ypres in the gloom of smoke and pulverized buildings. Through the murk came an apparition running down the street. It was covered with whitish dust, the overlay of everything where high-explosives have been at work in a town. Its skin beneath the powdery covering was a deep, unwholesome blue, and it spat blood. We tried to halt the sorry figure to see if we might be of help, but it tore past with glazed and staring eyes to disappear in the acrid after-spume of the shell.

"Looks like he's had it!" commented Ivor briefly.

We continued on our way, and a few moments later came upon two thoroughly shaken ambulance orderlies. They had, they said, been thrown nearly across the Grand' Place by the concussion of the last 420, just as they were about to remove a wounded man from the Cloth Hall.

"Our driver was standing quite near us," one of them added. "So help me, he was blown clean away! We couldn't find no trace of him!" Presumably he was the wretched object that had passed us on the run.

Neither of the orderlies knew how to drive a car, nor was disposed to remain longer in that hell-hole for ten ambulances. We let them stagger back towards the dressing station on the Vlamertinghe road. They were in no condition to be of use, and another 420 was due.

We crouched under a vaulted archway while the horrid thing came with a scream that seemed to last for minutes. It burst at the corner of the Street of Butter and the little Place with the big name—Van den Peereboom—that once had been the dock and inner "port" of Ypres. This was exactly where we were headed. The last three bursts had all been in the same quarter.

"Don't much care for that concentrated pattern!" said Ivor.

When the coarsest of the downpour of bricks, roof tiles, stones and timbers had let up we made a dash through the fumes.

"Just seven and a half minutes to go," said Ivor.

We came upon the ambulance in the little Place. It was a Model-T Ford, a good deal smashed but seemingly workable. Fighting desperately with its crank I got the engine started after several kicks that almost broke my arm. Ivor had discovered the wounded man in the debris of the Cloth Hall. He was badly shattered but still alive. We managed to get a stretcher under him, fearful lest he should come apart when we lifted him. My watch showed that there remained thirty more seconds before the next 420 was due. We hesitated, standing in the roofless, ruined Cloth Hall by the stumps of two Gothic columns.

Precisely at the eighth minute the shell arrived. We tried to ease the tension by betting on the exact split-second of its burst. Its scream was the most unpleasant, menacing sound I have ever heard; interminably prolonged. It burst on the other side of the narrow little Place. The whole world seemed to rock and shake: most of the remnants of the Cloth Hall came down, though luckily the concussion blew them outwards. We were knocked flat, deafened, and all but strangled in the fumes and smoke. The two stout columns, nearly seven centuries old, saved us from annihilation. Our clothing and skin were riddled, and in some manner I was scorched down the neck and one side. A fragment all but severed a foot of the half-dead man lying on the stretcher beside us.

It took ages for the smoke and dust to settle so that we could see at all. Our eyeballs burned from the bitter fumes. The roar of falling debris continued, it seemed, for minutes.

"Five minutes to go!" Ivor signalled with his hands.

I scarcely expected to find a trace of the ambulance. But here it stood: an astonishing contraption, riddled like a sieve et still holding together. The engine was running, racing and spouting hot water from a score of holes through the radiator. We heaved our casualty aboard and lurched off. There seemed scant chance of clearing the mountainous debris. We did clear it, in the weirdest motor drive I ever hope to make.

Three of the tires were flat. The single front spring was cut completely in two—every leaf of it. A chunk nearly two-thirds the diameter had been bitten out of the front axle. Half the spokes were gone from one front wheel, four from the other, and pieces of broken spring-leaf kept working out to wedge themselves between the spokes that were left. Where the instrument panel had been were merely a few splinters vibrating to the racing engine. The steering gear was all chewed up. Of the steering wheel itself only a fragment some seven inches long remained. I found myself repeating the refrain from some comic song I once had heard about a Ford—"but the damn thing ran!"

We all but upset innumerable times, lurching around the edge of shell-craters, rocking over great piles of wreckage. Ivor had strapped in the unconscious casualty. He himself hung way out as a counter-balance on one side or the other, as on an ice-boat; pushed and heaved, pried big chunks of Gothic carving out of the way. Twice more we were hit by shrapnel bursting almost overhead, and again it was our ill-fated passenger who bore the brunt—this time in the thigh. Thirty seconds after we had cleared the little Place another 420 burst just about where the ambulance had stood. In some manner I got that shambling wreck through to the casualty clearing station on the Vlamertinghe road, shouting rather inanely: ". . . but the damn thing ran!"

"Twern't possible!" Ivor yelled back. "And I can prove it! Just take a look at the damn thing now!"

That was the first time I ever drove a Ford.

A few weeks later I was summoned to a conference of Generals at Second Army headquarters. General Atcherly, of Vth Corps, introduced me. "This officer," he announced, "knows more about Ypres, above ground and below, than anyone in the British Army." I believe I did, at that time.

Second Army staff had decided that the only practicable

manner of protecting the Ypres salient was to maintain a strong reserve for counter-attack within immediate striking distance of the encircling lines. For this there was no other feasible location than underground in Ypres itself, unattractive as the position certainly was. After some figuring on ancient town plans, and recent notes that I had made, it was estimated that four thousand men could be maintained with some degree of comfort and security in the cellars of Ypres without too extensive engineering work being required. The matter of getting ration parties through to them without excessive losses was something else, but that was not my responsibility.

Many of the older cellars, as well as the casemates of Vauban's massive seventeenth-century fortifications, were large and strongly built. The vaulting of the casemates was three feet thick in stone and brick with some thirty feet of earth above; yet it was recognized—for we had suffered unpleasant experience in this regard—that none would stand up against a direct hit by a 420. This was a risk one would have to accept, said General Wintour of Second Army.

I was ordered to make a detailed reconnaissance with plans and a report on the condition of all the cellars in Ypres, showing the number of men that could be accommodated in each, the necessary clearing, repairs, strengthening and underground connections required; along with sanitary, lighting and signal arrangements which were made the responsibilities of two other officers on our team of three.

It was headachy work, burrowing through great heaps of calcinated brick and rubble for hidden openings beneath, being shelled continuously in the process. The cellars reeked of lyddite gas. They were full of mosquitoes, gigantic rats and beetles of peculiarly unamiable form. Many were choked with wreckage, half full of stinking water, along with very dead dogs and cats and bodies that the burial details had not found. Only good-sized cellars with barrel- or cross-vaulting, reinforced with iron beams or brick and stone piers, could be considered for the purpose. Most of the old ones were like that, but every one had to be inspected. In certain of them I carried out the excavations that kept our cellar at the Poperinghe mess well stocked with wine.

Some of the best cellars, such as the Post Office vaults in the seven-hundred-year-old Templar House, were even then capable of being utilized by battalions in support. They were strong, clean and airy, and a few of them had been fitted out with "rescued" chairs and tables, beds and mattresses, writing desks, lamps, china and a useful supply of wine. But many of the lesser ones, though as strong in their construction, required no little work to render them habitable, and it was work that would have to be carried out in a singularly uncongenial atmosphere.

The larger scheme of connecting up groups of those cellars, of maintaining a full brigade in support, underground in Ypres, was never put into effect. An unfortunate episode caused Second Army staff to defer that project. On the 12th of August, 1915, I was summoned to Château Lovie, where VIth Corps headquarters was then located. The British Commander-in-Chief, Sir John French, was there. General Ludlow took me to him. It was the first time I had met the "C-in-C," though I had seen him before at a respectful distance. His not very closely cropped greyish moustache was drooping more than usual.

He had just received advice that one hundred and eighty men were missing under the wreckage of Saint-Martin's cloisters, our very best large cellar in Ypres. "It was a direct hit by a 420," said General Ludlow, "and thus far no parties have been able to approach the spot because of continuous heavy shelling."

"There is hope that some of the men may still be alive under the wreckage," interposed the C-in-C. I was struck by his look of a very tired, grey old man. General Lord Locke, commanding VIth Corps, then asked if I would lead a rescue party to tunnel into the debris. I said that I would, of course.

General Ludlow went out with me to organize the party. I knew that cellar in the dark, every inch of it. But the 420 had done an astounding job. We struck in from three points, digging ferociously. I have never in my life been so time-conscious.

For every three minutes there came a 6-inch shell, every six minutes a 12-inch, every twelve minutes a 420; with a rain of lesser projectiles between. The men of the rescue party worked as I have never seen men work before or since.

Unexpectedly the Germans dropped a 15-inch shell on us off schedule. It wiped out one of the three groups—I think not a man escaped alive or without mortal injury. I had just left that group. The concussion caught me and I remember nothing clearly of what happened afterwards, though we kept going for a while longer until the shelling made it impossible to continue. But just before that 15-inch shell burst we came upon an example of fortitude such as one does not soon forget.

We had not been very successful in our quest. The tunneling was rightly directed but the few men we got to under the debris were dead. One, however, we partly uncovered who was still alive. He was a corporal, I remember. He was squashed flat from the waist down, held fast between great chunks of fallen stone that we could not budge. With clear mind and voice he directed the digging, telling us where the men had been located in the cellar when the shell which buried them had hit. Vigorously he protested at risking life to get *him* out.

"I'm cooked," he said. He said it in a perfectly matter-of-fact tone. "Don't waste time on me. Get after the lads who may still have a chance to live. I haven't." He drove us. With such intensity of spirit as made light of the impossible, that half-figure of a man, held up by the stones that had crushed the other half, drove us, his thoughts entirely on others.

He died there, still directing. We could not get him out, striving feverishly against his continuous protests: what with the enormous weight of thirteenth-century architecture pinning him down, and the fierce shelling. Perhaps it was better so. He was right, there was no chance of his living much longer. Up to the very end he—the half of him that was still alive—continued to direct the rescue work. He died upright in the stupendous upheaval of masonry. I regret that his name was blotted from my memory in the burst of the 15-inch shell. Corporal X of the D.C.L.I., a very gallant soldier.

THE JABBERWOCK

WHEN THE ANCIENT city of Ypres had succumbed to its multiple wounds, though the salient was still maintained around it, I fell back on Poperinghe. Here one could live above ground; in a sand-bagged house, to be sure, but with its roof comparatively intact. In this I also established a mess that was entertaining in its blend of racial components. There were, over a period of time, three Frenchmen, a Scot, an Irishman, three Belgians and two Americans—one, myself, in British uniform, the other, Franny Colby, in Belgian.

We did ourselves well, in the light of circumstances. I had grown a bit tired of eating salvaged rations from burning dumps in Ypres with a folding knife-fork-and-spoon and a tin cup. We sequestered a highly capable Belgian soldier-cook who had been chef of a restaurant of repute in Brussels; and our wines from the well-stocked cellars of Ypres were very good. Occasional mess guests coming from the coast at Dunkerque would bring us fresh fish; others from G.H.Q. brought whisky or gin, and sometimes a tasty cheese. We had reasonably good tableware, salvaged from the ruins, and even napkins. All in all we didn't do ourselves too badly for a mess that was fairly regularly under shell-fire.

One evening Lieutenant Sandeman, of the family of vintners that has maintained its English nationality in Portugal for many generations, and during that time helped to bring the drinking of port to a ritual among the British, arrived with a bottle of port that bore the Sandeman label. Lieutenant Sandeman was himself rather Portuguese in appearance, swarthy, brown-eyed, with dark hair and traces of an accent from the land of his birth though not his nationality. He carried the bottle in a basket, like a dozen new-laid eggs.

When we came to the drinking of it, Sandeman beamed. "Now *this*," he announced, carefully decanting the ruby liquid into a rather mixed assortment of glasses—pouring clockwise, of course, from left to right—"this is a *Port! This* is none of your thin, sharp, nasty, weak, immature, sickly ports one gets nowadays in most parts of the continent, and too often even in England itself!" He grew expansive. "This is a rare . . . rich . . . mellow . . . fruity . . . noble . . . beautiful . . . old Port!" Holding his glass aloft by the stem, with a reverential light in his eye, he purred on, his voice vibrant with emotion, "*This* is a . . ."

Ivor McClure, having come unexpectedly from Bailleul, was dining with us that night. He had not lately enjoyed the advantages of quite so well set-up a mess. As Sandeman pattered on, Ivor could stand the strain of waiting no longer. His mouth was watering, his eyes agleam. He reached for his glass, grasping it firmly around the bowl, close to the rim; not delicately as he should have done, with finger-tips low down on the stem. I saw a horrified look pass across Sandeman's face.

"Jesus Maria, man, don't do *that!*" shrieked Sandeman. "*You'll smell your fingers!*" Ivor snatched away his hand, but it was too late. Sandeman wept openly at the desecration of his splendid, rare, rich, noble old Port.

Franny Colby, the other American, could have been the original of *The Man Who Came to Dinner*. He came for dinner, and stayed for a year. He and Eugene Kuhlmann, who later served as a liaison officer on General Douglas MacArthur's staff, did not always hit it off too well together.

Kuhlmann spoke four languages with almost equal facility. His knowledge of Gothic architecture, of the masterpieces of the Golden Age of Painting, of heraldry and of wines has already been mentioned. He knew most of the great libraries of Europe, as far as their ancient volumes were concerned, as well as he knew his own library in Colmar. I ran into him ten years after the war, at Monte Carlo, recataloguing the library of the Prince of Monaco.

He had escaped from Colmar into Switzerland at the outbreak of the war in 1914 one jump ahead of the Germans, who, among other things, looted some of the best books from his library. He reached Paris and there, as a sergeant of the reserve whose class had not yet been called up, reported for military service. Because of his special qualifications he was immediately mobilized and assigned to herding the cattle that had been gathered on Longchamps race course to supply Paris with meat during the expected siege. He could speak to his charges in four, or perhaps five, languages. They did not understand him in any. As to their habits and care, their feeding and the manner of their slaughtering, his knowledge was confined to the descriptions he may have read in illuminated manuscripts dating from medieval days.

Kuhlmann was an amateur cook of no mean ability. His sauces were the inspirations of a genius. He taught me a number of things in culinary refinement. But Franny Colby took delight in tormenting him.

Franny had "borrowed," when I was out on a patrol, my most treasured Scott Adie camel-hair blanket, light as a feather, in which to wrap up a few odd items of his collection of unexploded German shells and bombs, heavy howitzer shell-bases, grenades, fuses, rifles, side arms and other trophies. He deposited these in my father's office at 30 Avenue des Champs-Elysées in Paris. I heard the repercussions of that deposit for twenty years. There was enough uncontrolled high explosive, my father maintained, to have blown his office and himself clear over to the left bank of the Seine.

Franny Colby returned from Paris with a collection of dead birds wrapped up in the frayed remnants of my blanket. He said that the birds were young pheasants he had shot when passing by the estate of the President of the Republic at Rambouillet. All but one *were* young pheasants, though he admitted later that he had acquired them in other ways than by shooting in the President of France's private preserves. One he had shot, himself, somewhere on the way up.

He took much concern over the preparation of those birds, and was careful to direct their serving so that the one shot by his own hands went to Kuhlmann. Ours were delicious, but I remarked a curious expression on the face of Kuhlmann as he sampled the dish served him. His keen blue eyes noted the gusto with which we were devouring our pheasants. Once more he tried his, then laid aside his knife and fork.

"*What* is this animal?" he asked coldly.

"That?" chirped Franny, digging into the other half of his pheasant. "You don't like pheasant?"

"I *do* like pheasant," said Kuhlmann. "This is not pheasant. I don't know what it is, except that it is very nasty and it is *not pheasant!*" He leaned back from his plate and glowered at Franny Colby.

"Not pheasant?" Franny remarked pleasantly. "Oh, then it may be there was some mistake; for on the way up I did kill a crow." Kuhlmann was less than mildly amused.

That evening, after Kuhlmann had left us in a dudgeon, I received a summons to report to St. Omer by nine the next morning for a conference with another group of Generals who wished information on the cellars and underground works in Ypres. Very early in the morning I set off with Franny Colby, who wanted to see some friends at G.H.Q., and my small black griffon-terrier mascot dog, presented to me by the part-griffon bitch I had saved from the flames of Ypres, known by the name of "Dicke-busch."

As dawn was breaking we zigzagged over Cassel hill. I knew that road well. In the wet, grey ground-mists I drove down the zigzags on the far side with confidence and precision. The eleven ancient windmills crowding one another for the breezes that fan Cassel hilltop signalled through the mist with gaunt wooden arms. They seemed to point the way, and whatever way they pointed would have been right on that zigzag road.

As we wound around the last hairpin bend I looked through the bordering poplars and could see that the road was clear. It was wet and slippery, but without traffic beneath the dripping fringe of trees. The car had begun to pick up speed down the straight lower slope when suddenly there came into view, close ahead, the profile of a horse shuffling onto the road from off the hillside; a dingy grey horse that appeared without warning out of the grey mist between the poplars.

I tried to guess what it would do—stop, turn, or continue across the road. A skid was sure to result if the rear-wheel brakes were sharply applied on that wet and greasy slope. My guess was that the horse would continue on across the road, so I aimed behind it. My guess was right.

But as we approached at a speed which made it unlikely that I could hold the car in control on any abrupt change in direction, I observed with acute pain a length of rope dragging after the horse. The rope was attached to the front of a little three-wheeled cart which a peasant steered by a pole sticking out behind. And I knew what little three-wheeled carts of that type in Flanders usually contained.

"Oh my God!" cried Franny Colby, " 'ware the Jabberwock!"

There remained the choice between hitting the horse or the cart. But in edging out a bit from the latter the car began to slip sideways, and I managed to get them both. The horse came suddenly rolling, I don't know how, up over the front of the car, carrying away the right front mudguard, the windshield, the upper segment of the steering-wheel and the canvas top. There was a heavy thump as the animal fell back on the road behind us. I saw "Dickebusch" sailing out overhead, small black beastie with a brilliant white vest and all four legs set like airbrakes, catapulted into the grey vapors of the morning that hung low between the poplars, and in those mists disappear.

We continued sideways with the cart thrown against the

right of the car. Franny Colby was slumped in the seat beside me with blood pouring down his face from cuts by the windshield glass. We had no shatter-proof glass in those days.

And then, like a slow-motion picture, the cart began to rise by our side, until it overtopped the edge of the car and slowly, quite deliberately it seemed, poured its contents upon us. Its contents, as I had realized only too well when the cart's single front wheel first appeared in view, were the ripe evacuations of Flemish cesspits—the rich liquid manure so prized by farmers for fertilizing their truck gardens.

The cart was about three-quarters full. With deadly precision it poured every drop in a localized Niagara over our helpless forms. I received most of it, on the right side behind the broken steering-wheel of the "Sunbeam." We came eventually to a stop across the main road between G.H.Q. and Second Army Headquarters. The tangled wreckage of car, cart and horse—the last by now quite dead—blocked the road completely. The peasant, aroused from his usual lethargy by the odd positions of his horse and cart and the spilling of his precious substance, began to yowl invectives in guttural Flemish. Franny Colby was in a bloody daze. I could not imagine that liquid manure was the best treatment for raw cuts.

Clambering out of the wreckage I mopped off Franny's face with a handkerchief that had escaped the septic bath, then plodded up the hill while the farmer howled throaty imprecations after me. On top of the hill there was stationed an M.P. from Second Army Headquarters. I summoned him. He saluted, but it seemed as though he noticed something peculiar in my appearance.

"I've had an accident," I said. This must have been fairly obvious, though perhaps not just what sort of accident. Certainly I smelt to high heaven.

"Go at once to Colonel Trevor"—Colonel Bill Trevor of the Buffs was Provost Marshal of Second Army and my friend— "and tell him that Captain Hall" (I had been promoted by that time) "has had an accident on the St. Omer road. Get an ambulance, a doctor and an orderly with antiseptics to go immediately half-way down the hill and pick up an officer who has been hurt. Get a wrecking crew to remove my car and unblock the road. And tell Colonel Trevor that I need a uniform, complete with undergear—any old things will do—and a large carriage-sponge, and a bucket. I'll explain all this to him later."

The M.P. saluted, went off at the double and carried out all his instructions swiftly and efficiently. Franny Colby was removed to hospital with a cut eye and face, from which he came out intact some ten days later with a new repertoire of stories of his Australian ward-mates. The farmer was quieted and ultimately reimbursed for damages to one horse and cart and the loss of a load of prime truck-garden intensifier. The car was dragged away for repairs. While all these things were happening, two more M.Ps. met me with a basketful of Bill Trevor's clothes, a large sponge and a bucket.

They led me, keeping at a respectful distance, to a well. There I stripped, flinging aside everything I had on, and they sluiced me down with bucket after bucketful of water. After this I made my way to Bill Trevor's office, garbed in a Colonel's uniform, very loose and sporting Boer War medal ribbons and other insignia which had no particular relation to my status at the time.

The Provost Marshal was seated at his desk. On top of this, anxiously waiting, sat Dickebush. He had been there on occasions before, and had found his way through the mists on the hillside to wait for me in a familiar setting.

I thanked Bill Trevor for the uniform and for the carriage-sponge. He telephoned G.H.Q. that I would not be able to meet the Generals by 9 A.M., adding a postscript of his own. "Tell 'em," said he, "that I don't suppose they'd want him there anyway, so soon after breakfast, if they knew he'd just bath'd in liquid manure!" He sent for some breakfast for me, but made me eat it outside.

"When you've had as much service as I have," he said with mock solemnity, "you'll appreciate that there are certain delicacies to be observed in the presence of senior officers. Such as—er—personal cleanliness. I *hope* my men sluiced you down quite well? One can get uniforms deloused and that sort of thing out here, but not readily dry-cleaned, you know."

I enjoyed Bill Trevor's hospitality a good many times after that, but he would always wrinkle his nose and sniff as I came in.

"It *may* have worn off," he would say. "But, now tell me, would you call taking a bath in liquid manure, and then coming to breakfast with the Provost Marshal, in the Provost Marshal's own uniform, 'conduct becoming an officer and a gentleman'?"

YPRES CLAY

"THIS SOIL HOLDS WATER like a sponge." So wrote the Maréchal de Vauban in the seventeenth century to Louis XIV, for whose greater glory he was then rebuilding the fortifications of Ypres and other strategically located towns of Flanders.

The outcroppings of subsoil known as Ypres clay, when wet (and the weather rarely remained dry there for any noticeable length of time), were among our major tribulations in the Flanders sector in the 1914–18 campaign. Where the wet surface had been ploughed by shell-fire, men attempting to cross it floundered helplessly in the morass. In the Battle of Passchendaele many walking wounded slithering toilsomely to the rear bogged down and expired in its sticky embrace. One would have been hard put to find a terrain less suitable for the prolonged operations of huge masses of men.

Yet the Ypres clay provided the background for certain episodes that served in their way as comic relief.

There was a Frenchman who had designed a new type of hand-grenade. This was in the early days of the salient, when the British were still heaving "jam-pots" full of iron scraps and explosives, ignited by a slow fuse like a fire-cracker. Quite often the Germans picked up these primitive weapons before they burst and flung them back to explode in the lines whence they had come.

A demonstration of the Frenchman's grenade was arranged to be given before an impressive gathering of British commanding and staff officers. This grenade, antedating the Mills "pine-apple," embodied some of the features of the latter. It had a safety release, a time and contact fuse and, its inventor claimed, would explode on falling in the softest mud. In order to show off its advantages properly the trial was held on an exposed stratum of Ypres clay which the rains had turned into a bottomless morass.

Over the slimy surface there had been laid a T-shaped platform of duck-boards. Corps, Division and Brigade commanders, staff officers from G.H.Q., Second Army and various lesser units, gathered from near and far. From Lieutenant Generals down to Staff Captains they came in their brass hats, their red tabs; in polished field boots and fawn-colored British Warms, with soft fur collars of opossum or beaver. They strolled out on the duck-board approach, lining up along the head of the T as at a pigeon-shoot. The demonstrator stood in the center armed with several of his new positive-action grenades in a haversack.

To the assembled Brass Hats he explained the mechanism, the deadly efficiency of the delicate contact fuse. "And now," he announced, grasping a grenade in his right hand, "you veel see how she explode ven touch even such *potage* as zees!"

He released the safety catch, made one rearward motion with his arm like a cricket bowler: and the grenade slipped from his hand. It shot upward in a puny arc, to fall with a soft *plop!* in the ooze a few feet behind his right shoulder. It did not explode.

But the Generals and the staff officers beat the grenade to the bog. With one accord they plunged, dived head-foremost in hearty abandon, flinging themselves deep into the mire. From this they emerged a little later, richly plastered with wet Ypres clay—in their eyes, in their moustaches, in their hair; over their boots and fur collars, coating their fine British Warms and whipcord breeches a dismal grey. Like water-buffaloes from a wallow they emerged, dripping, incredibly bedraggled, incoherently blasphemous. Some had difficulty clambering back onto the slippery duck-boards. Others had first to stir around in the slough to retrieve their red-banded, gold-leafed caps and rattan swagger-sticks. But once they had squirmed slug-like onto the cross-piece of the T, they stood not a moment on the order of their going.

I do not mean to give an unsympathetic picture of the British "Brass" at that demonstration. They felt that there were other and more useful ways of getting themselves annihilated than in the course of a display of some inventor's brain-child. They were not particularly keen on being carried from the scene on stretchers, and they took a very dim view of the result of the initial experiment. For this one could hardly blame them.

Alone in the mid-point of the clay-covered platform they left the demonstrator, confused and weeping. They ducked past that plaintive little man as though he had bubonic plague. He waved his arms. Tears welling in his eyes he cried aloud: "But nevaire 'as eet 'appen so before! Nevaire, nevaire zat *grenade* she not go off! Eet vas somezing wrong viz ze making of zat one *grenade!* But it veel not so 'appen evaire again: see, I try an-ozzer . . ."

"Stop him!" bellowed the Generals over their shoulders. "Shoot him! For the love of God will someone stop that damned lunatic before he has blown us all to bits?" Two or three of the younger staff officers edged gingerly up to the sobbing inventor— sobbing because his grenade had failed to explode and probably wipe out a not inconsiderable galaxy of British military seniority along with himself. They seized his arms, pinioning him to in-action.

"Please!" he shrieked. "Oh *please* do come back: zees time I *promise* she veel go off!" But the Brass Hats were jostling one another on their way back to the road over the narrow stretch of slippery duck-board, spluttering invective through the Ypres clay that stuck to their moustaches. They had the appearance of a party of tunnelers having just completed the clearing of a particularly slimy drain. That was what made them the angriest of all.

"Admiral" Smith, as he was known in British 6th Division, was a decidedly quaint fish. His khaki uniform bore the stripes of a Naval Lieutenant. He belonged to the Royal Naval Division formed by Winston Churchill for the defense of Antwerp and which, after the fall of that city to the Germans, had been broken up and its components integrated with various infantry divisions in Flanders and northwest France. The first time he had ever been at sea was when he embarked on a troop-ship from his native soil of Australia to rendezvous with the Royal Naval Division in Southampton and proceed thence to the relief of Antwerp. He never got to Antwerp.

He was carried on 6th Division's headquarters strength as Liaison Officer with the Royal Naval Division, then no longer in existence as an entity. He spent his time experimenting with weird gadgets and devising curious and improbable ways of enlivening trench warfare. Eventually he blew himself up along with half a platoon of Sherwood Foresters and no part of him was seen again.

Among some of the brighter issues of his restless brain was the planting of a Canadian bear-trap between the lines, when Second Army staff urgently wanted new prisoners to check our knowledge of the enemy's order of battle. "Admiral" Smith baited his bear-trap with a very plausible simile of a freshly-killed British corporal. The German night-crawling patrols, and ours also, would rarely pass by a new cadaver without examining it. The Admiral's bear-trap caught a German patroller by the arm, the man's co-patrollers being driven off from rescuing him by one of our patrols lurking nearby. The German's arm was badly mauled in the process, though he could still talk, which was the object of the endeavor. Admiral Smith's ideas on further exploiting his project were nipped by someone higher up who ruled it out as not quite in the spirit of the Geneva convention.

The Admiral was highly receptive to a French gadget conceived by some fertile mind at the Schneider munitions plant. This was in a way like a miniature "tank"—well before full-scale tanks had appeared—though it had no armor. It was about two feet wide by five feet long, with caterpillar traction. It mounted two sizable reels of strong cord which actuated its mechanism; and was fitted with a tail of flexible metal pipe three or four inches in diameter, thirty yards in length, filled with TNT. The forward end of the tail, carried under the chassis, had a small wheel in front.

It was a quaint piece of mechanism, both in appearance and in action. One had the impression of a toy designed for adult children, a Rube Goldberg contraption carrying a vicious sting in its tail; mixed with a medieval tinge of days long past when curious machines were dragged cumbrously to the assault of forti-fied places, and stones and boiling lead were poured down upon them from the ramparts. Its purpose was to blow a path in the enemy's barbed-wire through which our raiding parties could at-tack without having first to cut the wire with hand-clippers, a task that few men ever grew to relish.

The employment of it, as its designers saw the matter, was beautifully simple. One placed the caterpillar-chassis on the business side of one's front-line parapet, facing the enemy trenches; after having opened a path in one's own barbed-wire through which the mechanical dragon might crawl. One then at-tached the thirty-yard tail to the caterpillar from the parados behind, across the trench; not wholly unaware, though with fatal-istic disregard, of the fact that this was packed with TNT. The contrivance was now set for its trip to the enemy line.

The operator pulled on a cord that unwound one of the reels and so actuated the caterpillar tracks. Like an obedient dragon the tractor then crept solemnly forward, dragging its tail behind. If all went well it might crawl along the path that had been opened for it, without getting fouled up in the wire on either side and having to be realigned by hand out in front of the trench. Once clear of the "friendly" wire it would creep across no-man's-land, a determined little dragon forging slowly ahead as one pulled back on the cord. It was designed to take shell-craters and similar obstructions in its stride without deviating from its course.

On running against the enemy wire, it would be halted. The operator then started pulling on the other cord. The second reel, free-wheeling up to this moment, thereupon activated the tail, which was pushed forward between the dragon's legs, or tracks, and out in front to its full length. When this also stuck it meant that the whole thirty yards of the tail, its forward wheel leading the way, had advanced under the enemy wire.

The activator had still a third connection with the dragon. This was an insulated electric wire carrying a charge from portable batteries which would detonate the TNT-filled tail. The resultant explosion would clear a reasonably wide path in the enemy's wire defenses, through which the waiting assault party would pour to overwhelm the astounded Huns in their lair before they knew what it was all about. The last six-foot section of the tail was empty so as not to blow up the tractor, which could be salvaged and used over and over again.

Such, at least, was the idea, and it was not without merit in that peculiar phase of trench warfare: where the opposing forces faced each other for several years on a rarely changing alignment, and our raids were primarily to take prisoners for intelligence purposes, and to carry out local demolition of annoying enemy positions. But the best-laid plans of dragons and men "gang aft agley."

We tried our dragon out on a limited scale, which probably was just as well, from a trench to the north of Ypres. Admiral Smith staged the trial. His enthusiasm was not shared by everyone concerned. The infantrymen holding the trench viewed the procedure with acrid distaste: an undertaking of dubious sanity which was bound to bring enemy retaliation down upon their heads and quite likely speed a certain number of them to their graves.

We went out on a dark night, lighted by fitful star-shells. Four men in relays of two toted the tractor, like a corpse, on a litter. The tail was borne shoulder-high by ten others, in the fashion of the canvas dragon in a Chinese New Year's procession. They were not especially joyful in their task and treaded gingerly under their load of TNT. The sentries manning the fire-steps muttered virulent oaths as we filed through the trenches. At the traverses the carrying party had to hold the tail at arm's length overhead to get around the right-angled bends.

When we came to the point where the wire had been opened for the essay we hitched the tail to the body, as prescribed, across the trench. The dragon was then started off down the path, but it did not run straight and fouled the wire on one side before the tail was clear of the trench. While four of us were resetting it on its course, out in the open lighted by ambient star-shells, the enemy opened fire with trench mortars on the traverse just beyond. This might have been a coincidence, for we worked in tense silence, but the Captain in command of this section of the trench—which was now bridged with a flexible metal tube thirty yards in length filled with TNT—became coldly blasphemous. His invective was none the less biting for being uttered in a carefully modulated tone just above a whisper.

"Get that bloody bag of tricks away from my trench as fast as Christ will let you!" he murmured. "And by the beards of all the Apostles don't ever bring it back!" This was a very small part of what he said, in a quietly pitched voice. He must at one time have been in Serbia or have had Serbian friends, for he consigned us all to the devil's grandmother. We got our "bloody bag of tricks" moving out across no-man's-land, but his admonition against any return was frustrated by Ypres clay.

Because of the mortar fire we deployed our party along the trench, stationing the manipulator of the ropes in a traverse on the left. Beyond the "friendly" wire there was a depression, into which the dragon disappeared. The man on the ropes kept pulling steadily. For some minutes there were no star-shells and we were in inky darkness. At length a brilliantly glowing one lobbed into the sky overhead. In its light I saw something creeping up to our trench, and a split second later heard the tense whisper of the Captain over my shoulder: "What in Christ's name is *that*?"

It was the dragon, complete with tail, coming back home.

It had tried out no-man's-land and didn't like the pasture. It was now forging slowly but determinedly back to the point whence it had taken off.

For a second or so we stared with incredulity while the automaton advanced straight towards the opening in the wire. There followed a moment of confusion. The light of the star-shell was waning, and we couldn't locate the man who was pulling on the ropes—he had betaken himself from his appointed station to another point for a better haul on his cords that were now bringing thirty yards of TNT up to our expectant faces. We finally found him, pulling heartily from a point on the fire-step from which he could not see the dragon. He was dissuaded in whispers from further operation of the cords. This left the dragon, with its tail of TNT, facing us morosely just in front of our position. The trench mortars were touching up the traverse on the right. No one thought any of this really funny at the time. The Captain in command of the trench was the least amused of all.

"Now isn't that bloody jolly!" was the tenor of his remarks, but the remarks themselves were not conventionally printable. He intimated that the sooner we blew ourselves to hell, dragon and all, the happier he would be; though he wished we had picked another place at which to commit mass hara-kiri rather than the front of his parapet. If by some curious misdirection of God's benevolence we happened to live and still retained the urge to plant a load of explosive dung in front of anyone's trench, he suggested in terms lacking cordiality that we choose another trench. He thought that his sentries would probably shoot on sight, without awaiting an order, on any reappearance of our party; but he would be quite prepared to give the order if necessary.

Working under the sporadic light of star-shells, with large clods of trench raining on us from the mortar explosions on our flank, we managed to salvage the recalcitrant dragon and its unpleasant tail. In the early hours of the morning we went back in the same manner in which we had come out, in no less an atmosphere of seething unpopularity.

The next evening at dusk the Admiral and I went out once more to look over the ground. Not having our dragon with us we were not shot at, and the Captain was almost affable after being assured that we had no intention of bringing that ill-esteemed anachronism back to his trench.

We found, from the tracks, that the dragon had hit a shell-crater in the midst of an outcropping of wet Ypres clay. It had slewed around this and made a 180° turn without losing its forward momentum. As the reel was further uncoiled by continued pulling on the cord, the dragon returned on its tracks to menace its guardians who had sent it out into the night.

The experiment was not considered an unqualified success.

Two years later I was still in and around the Ypres salient. Ypres as a town had ceased to exist: it was now nothing more than an incoherent mass of rubble. Yet the general aspect of the salient showed little change. In June, 1917, came the attack by Second Army on the Wytschaete-Messines ridge which supported the Germans' eastern flank in the salient and from which they could look down into the British trenches below. This was far and away the most perfectly executed limited objective operation by the Allies until the nipping off of the salient of St. Mihiel.

Before the attack the 17,000-yard front, including the whole top of the ridge, was subjected to ten days' continuous bombardment of extraordinary intensity. Some seconds before the assault itself nineteen deep mines laid under the German lines went up together—one was ten seconds late—with blinding spouts of light such as might signal the final disintegration of our planet.

There was nothing much that resembled an enemy trench-line where we went through, nor any opposition, that I saw, from human elements. Our guns and tunnelers had not left that sector a place to support life. But the physical going over the up-turned ground was incredibly awful. Until the sun rose above the ridge I had a curious yet persistent feeling that I was on the moon.

The tanks, seventy-two of them, waddled into action after

the assault had reached its first two objectives—the "Red" and "Blue" lines. They deployed then through the slowly advancing infantry. Their commanders had been briefed on the outcroppings of Ypres clay, which were shown on a topographical report I had prepared. These locations had been overlaid on the maps they carried, and were to be avoided as absolute death-traps. But three of the tanks went astray and got stuck. The first mistook the course, which was easy enough to do with all recognizable landmarks effaced by the bombardment. The second went to help out the first, though this was against Tank Corps orders. The third thought the other two were on the right track and wallowed in after them.

I carried some chopped-up paper in a haversack, against just such an event. With it I laid a little paper-chase for other tanks to follow. This may have saved some from a similar sticky end in the clay outcroppings. Yet I was none too sure of the ground myself.

Eventually working to the south in the New Zealanders' area, after having "gone over" with Ulstermen, I tried to locate Messines. But I could see none of the familiar landmarks: neither the oak woods and brooks that once had indicated the lay of the land, nor any suggestion of where the town might have been. This seemed very odd, since I was then on the highest point of the ridge.

I had strolled around in Messines for several hours in October, 1914, before the Germans captured it. Later I often looked at it from Kemmel Hill and from the Wulverghem road. Quite recently I had flown over it in clear weather. During the ten days' bombardment the top of the ridge was invisible from ground or air owing to the constant cloud of dust and debris. But one could scarcely conceive that the massive ironstone remnants of the eight-hundred-year-old abbey church could have disappeared completely. They had, though. For even while I was musing as to where Messines could be, I was standing there. The bombardment had simply removed the whole outer shell of the ridge.

Returning a little later, after waving god-speed to a small

group of tanks wallowing towards the Oosttaverne Line, a momentary but intensely concentrated barrage of enemy shell-fire caught me quite alone and not at all expecting such attention. The suddenness and violence of the strike made it highly disconcerting. I found myself plunging head foremost into a small shell-hole in which there was a dead German, and lay as far under the fortuitous protection of that poor body as I could squirm. The concentration did not last long. I crawled out thoroughly shaken and exceedingly thirsty. Several wounded men near the Green Line had drunk up the last of my water.

I headed back to where the three tanks had been stuck in the clay. Their crews squatted, as some protection against the sporadic enemy fire and yet out of the cramped discomfort of their metal leviathans, under the tail of the first one that was nose-down in the mire. They were drinking from a two-gallon gasoline tin. This they drained bottom up as I approached. I tried to speak, but no sound came out. By gesture I indicated that I was badly in need of water.

"Ho!" cried one of the tanks commanders. "We have just what the doctor ordered for you, and a damn sight better it is than the stinking, chlorinated H_2O from the water carts! Here, this is half whisky and half spring water: go to it!" He handed me another two-gallon tin. It was about two-thirds full. I cocked it to my lips. It was heavy, and under the pressure of all that liquid my throat automatically kept on swallowing once it started. With six or seven swallows gone down I dropped the tin. There was a sudden reversal of process and the stuff spurted back up again from my revolted system. The generous but somewhat distrait officer had handed me the wrong tin. It was not half whisky and half water. It was half gasoline and half benzole.

"Mither of God!" cried out one of the crew in a thick brogue. "Ye've kilt him!"

Contritely they repaired the damage, those cheery, stranded lads whose visions of military glory had sunk with their clumsy tanks in the Ypres clay. With doctorial enthusiasm they poured down my half-opened mouth and over my face the contents of yet another tin that did hold whisky and water. The first gulps of that came up, too. But in their persistence they managed to bring me to my senses and then almost out of them again. I began to feel considerably better. The three crews were genuinely sorry over the mishap. Their sorrow induced them to dispense rather more whisky and water than I absolutely needed on a nearly empty stomach, after having been afoot for thirty-six hours. I weaved my way back across the battlefield, gurgling a trifle incoherently to myself. And for some days I was unable to taste any difference between bully-beef and plum-and-apple jam.

SANCHE

I FIRST MET SANCHE when he was the French liaison officer with the British 6th Division. We were of the same age, the same height and weight, and we could have exchanged uniforms with a completely satisfactory fit on either side. His well-shaped, oval head showed race and breeding. His keen and handsome face, with thick, dark hair brushed straight back but not too sleekly, vivacious brown eyes and sensitive, humorous mouth with very white teeth, expressed the zest for living that he felt as intensely as any person I have ever known. Life for him was a gorgeous adventure. He filled it very full while it lasted.

Sanche allowed himself a certain latitude in his uniforms, being attached to a British Division. His breeches were fashioned by an English breeches-maker, his field boots by an English boot-maker long established in Paris. He spoke English without effort or noticeable accent, having been brought up partly in England. He was very popular with the 6th Division staff, but he preferred my mess at Poperinghe to the Divisional headquarters mess because of the former's continental cuisine and diverse composition, as well as for its supply of excellent French wines retrieved from the cellars of Ypres.

Though heart and soul a Frenchman his point of view was international. He had a maturity for his age that few American youths attain at twenty-four, a ripeness of mind resulting from a different type of education and environment. Like many young Frenchmen of cultured upbringing he had a keen appreciation of the more gracious expressions of life—architecture and painting, literature, music, good food and wines: all the things that make for a fuller existence. Unlike many Frenchmen, he had also an appreciation of geography.

French aristocrats, as a class, have never completely got over their fear and dislike of the common man which was engendered by the Revolution. They find it difficult to talk to their social inferiors on a basis of equality. Most of them—it is rarely wise to generalize—look down upon the lower classes, yet fear them because of that hideous manifestation of human passion which the Revolution brought in tow. They are polite but distrustful.

Sanche was not like that. His manner towards his military and social inferiors was a blend of *camaraderie* and equality with a keen appreciation of the fitness of things and a total lack of self-consciousness. I doubt if he ever sensed fear as such, though his reactions were anything but bovine.

Sanche was self-assured in an agreeable manner, a diverting and intelligent conversationalist. He was in no wise awed by Henri Bernstein or Francis de Croisset, each some years his senior and neither of them what one would have called a shy man nor unconscious of a reputation for brilliance in the use of the spoken as well as the written word. These two dramatists, de Croisset a Captain liaison officer, and Bernstein then a sergeant interpreter (we had no distinction of rank in our mess, though our messmates and guests were hand picked), occasionally dropped in on us—separately—for a meal. Only once were they there together. This resulted in a highly entertaining evening.

It became fairly clear as dinner progressed that Bernstein harbored no profound respect for de Croisset's contributions to dramatic art, any more than for his military attainments, though mentioning neither specifically. De Croisset, while avoiding reference to Bernstein's successes as a playwright, managed to convey the impression that the latter's plays were overrated.

De Croisset's wit was sparkling but frothy, like the acrobatics of an aviator performing tricks before an impressionable group of women. I had heard that his scintillations had their greatest success with women. Bernstein brought his heavy anti-aircraft guns to bear with relentless and calculated skill. Sanche kept circling round the fringe of the combat, happily firing spasmodic bursts at one or the other major contestant. Before we broke up at a late hour, de Croisset—or in any event his opinions on numerous phases of human endeavor or disintegration—had been shot down in flames. He was still burning when the contest ended with a last, sonorous boom from Henri Bernstein departing into the night. That was the only time I ever heard Francis de Croisset silenced. It was also the last time I ever saw him at our mess.

Our evenings were not always so entertaining. Two or three nights later the Germans dropped a 6-inch naval shell, fired from a railway mounting, into our lounge. I returned late that night, to find the house a shambles. Georges Bloch, one of our Belgian messmates, had been killed. A French colleague, Bernard d'Hendecourt, found himself in the street, blown clear through the wall, though only superficially hurt. George Barclay, a Scotsman and son of my father's friend Sir Thomas Barclay, had been playing L'Après-midi d'un Faun on a "rescued" Belgian violin. He was flung through a sandbagged window, all in one piece, along with the sand-bags; spared to be killed on a later occasion. The Belgian griffon-terrier bitch I had saved from a burning house in Ypres, who had presented me with four pups in token of her gratitude, had disintegrated into small splashes along with two of the pups.

This all had happened before Sanche came in. When he did he took charge of the situation, restoring the mess to something approaching normalcy. We buried Georges Bloch in the morning, rebuilt the side of the house with rubble and fresh sand-bags, and "rescued" some more abandoned furniture for the devastated lounge. That was standard operational procedure, oft repeated with minor variations.

Sanche was an enthusiastic horseman. When occasion permitted we would go out on a restricted paper-chase mounted on

"Class 3" cavalry chargers borrowed from the British Cavalry Corps. Neither our hunting country, with its frequent barbed-wire defenses, nor the quality of our hunters was quite up to Pytchley tradition; though I do not mean to imply that the Pytchley Hunt is a paper chase. Sometimes we attempted to play polo on these same animals, or others like them, with officers of the Divisional staff and artillery on an improvised field under direct observation from enemy sausage balloons. That game, though its resemblance to high-handicap polo under normal conditions was remote to say the least, had a certain quaint zest of its own, played with untrained mounts on a field where the sport was frequently disrupted by sundering charges of high-explosive shells.

As was entirely normal for a warm-blooded young warrior in a time of violent stress, Sanche had an ardent love affair. This he discussed delicately but without inhibitions. The object of his affections was a lady of high degree then serving with the French Red Cross in Paris. Sanche occasionally slipped away to meet her in Boulogne, a debarkation and base hospital center in the back area which she could reach without too great difficulty in her Red Cross uniform. Once or twice I abetted his project by taking him there in a car, appropriately called a Sunbeam, that was now and then assigned to me and as frequently withdrawn. From personal observation I was able to report to the Poperinghe mess that Sanche's taste in feminine charm was well up to his high standard in other regards.

His beloved lived on the Place des Etats-unis in Paris, which later became the focal point of Sanche's aerial guardianship of the two things he held most dear: his lady, and the loveliest city in the world.

Sanche told entertaining stories of other and different adventures before the war, especially of shooting izard, the small Pyreneean chamois, in the mountains along the Spanish border. There, on the Spanish-speaking side, he was known as Don Sancho de Agramonte. He had an old Basque guide, a sort of family retainer, who despite his years had the agility and the

muscles of a chamois in the mountains, and who led Sanche
over the precipitous heights coated with the snows and ice of
winter in search of the elusive mountain goats.

Though endowed with excellent coordination and balance
Sanche suffered none the less a number of bad falls in these
ventures, for hunting the chamois is a tricky sport. Each time he
slid off a Pyreneean alp the old Basque guide carried him back
to his base camp, with a broken ankle, arm or collar bone. The
ancient tracker would report to Sanche's family: "He is not
badly hurt; only a little broken, and he will mend. Such things
are bound to happen to an impetuous youth, though I do my
best to watch over him. He will recover and be none the worse.
He will live for a long while yet, and when he dies I will die."

Sanche said that his shooting accidents did not unduly upset his family, but that the repetition by the Basque guide of the
remark after each fall, "He will live for a long time yet, and
when he dies I will die," gave them scant gratification. The
Basque guide had fought in the Franco-Prussian war of 1870,
and not as a mere youth. Sanche, who was more than forty years
his junior, had with normal life expectancy good reason to as-
sume that he might outlive his guide, hardy as the old man was.

The ancient Basque loved Sanche like his own son. Also he
retained an undying hatred for Germans because of his experiences in 1870–71. So when the Germanic hordes invaded France
anew in 1914, and Sanche was mobilized, the old man volunteered for combatant service. Being then more than sixty-five
years of age he was turned down, but through his insistence and
Sanche's intervention in his favor he was, some months later,
appointed a *garde-barrière*. In this capacity, outfitted in wooden
shoes, working clothes with an arm-band, an ancient military
cap and an Austrian rifle of a model of about 1864, he stood
guard on a railway crossing outside of Bayonne. There were no
Germans, there was no shooting nor even attempted sabotage
in the vicinity of the crossing, and the old man became bored
with inaction.

"He wrote me several letters," Sanche said, "protesting that his capabilities were not being made full use of in the war against his ancient enemies. Of course he doesn't know how to write, but he gets someone who does to do it for him. I managed, through a friend of mine stationed down there, to have him assigned as a *garde-convoi* in Bordeaux. He was given a uniform and a somewhat more modern rifle, and sat alongside the driver of a truck running ammunition from the port of Bordeaux up to railhead.

"But he still wasn't happy," Sanche went on, "because there were no Germans and there was no shooting around Bordeaux. So a couple of months ago I succeeded in getting him transferred to an ammunition truck-train running shells up to the front in the Champagne sector. He's happier now because he's being shot at, by artillery fire in any case, and he likes the sound of the guns. Also he feels that he's really doing something, delivering the ammunition to the dumps to hit back at the Germans who have again invaded our country. But I'll wager he'll end up in the infantry yet! He's a Basque mountaineer, and at sixty-six he's a damn sight tougher than a lot of youths from the towns."

Shortly after I was ordered by British Second Army staff to make an underground reconnaissance of Ypres, I came upon, in one of our rest areas, a Belgian refugee who had succeeded in saving a considerable part of his library from the flames and disintegration of what had been Ypres above ground. Among the volumes he had managed to take away with him was one called *Histoire Militaire de la Flandre*, published in Belgium in about 1880, as I recall. Accompanying this was an annex, in a separate album, containing plans of the fortifications and defenses of the towns of Flanders covering nearly a thousand years. The earliest one of Ypres dated back to 930, when the town was but a mean village of poor houses grouped for protection around the chateau of Baudouin-the-Bald, Count of Flanders, on a narrow island in the little river Yperlee.

Later and very detailed plans showed the formidable fortifications built by the Maréchal de Vauban, one of the greatest
military engineers of all time, in the reign of Louis XIV. A large
part of the defensive works he erected, with their heavy casemates and wide outer moat, still existed and served a useful purpose in 1915. The album also had diagrams of the many battles
fought for and around Ypres.

There was a village called Vlamertinghe—most of it disappeared in 1915 and the years immediately following—midway
between Ypres and Poperinghe. On the edge of it was a farm
known as La Ferme de Vlamertinghe. It was a very ancient farm,
but all of its buildings, save only one, had collapsed under the
impact of recurrent wars. The single one then extant was a
splendid, Gothic-vaulted stone barn. It dated from the sixteenth
century.

In this I established, while making my underground reconnaissance of Ypres, an advanced headquarters—in a manner of
speaking. Ypres itself was then utterly uninhabitable, and my
mess and quarters in Poperinghe were a bit too far back for my
purposes. There on occasions I was visited at dinner time, and
relardered, by some of my messmates from Poperinghe; expecially
Sanche and Bernard d'Hendecourt.

One evening the three of us were there, dining not too
frugally. They had brought food prepared by our Belgian chef
in Poperinghe, and I had several very good bottles of burgundy
retrieved from the cellars of Ypres. The enemy shell-fire was
moderately heavy, but we were well sandbagged against anything but direct hits.

During the previous evening while reading the *Histoire
Militaire de la Flandre* I had come across a description of the
assault of Ypres by the Maréchal de Grammont, an ancestor of
Sanche's in the seventeenth century, who captured the town in
four days. The album showed the plan of his saps, which took
off from beyond La Ferme de Vlamertinghe. They followed
almost exactly the line of one of the British communication
trenches of 1915, then used only in emergencies since the main
road was passable though often unpleasant.

The Maréchal had set up his headquarters in the same Gothic-vaulted stone barn which we were then occupying. The description of it in the *Histoire* was extraordinarily precise, varying little from our setting except that the Maréchal had not deemed it necessary to sandbag the arched windows. The barn had not changed notably in close on to three hundred years. Sanche was entertained by the thought that his remote great-grandfather had eaten his meals, drunk his wine and planned his attack in the same barn where we were now drinking our burgundy three centuries later.

"He was a hard egg, from what I've read about him," said Sanche, "but a damn good soldier. I don't believe that he would have milled around in quite so unimaginative a fashion as we seem to be doing now." Sanche lighted a cigarette on one of the long-tailed "trench" briquets which need no fluid.

"Forefathers of mine," he ruminated, "have served in whatever was the newest arm in all the wars of France. When crossbows were introduced, one of my ancestors was in command of a crossbow company. There have been many other pioneers since. Today the new arm is aviation. I have decided to go into aviation."

Bernard d'Hendecourt pulled a ring from his finger. "This," he said, "was cut off the finger of a dead d'Hendecourt after the battle of Agincourt in 1415. He foundered in the mud with his heavy armor, and was slaughtered by the English. I'm all for lightness. I, too, am going into aviation."

"That makes it unanimous," I contributed. "I don't know whether any of my ancestors wound up a crossbow, but I, also, dislike mud, particularly Ypres salient mud. I am going to take to the air. Let me fill up your glasses." We drank to our future in the new arm.

It took considerably longer than we had foreseen at La Ferme de Vlamertinghe to effect our transfers. Instead of going into the air, I went into the cellars of Ypres. But we all got out of the mud eventually.

Sanche was the first. He took his flying training at Buc, not far outside the gates of Paris. After receiving his brevet he went in for further training in night flying, and was then assigned to the night defenses of the capital. While on this duty he wrote us at the Poperinghe mess, where we were still flopping around in the mud, a charming and poetic description of his sensations guarding the two things closest to his heart: the City of Light and his lady of the Place des Etats-unis. The City of Light was dimmed, but he knew it exceedingly well. As he patrolled above it in the dark in his Breguet, watching for enemy raiders, he could see below him the tracery of the avenues and boulevards, the streets and parks, a network of veins and arteries centering on a heart that beat in the Place des Etats-unis.

Like a feudal knight he patrolled the approaches to his lady's castle, the trigger of a machine-gun in one hand instead of a lance, the stick of a Breguet rather than the reins of a bitted charger in the other.

Sanche must have been a first-class night pilot, for he was appointed to command the first night-fighter squadron of Spads formed in the French Army. This was based northeast of Paris not far behind the front lines, to intercept the enemy raiders before they could reach the capital. He was still protecting his lady and her castle.

He was in command of this squadron in July, 1918, when he was killed. At first he was reported missing in action, but there was a certain chivalry between the combatting Air Corps in those days. The Germans dropped a message on his airfield, with his gold identity bracelet. It said: "Captain-aviator Count Sanche de Grammont was killed in aerial combat over"—I do not now recall the name of the spot—"and has been buried there with military honors."

I was then in command of 1st Observation Group in the American Army, stationed at Francheville, not far from Chateau Thierry. As soon as I could get away, after hearing of Sanche's death, I flew to Paris and went to see Sanche's father to offer my condolences. The old Count was deeply affected by the loss of his son; yet he was philosophical.

"Sanche died, if it had to come," said his father, "as he would have wished: defending his country and his beloved city of Paris against a ruthless invader." I talked of various memories of Sanche, of his intense zest for life, of some of our experiences together in the Ypres salient.

"Did he ever tell you," his father suddenly asked, "about his old Pyreneean guide?"

"Why yes, sir, he did," I said. "I remember his stories about the old Basque very well. And also of how much the old man wanted to get into combat service in the war."

"Did Sanche ever happen to mention," asked his father, "how the old guide, whenever Sanche slid off some precipice and broke an ankle or an arm, would say: 'He's not badly hurt, only a little broken. He will recover and live for quite a while yet, and when he dies I will die?' Did Sanche ever tell you that?" There was a curious expression on the Count's face.

"Yes, sir, he did," I said. "And I recall his saying that the family were not greatly reassured by the last part of the old man's assertions."

"Well," said Sanche's father, "then I think this will interest you." He pulled out of a folder a notification from the French War Ministry. "This came to me," said the Count, "because the old Basque gave my name as his next-of-kin to be advised in case of his demise. He finally got himself into the infantry, you know. It reports, as you see, with regret that he was killed in an infantry charge near Verdun on the morning after the night that Sanche was shot down."

IV

PERSIAN FAÏENCES

"A Moment's Halt—a momentary taste
Of Being from the Well amid the Waste—
And Lo!—the phantom caravan has reach'd
The Nothing it set out from—Oh, make haste!"

LAND OF THE SUN

Ⅰ T IS SPRINGTIME on my hillside. The fruit blossoms have mostly passed, but the lilacs and wisteria, the irises and syringa, are superb. The farmers are ploughing irregular strips of field with yokes of cream-colored Charollais oxen, shouting an endless flow of encouragement or abuse. Huge two-wheeled carts full of manure, pulled by three heavy Auxois horses in tandem, creak over the rough country roads and out onto the fields. Crows and rooks are arriving in great bands to snatch up the seed as soon as it is scattered, and launch lusty assaults on the gardens and the barely forming young cherries.

Offsetting the rich brown strips of ploughed earth are other strips flaming with the yellow of mustard, and yet others where the red-top clover is taking on its brilliant crimson shade. Along with a wide variety of greens they make up the constantly changing patchwork-quilt of the slopes and the valleys, the patches stitched together with the deeper green of the hedges and framed by the dark borders of the forests beyond.

Cuckoos call back and forth from the hedges. The air is fragrant with the fresh perfumes of spring. It tinkles with the burbling songs of nightingales, their singing by no means confined to the night. There is also an evening chorus, in one localized area on the hill, of little grey toads that live in the crevices of the walls. These do not trill like the spring peepers, the tiny frogs of brooks and ponds in the States. Each utters one short peep of even pitch, over and over again at intervals of a second or so; but the pitch varies among the toads, and the choral effect is ludicrously like a lot of penny whistles.

Now is the uncertain period of the spring: *"la lune rousse"*—

the April moon—which may spell success or disaster for the fruit crop, benefit or tribulation for those who grow it and the many others who rely on its products to supplement their diet in summer. For a frost may strike at any time up to the fifteenth or twentieth of May, and should it be a heavy one, like that on the 6th of May, 1945, all the fruit will be lost. That year following the "liberation" is painfully remembered by the people of the hillside. The fruit was killed by the frost; the vegetables and spring-sown cereals were dried up and grilled in the drought of the summer; the wine-grapes, which flourish in the sun, were destroyed by hail just before they were about to yield one of the great vintages in Burgundian history. The life of a husbandman in these parts, as indeed in most others, is a never-ending gamble with Nature.

Many of the apple and pear trees are *espalier*—trained low to the ground and along the sides of walls, so that the fruit is easy to pick by hand and has not so far to fall and bruise itself should it drop. But a frost will kill off the budding fruit just the same.

"*La lune rousse*," say the people of the hillside, "is like a red-headed woman. She is highly temperamental. She may be very amiable, very gentle and warm. But she may suddenly change her temper and fling upon us a cold and devastating fury. She is born in the north, you know, where the ice-bergs are made, and from these she brings the icy blasts to freeze our budding fruit when her temper turns evil. Like a red-headed woman, she is unpredictable."

Devastating and unpredictable as a red-headed woman, this one understands; but *la lune rousse* would seem an exception among red-headed women in expressing her temperament frigidly.

Père Olart is stolidly spading the ground, spitting on his hands as he works. Now and then he rests on his spade, staring contemplatively beyond the horizon even though his thoughts may fall within the enclosure of the garden walls. He wears a battered felt hat, which he sometimes alternates with a tweed cap that might first have seen the light of day around about 1912, and mutters in his week's growth of beard through a draggly moustache that surely has never felt scissors. I do not know how he keeps his pipe in his mouth or manages to mutter past it, for he has no teeth that bear against each other as far as one can observe. Civa, his ancient female hound, lies at no great distance from him as he works, contemplatively scratching fleas.

Père Olart, though at seventy-four he has attained a reasonably ripe span of human existence, does not particularly appreciate one of the oldest things in my house. This is a massive china platter, roughly eighteen inches in diameter and an inch and a half thick in its central part. It is of hard-fired stoneware, heavily glazed and weighs almost the same as so much lead.

Its central section is enlivened by eight cheerful, five-toed blue dragons with heads rather like pandas and tails that resemble palm-leaf fans, cavorting through scattered blue foliage on an oyster-white background. Around this is a border of varied geometrical pattern in blue and oyster-white, in the style of Assyrian brickwork. On the back are conventional Chinese designs and what appears to be the signature of the artist, but which no one so far has been able to decipher.

The platter dates from the Tang dynasty of China and is of ninth- or early tenth-century origin, according to my friend the late Professor Ernst Herzfeld, one of the most eminent archeologists of our time on the Middle and Far East. Professor Herzfeld esteemed it the earliest example of its kind that he had seen. He tried, some twenty years ago, to induce me to send it to the Berlin Museum, a suggestion that I am glad to say I resisted. But Père Olart does not understand why I keep such a dish, all broken around the rim, which he feels is an unsuitable ornament in my establishment—simple as the latter is—and should only be used to serve food to his undernourished hound.

It did not occur to him to remove the platter to the temporary security of his cottage on the hill, during the German occupation, along with the many other objects—M'sieur Buddha, Persian brass trays, mattresses, blankets and so on—that he transported on his wheel-barrow out of reach of the Nazi invaders.

And the Germans, happily, seem to have been no more interested in it than Père Olart.

High up on the top shelves of the bookcases that flank M'sieur Buddha are two Omar Khayyām wine jugs. These are kept there away from the casual touch of the *femme de ménage* who comes in her good time to clean the room and those that adjoin it. The jugs are twelfth century Persian faïence, shapely little clay jugs about eight inches tall, with trefoil tops and a graceful single handle in the back. They were covered with rich blue glaze which has oxidized into silver in the course of eight centuries under ground, though the original blue still shows through in streaks and splashes.

One of the jugs is intact save for a small nick in its top and one in its base—the other is more damaged—which is remarkable in view of the manner of the jugs' burial some eight hundred years ago and subsequent disinterment in 1923. There is, I have been told, perhaps no other extant example of an Omar Khayyām wine jug in such good condition, authentically from the town where Omar lived and died. Nothing now remains of that town, nor has anything of it existed above ground for the last seven centuries or so save for a wind-swept and eroded mound.

It is a curious thing that the two Persian jugs and the Chinese platter came out of that same mound.

Khorasan, the great eastern province of Persia, comprises a very large area. *Khor*, in old Persian, means the sun: Khorasan, the land of the sun, or where the sun rises—the east. I first went to Khorasan from Teheran in a Russian-built *kaleska*, a kind of landau swung on leather straps in lieu of springs, drawn by relays of four underfed stallions, travelling day and night for ten days. There was no other way of making the trip save by caravan, since the track was then impassable to motorcars.

I had been appointed Administrator of the Finances of East Persia, an area about the size of France though with less than a tenth of France's population and served only by animal transport. Among the responsibilities of the office was the administration of the Public Domains. At Nishapūr I found that the Public Domains of the district included—a minor item on the government's register—the site of the town once known as Shahdiakh, one of the earlier predecessors of the present town of Nishapūr. Of Shahdiakh no vestige is left save for the low and barren mound rising above the level of the Nishapūr plain, though the outline of its former walls is still fairly distinct. The mound was at that time under lease by the government to an illiterate donkey driver for an annual rental of sixty tomans, the equivalent of sixty dollars.

The donkey driver took earth from the mound in diminutive loads carried in panniers on the backs of his eight donkeys. This he sold to the opium cultivators as top soil for the opium fields. For though the town had been buried and wind-blown for eight centuries, the soil from its remnants retained some fertilizing element which was valued in a land where fertilizer, either natural or chemical, is scarcely obtainable. Since there were many opium fields needing enrichment in the vicinity of Nishapūr, the donkey driver found a steady demand for the product of his labors.

Shahdiakh was established by Abdullah ibn Tahir in the ninth century as a palace and garden. Other constructions were added, and it became a popular residential suburb. The original town of Nishapūr dates back to the reign of Shapur II or that of Shapur I, five or possibly six centuries earlier. But the history of the towns called Nishapūr and the others spattered over the same broad plain including Shahdiakh, which supplanted them as each in its turn flourished and expired, has been a continuous sequence of alternate affluence and misery, of devastation by earthquakes, of ruthless slaughter and destruction in the recurrent invasions of Turkomans and Mongols, Uzbegs, Kurds and Afghans. The present town is said to be the ninth in succession since the first foundation in the third or fourth century, which does not include rebuildings after partial demolitions.

There is evidence that Omar Khayyām, the mathematician,

astronomer, freethinker and poet, lived and died in the town
called Shahdiakh. His death is placed in 1123. Thirty years later
the Ghuzz Turkomans overran the country and destroyed Shahdiakh. It was reinhabited subsequently and in about 1220 was
the capital and finest city of Khorasan. But it was again completely destroyed by the Mongols in 1221, ploughed under and
the site sown in barley; and later in the same century an earthquake wrought its final end.

I rode out on an ill-mannered stallion to look over the mound
with the donkey driver-lessee. Though illiterate, he was an intelligent man of good appearance, who did not seem to be an in-
dulger in the product of the opium fields for which he provided
the top soil. The Nishapūris of our day are prime opium addicts,
but the donkey driver lived in a nearby village and the villagers
are far less addicted to smoking the drug than the townspeople.

It appeared most improbable, after such a sequence of events
as had befallen Shahdiakh, that anything of interest in the way
of pottery dating from Omar Khayyām's time would remain in
that shaken and eroded mound, seven hundred years or more
later, except in small pieces. The donkey driver said that he often
came upon fragments in his digging, but nothing bigger. I suggested to him that in wielding his pick and shovel he go easily,
for should he uncover any reasonably intact objects that had been
fashioned by human hands, and not break them further in getting
them out, I would give him five tomans for each one. In such
way, if he happened to find a dozen items, he could reimburse
himself for his year's rental of the mound.

He promised to dig with great caution, but I think neither
of us had much hope that anything other than bits would be
retrieved. I gave him a small advance as a token of good faith,
and rode back across the plain to the latest of the Nishapūrs,
which is a mere five hundred years old. The fields were full of
quail, it being springtime, and of big black-breasted sand grouse.
In some places cultivation was being carried on in small basins
terraced in concentric circles like shallow Roman amphitheaters,
and around these many fat sparrows chirped with throaty, buzzing voices that sounded exactly like radio transmitters.

There were men squatting on their haunches, pulling up and eating leaves of *tulleh sabzi*—something like violet leaves—which recalled the story of Nebuchadrezzar eating grass. It may have been that Nebuchadrezzar appreciated the taste of *tulleh sabzi* and has been maligned in biblical history. The leaves are also eaten boiled, with curds, like spinach.

The foothills of the mountains behind Nishapūr were marvelously colored, with yellow and deep reds predominating, and on their crests the ruins of ancient villages and forts and towers stood out against the background of the evening spring sky.

It was some months before I returned to Nishapūr. The opium fields had flowered and produced their noxious crop. The donkey driver was still digging in the remains of Shahdiakh. I looked for him, and he told me that he had unearthed something that might possibly interest me. It was a blue plate, he said, broken around the edge, but there was quite a lot of it in a single piece and it was very heavy.

When he brought it to me I was surprised to find that it was not Persian but Chinese. After I had cleaned it of the deposit its surface had acquired in some seven centuries underground, the decorative blue dragon and foliage design come out as clearly as when the platter had first been fired. I thereupon doubled the donkey driver's stipend.

How a ninth- or early tenth-century Chinese platter came to Shahdiakh is, of course, a matter of conjecture. But it would seem a reasonable supposition that it was brought there by the Mongols after their conquest of China, when Tulē, the youngest son of Jenghiz Khan, invaded Khorasan and destroyed Nishapūr and Shahdiakh in 1221, slaughtering all the inhabitants. Perhaps it was Tulē himself who scooped up his mutton and rice with his fingers from that large and impressive platter. Possibly the platter was partly broken and abandoned, or was lost in the orgy of destruction. At all events it had been buried in the ruins of Shahdiakh for seven hundred years before the donkey driver dug it up in 1924.

He unearthed a few other pieces of Persian origin but all very broken; and some while later uncovered the two Omar

Khayyām jugs. These, though at least two centuries more recent in date than the Chinese platter, had been below ground for nearly a century more. They were found in a deeper part of the mound, protected against being crushed by an abutment of strong burnt brick. Most of the structures of that time except for the mosques, an occasional *madressah* (college) and a few governmental buildings, were made of sun-dried brick, which accounts in large part for the almost total destruction caused by earthquakes and the fact that a city could be "ploughed under" by invading barbarian hordes.

But the two little jugs, though buried in fallen earth, had been preserved by part of an arch of kiln-fired brick built in Omar's time. When the donkey driver showed me the one that is practically intact, after eight centuries of sojourn in an inhospitable, earthquake-rocked mound, his gratification was nearly as great as mine. The jug itself meant little to him. He could purchase a new and better one, for his purposes, from the potters of the present Nishapūr. But to have excavated from his mound, while digging out top soil for the opium fields, an unbroken piece of pottery which I esteemed, and not to have broken it in the digging, was for him the prime reward of an amateur archeologist.

The North Persian caravan track, sometimes called the Golden Road to Samarkand, wanders over the plains below the foothills of the Elburz Mountains. There are almost no trees on the southern slopes of the range save in occasional walled gardens, deforestation having been uncontrolled and furthered by the ubiquitous nibbling of goats on everything growing. The spring rains and melting snows run off unchecked across the plains, cutting innumerable water-courses which had then to be forded in an endless sequence. These tail out into the vast salt desert waste known as the Dasht-i-Kavīr. In summer they are dry and stony.

The Persian postal department operated a relay service of heavy, springless wagons drawn by four horses, always stallions. One could also hire a carriage of sorts and arrange to have it pulled by the postal relays, which were changed every twelve to sixteen miles. The stallions were quarrelsome, their harnesses completely rotten and continually coming apart, their drivers usually sodden with opium. The springs of those vehicles which boasted any were tied together with goat's hair rope and there was always a good chance of a wheel coming off or an axle breaking. In maintenance of its equipment the *Chapah Khaneh* —the postal service—was far from brilliant. But this was not entirely the fault of those in charge of the service.

When I went out to Khorasan the Administrator General of the Finances, Dr. Arthur C. Millspaugh, was having difficulties with the Persian Parliament over the enactment of a law for a consolidated budget. There had been no budget in Persia up till then. Though there was ample time for enactment of the law before the start of the Persian year on the 21st of March, the Parliament took an unconscionable while in considering it. The Administrator General, to force the hands of the dilatory law-makers, gave order that until the law was passed the Treasury was without authority to make appropriations from revenues, and therefore no payments of any nature would be approved.

I took over the post of Administrator of East Persia just before the New Year. The situation grew rapidly acute as time passed, but not the Budget Law. All that issued from Teheran was a multiplicity of telegrams and Treasury circulars stressing that no payments were authorized. The howls of salaryless functionaries, of the police and personnel of essential public services, grew desperate, and with an ugly undercurrent.

There came to me then the Chief of the *Chapah Khaneh* for Khorasan, a quiet little man with a sense of humor, whose responsibility was the service of transport that carried the post and "express," as well as all travellers proceeding otherwise than by caravan, over an area the size of France. He bore an armful of mimeographed instructions and copies of Treasury telegrams transmitted to him by my office in Meshed.

"I have written many reports," he said, "about the miserable condition of our harnesses, the total lack of harnesses in many places, the dire need for new harnesses, but all I get in reply are circular letters from the central administration instructing all Chapah Khaneh stations to keep their harnesses clean and in good condition.

"Then I received instructions not to expend any money at all until the budget should be approved. I wrote, and sent many telegrams, saying that I had no fodder for the horses and no means to buy any. The only response was more circular letters to the effect that *no* money could be spent for any purpose pending approval of the budget."

He waved the sheaf of circulars and copies of Treasury telegrams that he bore under his arm. "I have put these in the horses' mangers," he said, "but the stupid animals refuse to eat them! I have explained to the horses that they must wait patiently for the Parliament to pass the Budget Law. But they grow thin, as we have no fodder left and our credit is exhausted. Since we have to turn in the whole of our revenues to Your Excellency's Administration, and the horses will not nourish themselves on the Treasury instructions, we will have only dead horses to feed when the *Majless*" (the Parliament) "finally acts and the Treasury authorizes the purchase of more fodder. And dead horses will not carry the mails, no matter how much fodder we give them. So there will be no *chapah* service; for it will doubtless be another year before we get authority to buy new horses to eat the fodder we will eventually be authorized to provide for the dead ones!"

In the cold reality of such argument one develops a certain flexibility of one's own, or else the situation deteriorates rapidly. Though not in strict accord with my official instructions I authorized the immediate expenditure of the necessary sums to purchase fodder for the Chapah Khaneh stallions. Some three months later the Parliament voted the Budget Law.

When I came for the first time to Meshed, one of the most fanatical cities of Central Asia, it was in spring. The Persian New Year—No *Rūz*, literally "New Day"—is sensibly fixed at the time when the sun again takes over after winter, and the vernal season begins on the 21st of March. There were pilgrims on the road, heading for the Shrine of Imam Reza; travelling on foot, on horseback (often two to a horse), on donkeys, mules and camels. Many of these were women, heavily veiled, most of them riding folded up in *kajaveh*—wooden crates, one to a woman, hung on the flanks of the beasts of burden. Some of them had been many weeks on the way. As they reached the Hill of Salutation, from which the golden dome of the Shrine is first visible, they descended from their animals—the folded women had to be helped out of their *kajaveh*—and built little cairns of stones beside the road in token of their prayers.

Going in the opposite direction was a big drove of donkeys, many of them white, all in New Year's garb: their foreheads and chests daubed with orange, light green, red or blue color. In the villages and the outskirts of the town other animals—goats, sheep and chickens—were similarly splotched in festive array. The color is left on until the fourteenth day after No Rūz, then removed. On this day the streets of the towns are full of faded New Year plants, mostly a kind of quick-growing grass, thrown out at the end of the holidays as we discard Christmas wreaths after our Twelfth-night.

The No Rūz festival is a season of feasting and of gaiety, of innumerable rounds of calls in the course of which one consumes vast quantities of tea in small glasses along with far too many sweetmeats, and of very little work. But when it happens to fall in the lunar month of Ramazan, the month of fasting, or Moharram, the month of mourning, there is no gaiety at all. Particularly at Meshed, a city as much of the dead as of the living because of the enormous number of bodies of the Faithful buried in the sanctified soil around the Holy Shrine, people go about with lean and doleful faces. The Moslem clergy can be quite unpleasant to any who make merry.

As the springtime flowered and waned, the mournful month of Moharram came upon us in the full heat of summer. While No Rūz is a fixed date based on the sun's orbit, the Persian lunar months slip gradually backwards since the lunar year is approximately eleven days less than the solar year. So Moharram begins eleven days earlier each year and thus in every thirty-three solar years, or thereabouts, completes the circuit of seasons.

My house in Meshed was located outside the walls on the outer Maidan, a large open space where great caravans of camels laden with wool knelt and off-loaded. Behind the walled garden was a *chai khaneh*, a Persian tea house, for cameleers and sundry travellers of the road. From this, as from several others in the vicinity, came sounds of lamentation throughout Moharram by day and by night, the dull thud of the beating of breasts in unison, interspersed with loud cries of "*Shah Hossein! Wah Hossein!*"

The month of Moharram is a period of religious fervor and penitence amongst the Shiah sect of Moslems which has no parallel, certainly as to duration, in any other faith. As elsewhere, the ignorant and fanatical are those who are the most violently swayed. The ardor of their devotions is nowise lessened in the thought, deeply imbued by their religious leaders, that every tear shed in memory of the martyred Imam Hossein washes away a multitude of sins. During Moharram they strive, as one somewhat cynical observer noted three-quarters of a century ago, "to lay up a reserve of piety on which to float through another year of iniquity." Even so, the emotional hysteria which they reach has an underlay of profound sincerity.

The Imam Hossein, grandson of the Prophet Mohammad, was killed at Karbala in Arabia with seventeen of his immediate family on the tenth of Moharram, 680 A.D. This slaying of the descendants of the Prophet by Shimr, Governor of Basrah, at the instigation of the usurping Khalif Yezid in Syria, split the Islamic world into two sects. The Shiahs, residing principally in Persia, refuse to acknowledge the first three Khalifs who followed after Mohammad as spiritual leaders of the Moslems, since they were not blood relations of the Prophet. Shiahs hold that Ali, son-in-law of Mohammad, and his descendants were the only true interpreters of Mohammadan tradition. They retain an undying hatred for the Sunnis, the orthodox sect, whom they blame for the killing of Hossein; and they execrate the names of Shimr and Yezid as the murderers of the Prophet's grandson.

Meshed was hot and dry in summer, but with three thousand feet altitude the heat was never really oppressive and the supply of water from the mountains flowed in abundance. It had an odd effect, therefore, to see people on the last day or two before the tenth of Moharram staggering as they walked through the streets, gasping and clutching their throats, crying loudly: "I thirst!" These gestures were in memory of Hossein and his party, who were cut off by Shimr from the Euphrates and were without water in the burning Arabian heat of early autumn.

On Asūra, the tenth of Moharram, the devotional manifestations reached a climax bordering on frenzy. My Persian servants, bare-footed and with staring eyes, carried out their duties perfunctorily while crying at intervals: "Hossein is dead!" Outside on the streets, most of the populace were chanting: "How full of calamity is today! . . . The head of the innocent Hossein is off its body today!" Only Mohammad-the-cook, who was not very religious though he, too, went bare-foot that day for appearances, took the tragedy lightly. "Hossein is dead," he said to me slyly, "but one still has to eat!" Mohammad also failed to take Ramazan, the month of fasting, very seriously.

In Teheran and elsewhere in Persia an extraordinary Passion Play, the Tazieh, is presented in which are featured the agonies of Hossein and his family in their last stand when surrounded by Shimr's troops and cut off from their water supply. Undoubtedly no other play in the history of mankind has so deeply stirred so many people. But in the Holy City of Meshed the religious leaders opposed theatrical representation in any form, so the Tazieh was not given there.

Rhozéh—recitations of Hossein's torments, by Mullahs— were permitted. One could hear the cries of anguish rising from the walled enclosures where these recitals were being held. But the main demonstrations in Meshed were the *testéh*, the parades, on the tenth day of Moharram. Probably nowhere else could one have seen—I believe the parades have been greatly toned down since then—such an amazing display of religious hysterics.

I went to watch the *testéh* accompanied by my secretary, Hadi Khan, and Sami Bey, the jolly and amusing Turkish Consul General who had twice been exiled from his country by the former Sultan Abdul Hamid for holding too liberal views. Sami Bey was a Sunni, though not an ardent practicer of his faith. He wore a *kola*—the round, brimless black hat of Persian officialdom, later abolished by Reza Shah—instead of the red fez which was then the customary headgear of the Turks, though shortly afterwards proscribed by Kemal Atatürk. The fez would have marked him as a Sunni, and he had no wish to be assaulted and torn to pieces by the impassioned Shiahs.

I, too, wore a kola. I was entitled to this by virtue of my official position with the Persian government, but the motive behind my wearing it on this occasion was identical with Sami's. Any unbeliever, were he Christian or of whatever other faith, faced quite as good a chance of an untimely end in the aroused passions of the tenth of Moharram as did a Sunni. Hadi also wore a kola, but being a Persian was not in disguise.

We went first to the covered bazaars and established ourselves in a window looking down upon the long, roofed-over passageway. The processions were marshalled in the central Maidan, the main square, by my friend Brigadier General Prince Mohammad Hossein Mirza, Chief of Staff of the Eastern Division of the Persian Army. He was in uniform with a black mourning band on his left sleeve, bare-footed, his tunic undone at the collar, a large V of his chest exposed, and with ashes on his head. It was a quaint picture to see him in such garb as he was one of the least fanatical Moslems I ever met, a hearty drinker of the alcoholic beverages which his religion forbids, and he had an Orthodox Russian wife.

The marshalling was essential not only to maintain orderly movement but to keep the *testéh*—the individual processions which together comprised a four-hour-long parade—from entangling with one another. Had they clashed, though all held the same religious views, they would have engaged in bloody battle with each other for the honor of Hossein.

The first *testéh* to approach through the covered passage came crab-wise in a long single line facing outwards, moving from left to right. It was composed of men whose parents had pledged them to Hossein in their youth when they were suffering from some serious illness, should the martyred Imam intercede for their recovery. They were bare-foot and garbed in white over-garments, belted around the waist, like surgeons on their way to perform an operation. Their heads were freshly shaven in a broad swath down the middle. Each shaven swath had been incised with several gashes by a razor blade so that the blood would flow more freely.

With tense faces the line of men moved slowly sideways, passing their left feet in front of their right, brandishing long knives, sabers and bayonets over their heads. The gloomy passage-way reverberated to the rhythmic chant of *"Shah Hossein! Wah Hossein!"* cried loudly in unison. As the excitation worked up to fever pitch the pace increased and they began beating their heads with the flat sides of their knives and sabers. The blood from their incised pates spurted forth, running down their faces, crimsoning the shoulders and fronts of their white shrouds.

With each few yards of advance the tempo grew more violent. The now rapidly moving line broke in many places where men with hideous grimaces suddenly swung around upon themselves as in a delirium, hacking savagely at their own heads. A few other men, without white shrouds and carrying heavy sticks, roamed up and down the line trying to prevent the more frenzied penitents from hacking themselves to death.

The head-hackers passed on, some seventeen hundred of them, though we saw them later and in greater dishevelment. After them came a *testéh* of men garbed in backless black cotton suits who leaped around in a weird sort of dance, flogging their bare backs with heavy chains until they became all raw and streaming blood. Still others followed, also in black, beating their bared breasts and heads with open hands or clenched fists in dull, monotonous thuds. The sum total of violent headaches that day and the next in Meshed must have been fantastic.

We moved on to the Bala Khiaban, the "Upper Avenue," and again took our position in a window looking down upon the procession, if it could now be so termed. The Avenue was a scene of utter confusion, with the head-hackers milling about in large, disorganized knots, their white shouds covered with blood, charging in to the center, whacking at their heads, withdrawing to charge in again. The men with sticks were working valiantly to restrain the self-slaughterers from annihilating themselves, but there were many lying collapsed in their blood-drenched shrouds along the sides of the road.

Through the mêlée and confusion, representations of the tragedy at Karbala were borne on floats on the shoulders of weeping mourners. One of these showed Hossein lying dead on the desert after having been decapitated by Shimr. The living man who portrayed the corpse lay stretched on the float, with his head hanging down below the flooring screened from view by side curtains. After more than four hours in this posture during the heat of the Meshed summer one would imagine that his headache may well have equalled the throbbings of the hundreds of pates that had been hacked to a bloody pulp. The anguished lamentations of the spectators as this float was forced slowly through the knots of head-hackers had the sound of a vast assemblage of keening women at an Oriental monarch's wake. A brilliantly caparisoned led horse, representing Zoldjanak, the horse of Hossein, followed behind the float.

There were other floats depicting the slaughter of the tenth of Moharram, 680, on the desert plain at Karbala. All wrung a flowing chorus of woe from the ranks of the watchers massed along the edges of the Khiaban. The scene of Hossein bidding farewell to his wife and family, when all hope was lost, brought paroxysms of weeping.

Hossein's son Ali Akbar, the first member of the family to be killed in the debacle; his brother Abbas, the standard bearer, and a dozen or so other descendants of the Prophet all slaughtered by Shimr on that fatal day, were portrayed by men dressed to appear decapitated who walked behind the floats carrying their heads on poles. There were also elaborately embroidered, three-cornered banners, some with long black skirts below and a metal hand at the peak in representation of Hossein's little nephew Kasim whose hand was severed by a saber blow early in the fight.

As the afternoon shadows lengthened the processions broke up in disorder and exhaustion. On the way back to my house on the Outer Maidan I counted fifty-seven men who had collapsed by the roadside in a welter of their self-drawn blood. They at least had fulfilled their pledge to Hossein. Whether their reserve of piety was now sufficient on which "to float through another year of iniquity," one hesitates to say. Some thirty of them, in any case, did not float through another year. They died of exhaustion and loss of blood on that tenth day of Moharram.

In that fanatical city of Meshed the American Presbyterian missionaries had established a mission. It was a gallant effort, even though one may question the desirability of attempting to convert people from one faith to another at a place where the converts—in the unlikely event of any being really converted— would, if they openly proclaimed their conversion, be gravely handicapped in earning a livelihood and face the constant threat of physical violence.

The founder of the mission, Dr. Esselstein, was a gallant man. I did not know him, as he was before my time, but there are many stories about him that illustrate his crusading spirit and his wit. He was a big man with a deep, powerful voice, a head as bald as an egg, and a bright red beard. He spoke Persian extremely well.

Against the advice of all who heard of his project, he proceeded from Teheran on a one-man crusade to Meshed. There he undertook to sell, for a few cents each, Persian translations of the Bible. (If one gives the average Persian medicine to cure his illness, and it be bitter, he will not take it; but if he has to pay for it, however little, he will swallow every drop or every pill.)

Dr. Esselstein took up his position to sell the Bibles in a street contiguous to the Sacred Shrine of Imam Reza, nearer to which holy spot no infidel might proceed and where unbelievers of the True Faith were accompanied, as they walked or stood, by the lusty expectorations of devout Shiahs. Even to offer his wares appeared somewhat ambitious, since only about five per cent of the Persian population could read, and what the literate read in Meshed was strictly controlled by the *ulema*—Moslem doctors of theology and sacred law. It was, moreover, an exceedingly dangerous undertaking.

He had no notable success in the way of sales; but with his deep, persuasive voice he managed to attract a considerable, though surly, crowd. It was not long before some fanatic stirred the latent passions of religious intolerance against what this agitator violently proclaimed to be an impious insult to the shades of the Holy Imam. Thoroughly aroused and screaming with hate and fury, many in the mob seized stones and began to bombard Dr. Esselstein where he stood with his back against an earthen wall, a little stack of Bibles beside him. At that moment his life was worth no more than the stones being hurled on him from three sides.

Dr. Esselstein saw two ulema approaching slowly, their heads clean-shaven under their turbans, their beards dyed red in sign of their having made the pilgrimage to Mecca. He raised his hand in the air and addressed the frenzied mob.

"Stop for one moment!" he bellowed in his deep, carrying voice. "Stop, while I prove to you that God in His infinite wisdom has showered His blessings upon me even more than upon your respected ulema!" He pointed to the two doctors of theology then approaching.

"They *shave* their heads!" he roared, removing the hat from his completely bald pate. "God gave me mine already shaven!" Again he pointed to the ulema, now standing stock-still in astonishment. "They *dye* their beards!" he cried, spreading out his own flaming red whiskers. "God gave me mine already dyed! Is not that proof of what I say?"

The mob hesitated and some snickered, for Persians are not lacking a sense of humor. They let Dr. Esselstein slip away with his Bibles, his life saved by the quickness of his wit.

It was not very long after this espisode that he established the mission in Meshed.

Meshed was not solely notable for its religious fanaticism. It was an important center for rugs, not only those woven on the spot but many brought in from Bokhara and Samarkand, from Herāt in Afghanistan, from the Yamūt, Balūchi, Taimūri and numerous other nomad tribes. And while the products of the Meshed looms are not always the most highly prized of Persian rugs, a rug being made on one of Ali Asgharoff's looms when I was in Meshed was said to be the finest that has ever been produced in all the history of rug making. Perhaps nowhere else in the world, in this century at any event, could such a rug have been woven.

It was comparatively small in size: thirteen feet four inches by about eight feet four. It had been on the loom for two years and would be there another year before it was completed. Four slim-fingered men, not boys or girls as was usual, were working on it, each tying with single strands an average of ten thousand knots a working day. Behind them stood a man with a large, heavy paper pattern in his hands through which were punched many holes, one for each knot on a given surface for the day's work.

There were notations on the pattern, from which the man chanted in a low, monotonous voice: "Eight light green, thirteen deep ochre, five rose of Shiraz, nine bull's urine . . ." and so on. The knotters worked from right to left, as in Persian writing, and their incredibly nimble fingers were hard to follow with the eye.

Ali Asgharoff informed me that there were 200 *moghatars*

per square *zar* in that rug. A moghatar is a group of 12,000 knots; a zar a little over forty inches. That made 2,400,000 knots, single strand, every one tied by hand and then sheared when several rows had been tied, for each square forty inches of surface. The rug was valued at $10,000 as it hung on the loom in Meshed, with a year to go before its completion. I have often wondered what became of that rug.

The Military Attaché of the Government of India to the British Consulate General at Meshed, Major "Tommy" Thompson, was tall and thin and undoubtedly had hollow legs, which fitted in nicely with a fairly substantial thirst. We played polo together twice a week, with Weldon, the Bank Manager, an Indian *sowar* of the Consular escort, and several Persian cavalry officers. This game, played on half-trained stallions that ranged from fourteen-three to seventeen hands, on a stony, irregular field, while not exactly reminiscent of Meadowbrook or Hurlingham, had a distinctive zest of its own.

Dekerkher, the Belgian Chief of Customs, could hardly get through an average door. If he had been cut in two laterally in the middle the exposed ends of his carcass where the cut had been made would have described two perfect and very large circles. He came by his dimensions honestly, as he had a colossal appetite and drank incredible quantities of beer and whisky-and-water, without any noticeable outward effect other than to his girth.

For reasons best known to themselves Tommy Thompson and Dekerkher decided to go together, though on separate duties, to Teheran. This, since the caravan track had not yet been made passable to motorcars, meant driving the six hundred miles in a carriage drawn by relays of the Chapah Khaneh for ten days and nine nights. Under the circumstances it was highly desirable to find a moderately intact and well-sprung carriage if such a one were available. But one rarely was.

Tommy Thompson and Dekerkher divided up the duties of

preparing for the trip. Tommy took on the commissariat, Deker-kher the transportation. On the day they were to start, the members of the "European colony" drove them out by motor about seven miles to Toruq in the pleasant Persian custom called *bad-raka*—"seeing the traveller on his way." Toruq was on the bank of the first of fifty-four rivers and torrents they had to ford to reach Teheran. The carriage was already on the other side, along with the first relay of scrawny, squealing, ill-humored stallions standing by under the attendance of a blear-eyed groom.

We had arranged to have two donkeys on the near side to carry the two departing travellers across the river, which at that time of year was wide but not more than waist-deep at the ford. One of the donkeys, specially picked, was a large white animal from Bahrein on the Persian Gulf, where the world's strongest and costliest donkeys hail from. No lesser beast could have coped with Dekerkher's bulk.

On the river bank we had set up a tent, under which were stacked, or hung on strings in wet shirts to cool by evaporation in the light breeze, a considerable array of bottles. Most of the colony and a good number of Persians forgathered there to bid the travellers god-speed, and the consumption of beer, Scotch whisky, cognac and champagne, well paced by the two departees, was not exactly negligible. The hour was about noon, since in Persia it was not considered well to make too early a departure. In the first place, what with all the last-minute things that came up, one probably wouldn't get off to an early start even if one planned it; while secondly, if one did, one would get too far along to send mounted men back to pick up the things one had forgotten.

About one o'clock, when preparations for the departure were finally getting under way, Tommy Thompson looked across the river. He saw the carriage standing there, a little black box-like affair with slats in place of windows and its broken springs tied up with goat's-hair rope.

"God Almighty!" cried Tommy, pointing to it. "Is *that* the carriage you've got to take us to Teheran, for ten days and nine nights—*you* with *me*?" Dekerkher was standing beside him. Their contours together were rather like a bat and a very large medicine ball.

"It is a very nice carriage," said Dekerkher. "Anyway, there is no better one to be found in Meshed, so there is no use grousing about it. And now, what have *you* done with regard to the commissariat, and, more especially, what do we have to drink?"

"We have a case of beer," replied Tommy sententiously, "six bottles of whisky, three of gin, two of French vermouth and one of Italian vermouth."

"And what else?" queried Dekerkher.

"Why, that's it," said Tommy.

"My God!" cried Dekerkher, his eyes wide, round and reproachful. "And what are we going to do tomorrow?"

OPIUM

My WALLED GARDEN on the slope of its Burgundian hillside has something of the atmosphere—a vague, hardly definable suggestion—of a Persian garden. This is enhanced by the rippling songs of the nightingales in springtime as one sits on the terrace under the moonlight and they pour forth their melodies on every side. Down below, by the edge of Asquins village near the foot of the hillside, a narrow strip of field planted in opium poppies, with white and pale lavender blossoms in the spring, carries on the illusion of the Persian scene.

There are occasional other strips of field hereabout cultivated in opium poppies, growing three feet tall and with larger heads than ordinary poppies. Their cultivation is not controlled by the State as it is in Iran, yet the areas so planted are of limited extent. Owing to the nature of the labor required in the harvesting and manipulation of the product, the opium poppy is not grown on any considerable scale outside of Asia. And the European offshoots of this anciently known Asiatic plant, striking as their blossoms are in spring and early summer, seem pallid compared to their Persian progenitors.

Back of my Meshed garden, in northeastern Iran in the 1920's, the ground rose gently up to the slopes of the Binalūd Range in a broad sweep of rich alluvial soil. This, in springtime, was ablaze with the flower of opium poppies. There were many fields in Khorasan Province and elsewhere in Iran cultivated in the crop that was at the same time the most valuable and the most sinister in Persia, but few so wide in expanse or so gorgeous in their vernal beauty as the one that stretched from behind my garden walls to the folds of the Binalūd.

By moonlight it turned to a foam-flecked sea, when the poppies were in full bloom: a sea of white and purple breaking against a malachite-green island of tall trees, where the walled garden of Hajiabad rose like an Isola Madre from a wind-combed, mystic Lago Maggiore. When the petals fell it became a seascape before storm, grey-green, foamless and deceptive. Then the itinerant harvesters of the sap, the "oakies" of opium, would wade through it waist-deep among the stalk-heads, by evening and early morning in groups of a score or more, armed with the instruments of their trade. Each carried, in the evening, a short, wood-handled scalpel with five pin-point teeth in line across for incising the ripened poppy-heads; in the morning a crescent-shaped spoon and small copper bowl for collecting the sap, called *shireh teriyak*.

They make the incisions in the evening so that the sap will exude during the cool of the night, for by day it liquifies under the sun's warmth and much would run off onto the ground and be lost. In the morning before the sun is high they again pass through the field, scraping the tacky sap-drops from the incised heads into their bowls. Each process is repeated some five times, a few days apart: up to ten separate operations on every poppy-head.

From the small bowls the collected sap is transferred into a large copper pot, or several if the field is great. These are taken to a government storehouse in the village, are weighed, and sealed under goatskin covers by excise inspectors who check the yield against advance estimates of what the field should produce. The sealed pots then are transported by horse or mule or donkey to the district excise warehouse, there to be worked into opium after a further check of the weight against a fixed tolerance for evaporation en route. This in theory, and to a fair extent in practice, is the government's manner of contraband control of a crop that yields a higher return per given area than any other in Persia, and for whose product there is a steady legitimate as well as ille-

gitimate demand. But if there is any other product of the soil
that lends itself so well to smuggling, to endless wrangling, to
every form of official and private malfeasance and abuse, I have
yet to find it.

Effective control of opium production in Persia was made
infinitely complicated then—and, I have no doubt, still is—by
a number of factors compared to which the problem of enforcing
prohibition in the United States seemed of almost puerile simplicity. The distribution of poppy culture was very wide, since
profitable cultivation can be carried out on small patches of
ground within the walls of private gardens, or land endowed to
religious benefices, where surveillance by government agents, in
a Moslem country, is all but impossible. The important opium
growers and merchants are amongst the wealthiest of the Shah's
subjects, and in the case of the growers include many of the most
influential members of the clergy, as well as of the landed pro-
prietors who either by themselves or through their chosen repre-
sentatives largely control the legislature.

The number of people who have a direct interest in the
harvest is very large. Local peasants cultivate the poppy until
harvest time. Then, many extra hands are drawn from neighboring villages and towns, from the itinerant nomads, and from a
horde of casual labor that moves with the harvest over great
distances. Their wages are paid in opium sap; or partly in cash
and partly in sap, but mostly in sap.

During the year small merchants and wandering pedlars
advance goods on credit to the peasants; in the harvest season
they receive payment in sap, with heavy interest, at the villages
and fields where the opium is grown. Many hundreds of other
pedlars of knicknacks and sweetmeats go out from the large towns
to the villages and the fields while the sap is being gathered, and
barter their goods for sap on the spot. So do story-tellers, musi-
cians, men towing dispirited trained bears or monkeys on chains,
dervishes with their begging bowls, and a horde of mewling beggars; to receive the scrapings of the opium spoon on the palms of
their hands or the edge of their bowls as recompense for the en-

tertainment they provide, or in pseudo-generosity through which
the offerer hopes to acquire merit for the hereafter.

The village mullahs, interpreters of the word of God and
Islamic law; the ironsmiths who shoe the donkeys and oxen and
the tips of wooden ploughs; the barbers, the carpenters and other
adjuncts of an agricultural economy, are likewise paid for their
yearly services, seasonally, in sap.

Then come the travelling buyers who purchase the sap from
all those who have acquired varying amounts of it in payment
and in interest, in return for services and distractions and for
hopeful potential influence in the life beyond; and also buy
directly from the peasant cultivators. Considering the thousands
of people who have a hand in the collection of the crop, as well
as the opium brokers and commission merchants, the manipula-
tors, packers, transporters and others concerned in the finished
product, it is not surprising that much of it evades governmental
control. Given the low pay and the venality of most of the government agents, the high value of opium relative to its bulk and
weight, and the consequent ease of transportation and of smuggling, there is little wonder that the complete suppression of contraband traffic is fraught with almost insuperable difficulties.

We had some experience of similar difficulties during prohibition days in the United States.

For my enlightenment in these matters it fell to my lot,
amongst a considerable variety of other responsibilities, to direct
the excise services of the two principal opium-producing provinces in Persia—Khorasan and Fars. Opium is one of the oldest
known Asiatic medicines. It is commonly used medicinally or
quasi-medicinally in Persia today, as a pain-killer and a stimulant
to offset fatigue and lack of proper nourishment. Though the
habit of eating opium to such ends has long been known in many
sections of Asia, the smoking of it as a narcotic does not appear
to have been prevalent before the seventeenth century.

The Koran specifically forbids the use of alcoholic drink,

which was a social evil in parts of Arabia when Mohammad received his revelations from God in the seventh century; but the Holy Book of the Moslems does not condemn the smoking of opium, doubtless because this was not practiced at the time. Whatever may have been the date when the opium pipe was first devised, and notwithstanding that there are people of strong will power who can and do smoke in moderation with little apparent noxious effect, the practice has spread in certain areas with disastrous social results. One of these areas was the Persian province of Khorasan.

I have had the curiosity to try out rather many things, some of which were good and some not good for me, but I have never smoked a single puff of opium. Perhaps I feared the result that many inquisitive experimenters have encountered on trying their first pipe—a deathly and disillusioning nausea. It may have been that I did not wish to put my will power to the test of not repeating the first experiment, should I try it and find it pleasant. I do know that after having seen certain things in Khorasan there is no likelihood of my smoking opium in this life.

When I first arrived in Meshed to be Director of the Finances of East Persia I found, as a minor but curious side issue under my charge, one of the world's largest opium "factories." It was a factory of unlovely aspect and singularly vicious character. Most of Khorasan's opium addicts—a formidable proportion of the townspeople—had acquired through long practice of their vice a taste that the standard type of smoking-opium failed to satisfy. They smoked *shireh-i-soukhteh*, "sap of the burnt," a baleful concoction made from the scrapings or "cake" of well-smoked opium pipes.

The excise service collected these scrapings from the licensed opium dens, and in theory from all pipes in private use. The factory prepared the noxious substance for reissue in the form of round, dark disks. These evil disks, like chocolate-covered peppermints or dark brown poker-chips in appearance, were loaded with a morphine content far higher than normal Persian opium —which itself is much higher in morphine than Indian or Chinese opium. Since there was insufficient *soukhteh* to meet the demand, the factory also bought up tens of thousands of dollars worth of raw opium each year to burn down into the noisome chips.

It is very well to say that one should abolish the factory, which eventually was done; but to stamp out a habit so deeply rooted is something else. I was not at all happy with that factory, the few times I inspected it before we closed it down. The very atmosphere around it was poisoned with the sickly sweet stench from its witches' cauldrons, its fuming pans. In this atmosphere men worked naked to the waist; sallow men with deeply sunken faces and burning eyes, with fleshless bodies of unhealthy color; every one an addict.

Some of them were Persian princes—*Shahzadeh*, "Son of Shah," or more precisely descended from a Shah. They had descended a long way. Persian princes were then nearly as current as Persian cats, for every son of every son of every son of a prince was a prince, and so on *ad infinitum*. Half-naked princes, cooking *soukhteh* for wages of six dollars a month, to spend on *soukhteh*.

Soukhteh was by no means the only form of morphine consumption in Khorasan. The sticks of normal smoking-opium called *louleh*, rolled from pure opium of the highest grade with ten to eleven per cent morphine content, were in large demand among the upper classes, temporary residents from other provinces, government officials and pilgrims. Some ate opium pills, others injected morphine subcutaneously. In general the use of opium other than medicinally was little current in the villages or amongst the tribes save for a moderate proportion of the tribal Khans or chieftains. But in the towns it was rampant. The excise agents' estimates for Nishapūr showed more than eighty per cent of the total population addicted in one form or another.

The habit is self-perpetuating, and spreads in a variety of ways. Mostly its use starts as a pain-killer, a palliative that takes the place of proper medical or dental ministration, very often of proper nourishment. Quite effective at the outset, if continued it soon creates its own after-pains that only more opium can relieve. Mothers frequently give opium to calm their fretful infants; smokers like to waft their smoke in the faces of non-addicted companions—especially husbands and wives—to the end of greater companionship in mutual addiction.

I knew a red-beaked, yellow-legged *zaghi* bird, about the size of a raven, that was a confirmed opium addict. It lived in the *chai-khaneh,* the tea-house, of Hauz on the road to Nishapūr, where wayfarers rested and smoked a pipe or so to relax from the fatigues of the road. All the smokers would blow a few puffs of smoke in the zaghi bird's face until it became thoroughly drugged and would lean against the wall with its eyes closed. When it didn't get its opium it would squawk reproachfully, until someone lighted up a pipe and breathed the smoke at the zaghi's red beak. The feathered addict, deeply inhaling each puff, would at once quiet down. It took almost no food.

The wretched, disease-ridden addicts of the lowest grade in the towns, the derelicts and casual laborers, existed on practically nothing but opium.

I had frequently to visit Nishapūr. It was an important financial agency, with extensive public domains including the remnants of Shadiakh where Omar Khayyām lived and died eight hundred years ago. Among other side issues there, I controlled the world's principal turquoise mine. This ancient working in the vari-colored hills was under lease to a wealthy opium merchant habitually in arrears in his rentals. The mining was done in a most primitive manner, in cavernous rooms and unshored traverses deep underground, reached by nearly perpendicular shafts with notches cut in their sides in lieu of steps. The floors were pitted with dangerous holes half full of foul, reeking water. In the light of open castor-oil lamps men with handdrills bored into the rock where the turquoises appeared in narrow seams and small patches, then blasted out the semi-precious stones with black powder.

The Nishapūris were a degenerate, unhealthy-looking lot, but their mile-long covered bazaar had an unfailing fascination. In some of its open-fronted booths wool was carded on big bows, the wire string of the bow snapping under the fingers of the carder with a dull, monotonous note. There were booths where rope was being made from twisted goat's hair; booths where wool was felted and crude little colored designs were beaten into the felts as they were sized; sweet shops selling a sort of yellow sugar candy and clay pipe bowls and thick pipe stems; dyeshops where long strips of coarse cotton cloth were being dyed dark blue in open vats with German-made synthetic indigo, and the dyers were stained deep blue up to their shoulders.

There were hat shops producing round felt hats of standardized shapes; the finer qualities in black for government officials and the gentry or near-gentry, the coarser ones in brown or dingy white to form the base for the peasants' turbans or to be used alone. There were soup and kabob kitchens; potters shaping wet clay on whirling wooden stands trundled by foot; shops selling pungent spices, saffron and pepper. There were coppersmiths beating interminably with little hammers on the metal they fashioned into articles of utility; ironmongers whose charcoal-fed forges fumed in the back of their seven-foot-wide stalls; shops selling printed cotton cloth produced in Manchester, Germany and Japan to veiled women in shapeless cotton prints who had walked in from the outlying villages; shops selling Russian-made lamp-chimneys which turbaned village grey-beards carried home in the folds of their turbans.

There were narrow booths in which were produced high-pummeled and high-cantled wooden saddles with embroidered trappings, and padded donkey saddles, and partly padded wooden cross-trees to hold heavy loads on the backs of camels. There were shops offering extremely unappetizing dried fish from the Caspian with large, empty eye-sockets, and the tiny red bodies of skinned baby kids whose pelts had gone into hats for the affluent. Throughout the length of the covered passages there swarmed like flies in their stickiness, or lay on the ground in postures to show their disabilities, a host of importunate beggars, male and female, who kept up a moaning chorus of woe.

"*Arbob! Na khush hastam!*"—Master, I am ill!—they would

wail. *"Yek cheezi bi man bidahid!"*—Give me something! But if
I offered one of them a chunk of bread there would be a cry of
alarm: "Nay, but I am *ill!* Naught but money will cure my
illness!"

Sometimes I gave a marked silver coin, the equivalent of a
dime, and by pre-arrangement with the excise collectors I would
time that small token of exchange back into governmental coffers
by way of the nearest licensed opium den. The average elapsed
time came to eight minutes.

There was one particularly repulsive beggarman who always
lay grovelling on the ground at the main intersection of the
bazaar. He appeared a helpless, distorted cripple, naked even in
winter but for a tattered piece of gunny-sacking. Over his re-
cumbent form on a November afternoon, when the cold should
have stiffened him into more repugnant shapes than ever, one
of my excise agents made a dispassionate but exceedingly rude
comment. The wretched cripple jumped to his feet, screaming
with rage. His sorrowful state of helplessness for the moment
forgotten, he poured forth a wondrous flow of invective covering
the matter of our ancestry. And then my agent handed him one
of our marked coins. In just four minutes and twenty-seven seconds it lay in the till of an opium den against its worth in
soukhteh.

Our own time from that point to the den, at a more leisurely
walking pace, was over nine minutes. But we were not so anxious
to get there.

I was not at all anxious to get there. Of all things I have
looked upon, aside from certain examples of human malevolence
during war, none has struck me as quite so unlovely as a low-
grade Persian opium den. Several I visited out of sheer curiosity
in China and Macao were rose gardens compared to those of
Nishapūr. And the Nishapūri dens were by no means unique in
Khorasan, though none could well be less inviting.

Nauseous dives they were, dark and fetid, festooned in cobwebs like witches' caves. Their atmosphere could have been ladled
as though it were a soup. It was rank with the sickly sweet fumes

of the drug, sharpened in the acridity of bodies long unknown to water; derelict bodies clad in verminous rags, stretched out on yet more verminous rags upon earthen couches that projected a few inches above the earthen floor. All was in silence, a sinister silence, but for heavy breathing and the gurgling of the pipes; in darkness save for one dingy oil lamp to each cave-room, and the tiny naked flames sputtering like tired exclamation points from the little lamps off which the pipes were lighted.

Behind the small lamps vague forms took shape as one's vision grew accustomed to the murk. These were the forms of smokers lifting themselves on an elbow to relight; the reflected high lights of the pin-point flames glinting dimly on round pipe-stems and dully burning eyes.

They were foul dives, indescribably repulsive. Yet it was no practicable solution merely to close them up. Not that the swift death of all the *soukhteh* addicts would have been any great loss to the community. But to suppress or even curtail a habit that has a hold on eighty percent of the population of a sizeable town is no simple matter. The Anti-Saloon League found that closing the saloons in the United States did not put an end to the consumption of alcoholic drink. It merely moved the consumption to other places, and changed the quality of what was consumed to something that might or might not prove lethal. And Persian governmental control of opium production and distribution was certainly no less effective than the control over "liquor" bootlegging in New York or Chicago.

The excise service was continually seizing contraband opium. This consisted both of opium produced, transported or held in private storehouses undeclared, without government supervision or seals, and of opium properly exported under excise drawback, then smuggled back into the country. It paid well to smuggle smoking-opium back into Persia, even though the regular export cakes were adulterated with up to twenty percent of a kind of gum called *ghonjedeh*, since the taxes and fees on smoking-opium for home consumption were about sixteen times those on opium for export.

Captured smugglers and possessors of the fraudulent product (who invariably disclaimed any knowledge of it) were imprisoned, their property, if any, sometimes being sequestrated to pay the heavy fines imposed over and above confiscation of the opium. But these were the little fellows. The big ones were seldom apprehended. When they were, they nearly always managed to "arrange" the affair by sharing the potential gain with the underpaid government authorities concerned, and with certain others. For in most cases they enjoyed the support of the more influential local clerics, of the mullahs and mujtahids, the guardians of the shrines of pilgrimage: a support which was in no manner of speaking purely altruistic. Since the Koran does not condemn opium addiction, the Moslem clergy has not to suppose that God looks upon the drug with disfavor. And with a few notable exceptions the Moslem clergy in Persia were unimaginative, reactionary and venal.

But there came a time when we netted some of the bigger fish. That unprecedented haul caused considerably more than a nine days' wonder in the sleepy old town of Torbat-i-Haideri.

I learned, shortly before leaving Meshed on an extended inspection trip in the southeastern province of Sistan, that my senior excise inspector had made a spectacular seizure of more than sixty thousand dollars' worth of illicit opium in Torbat. In this matter were involved half a dozen of the town's principal merchants and several of the most eminent clerics. The fines laid down by the law of the land, which would provide a substantial reward for the discoverer should they ever be collected (an improbable contingency), came to roughly three times the value of the opium. From the inculpated merchants and their associates loud howls of anguish resounded over the single strand of telegraph wire to Meshed and Teheran.

The offices of my administration in Meshed were flooded with telegrams of protest, expressing injured innocence and outrage, calling for immediate release of the opium and assuring me that only intrigue and sinister self-interest lay behind the actions of the government officials charged with carrying out the law. Similar cries of distress went to the Governor General of Khorasan, the Commander of the Eastern Division of the Army, the Chief Guardian of the Holy Shrine, the Leader of the Friday Prayer and various other notables. When Persians send telegrams of remonstrance, particularly if sizeable sums of money are involved in their lamentations, they do not confine themselves to any specified limits of verbosity. Many of the telegrams ran to twelve or fourteen pages of flowing Persian script like shorthand, avowing astonishment at the charges of evil-doing, invoking God and the Moslem hierarchy of saints as witnesses to the unexampled honorability of those who were alleged to be at fault, and implying in no veiled terms that the excise inspector responsible for the seizure was a monster of singularly vicious habits and incredible avarice.

Telegrams to like effect poured into Teheran, addressed to the Sardar Sipah—Reza Khan, then Minister of War and Commander-in-Chief of the Army, who later was to crown himself Shah; to the rest of the Council of Ministers, the President of the Majless—the Parliament—and scores of other persons with governmental or religious influence. These were referred to Dr. Millspaugh, Administrator General of the Finances, some with the request that he dismiss and punish the malignant officials who had conspired to implicate the good merchants of Torbat and so had brought dismay and sorrow on the town. When such pleas failed to obtain release of the confiscated opium, articles attacking me and my administration, the American Financial Mission as a whole and Dr. Millspaugh as its head appeared in the scurrilous and venal press.

My chief excise inspector who had carried out the seizure—his name was Silver Heels—was a man of what might be called potential honesty. He was then working under an honest administration where he had neither to buy his job nor share its perquisites with his superiors. As to the persons charged with evasion of the laws covering the production of opium, with the illicit possession of a very substantial quantity of the drug whose provenance they were quite unable to explain, there was not the slightest question of their guilt. Nor was there any doubt that certain prominent ulema were implicated in the transaction.

Thus when I set off for Sistan, over the rugged track that passed through Torbat-i-Haideri, I was not uninformed on the situation brewing in the sleepy, mud-built town which was to be my first stop.

I had been in Torbat the previous year, just after a severe earthquake had devastated considerable sections of the town and completely flattened most of the outlying villages. The villages then, as the earthquake had left them, were curiously reminiscent of villages near the lines of the trenches in Flanders around 1915–16. There was the same formless mass of rubble, the same sense of meaningless and hopeless desolation, the same pervading odors—except for the absence of the smell of lyddite, like rotting pears, that prevailed in Flanders—of upturned earth and crumbled habitations, blended with the stench of decaying flesh and exposed cesspits. There were few if any cesspits in the Torbat villages, where the open air and the sun provided the sanitation; but there was an odor which none the less was a part of that blend of remembered smells.

The wretched survivors living under temporary shelters of goat's-hair blankets and pawing about in the ruins for anything they might possibly salvage, or squatting in mournful groups still dazed by the catastrophe, wailing and sobbing and beating their breasts, recalled also—save for the difference in gesture of the less demonstrative Flemish peasants—the expropriated villagers of West Flanders in 1915.

Torbat town itself, though many buildings had been shaken down, suffered less from the earthquake than the outlying villages. By the time of my second visit much of the damage had been repaired. New structures built of mud, like adobe, replaced most of those that had collapsed. The bazaars were well stocked: an index of recovery.

The town is pleasantly located in a fertile plain at an altitude of 4500 feet, with gardens all around and an ample water supply—the primary essential of any agricultural community in the Middle East where the rainfall is light and at best capricious. It is backed on three sides by vari-colored mountain ranges, through which the only road available to wheeled traffic—hardly more than a caravan track in those days—clambers over 6500-foot passes in the barren ruggedness of tier upon tier of upended stratification. Each tier has a different shade of deep blue-grey, lighter grey, dark purple, grey-green streaked with turquoise blue and red and yellow, topped off by white peaks beyond.

From this we descended into the broad, yellow-green plain under the plum-colored glow of the setting sun. As we drove into Torbat the moon rose behind the mountains, turning them to silver with deeply tarnished streaks, and the town to a ghostly cubist picture in superposed horizontal lines of flat roofs, broken by the rounded domes of mosques and upreaching shafts of minarets, all edged in quicksilver with rectangular white surfaces and purple shadows beneath. We dined at eleven o'clock in the house that had been placed at my disposal, complete with servants, by the Financial Agent of the District. Persian servants were not, then in any event, particularly time-conscious, though this worked both ways.

In the morning, before I finished breakfast—which, while my requirements are simple, I like to take in leisurely fashion— I received the calls of the Governor of Torbat, the Financial Agent who was my host and a member of my staff, the officer commanding the local garrison, the Chief of the Gendarmerie, the Chief of Police, the Chief of Telegraphs (who had a single wire connecting him with the rest of the world) and various other dignitaries. These formalities concluded—a recurrent test of one's patience, tact and sense of humor that had to be faced at every stop I made—I repaired to the Financial Agency to begin my inspection of its activities and accounts.

A few minutes after entering the office portals other callers were announced. These were the principal merchants of Torbat, now under accusation of having been caught red-handed in possession of a very substantial quantity of illicit opium, the origin of which they were unable in any satisfactory manner to explain.

I gave order that they should be admitted; whereupon there filed into the long, narrow room which was my Financial Agent's office six reproachful gentlemen whose leader was called Hadi-off—a name part Persian and part Russian.

After deep salaams and stereotyped inquiries as to my health they seated themselves on the floor along the edge of the wall, their white turbans of the merchant class pushed back on their shaven pates, their trimmed beards all neatly dyed black. They tucked their feet under their hams and bunched the skirts of their long *abbas*—sack-like outer garments—so as to conceal their pedal appendages as good manners require. Similarly they kept their hands with henna-dyed nails in their laps, motionless and discreetly covered by their *abba* sleeves; save when they waved them in the air in the excitement of their talking, and then would replace them and pull down the sleeves. Their countenances were mournfully downcast, but with eyes sparkling from the fear of losing their opium and their money.

The conference was long and largely unilateral. It began with deep solicitude for my welfare, assurances that my arrival at Torbat had vastly improved the prospect of the crops, the rainfall and the future prosperity of the area. With fulsome honorifics they gave me to understand that they realized I was far too noble, good, honorable and clever a person to be misled by the evil machinations of the self-interested and corrupt individuals who, unhappily, represented the government's excise service, and with real feeling assured me that until these latter were permanently removed there would be no peace or tranquillity in Torbat.

"And just how," I interposed, "did you happen to come into possession of such a quantity of undeclared opium?"

Their henna'd finger-nails smote the air as they cried in cracking falsetto that nothing could have been more regular, that the excise inspectors whose evil genius had brought them to this pass had misplaced the declarations, that the requisite taxes had been paid and the receipts destroyed, that God and Mohammad knew they spoke the truth. From this they went into effusive descriptions of the way they had acquired the opium, which would have defied the architect of the original labyrinth to follow, and said that if I would discuss the matter with them in some other place I would clearly understand how greatly they had been misrepresented. They added that Their Eminences of the clergy were deeply concerned over the affair and would fully support their contentions.

I eventually had them ushered out, doleful and dismayed because I was unable to appreciate their point. That afternoon they moved into the telegraph office, complete with servants, bedding, samovars, bags of charcoal, cooking utensils and all the essentials for setting up housekeeping.

Sit-down strikes were invented in Persia centuries before they were ever thought of in the West. In Persia they go by a different name, and do not take place in factories because there are, or there were then, neither factories nor labor unions. They are called "taking *bast*," or refuge, and are a recognized procedure.

The Persian *bastee*, the refuge-taker, is sometimes a criminal trying to escape punishment, but more usually one of a group of persons seeking redress from wrongs, real or alleged. Bastees take refuge in a holy sanctuary—the shrine of an Imam or a revered Moslem saint, or a famous mosque; in the grounds of Legations and Consulates; and in the Royal Stables in Teheran, in the hope of obtaining the Sovereign's ear to their plaints. From the person of the Shah, according to traditional belief, all life stems (and in former days, when the Shah maintained an enormous *anderun*, or harem, a great deal of life did stem from his person). The Shah, just below God whose shadow and Vice-Regent on earth he claimed to be, as well as the Pole of the Universe, was looked upon—quite fallaciously in most cases—as the protector of the oppressed and redresser of injustice.

It is not considered seemly to turn out the suppliants, or even the miscreants, from where they have taken refuge; just as medieval Church law secured from arrest and violence those who sought sanctuary in the holy places. So once having taken bast they remain for as long as they can support themselves—tradition does not hold it necessary to feed them—until their wrongs are righted, at least in verbal promise, or a compromise is reached, or the bastees' nuisance value attains the desired ends: again mostly in promises whose fulfilment is dubious at best.

When the telegraph was introduced in Persia it was believed by the Persians in the provinces that the wire led directly to the ear of the Shah. Hence the *Telegraf-khaneh*—the telegraph office —was, and I presume still is, regarded for purposes of bast as on a par with the Royal Stables in Teheran.

The six merchant-smugglers of Torbat took up residence in the Telegraf-khaneh with every indication that they had come prepared for a long siege. Their servants unrolled their rugs and bedding along one side of the Telegraf-khaneh's single room, lighted the samovars and arranged the small glasses on brass trays for the merchants to serve tea to their visitors, and set up the candle lamps with tulip-shaped glass shades for use in the evenings. At meal times they brought heaping pilaus of rice with mutton, chicken, raisins and spices, prepared outside, which were served on platters of long, thin loaves of bread, laid on the rugs upon the floor. After the repast the servants passed around copper basins and ewers with water to wash sticky fingers (for knives and forks were not in vogue), and bath-towels with which to dry them.

In addition to housekeeping equipment, the bastees installed branch offices in the room. Their clerks and scribes came in and out throughout the day, bringing letters, penning others on their knees in flowing Persian script, taking orders and reporting matters of interest. Clients and associates flowed in a steady stream, squatted on little rugs placed on the earthen floor, and transacted business in a never-ending rumble of voices. Through it all a steady barrage of telegrams of protest, many of them signed with twoscore or more names of sympathizers, was launched over the one wire that served Torbat.

Before I left for the south, three or four days later, the *Rais-i-Telegraf*—the Chief of the Telegraph, or more accurately the despatcher in charge of the office—came to me, wringing his hands. He had, by then, a space about five feet square left to him in which to conduct the normal business of the Telegraf-khaneh; and in this he was outflanked and surrounded on three sides by a welling horde of people who were not particularly helpful in the carrying out of his duties.

"My friend," I said, for I liked the little man, "I heartily sympathize with you and appreciate your predicament. But it was not I who devised the practice whereby miscreants may take refuge in the Telegraf-khaneh and not be ejected therefrom. That is purely a Persian custom. I like it no better than you, but it is a traditional practice that I do not feel I can oppose. And the fact remains that your uninvited guests were caught with a very large amount of undeclared opium, as you have good reason to know; and that the laws of your country, which by my contract with your government I am required to uphold, impose very heavy penalties in such a case."

The Rais-i-Telegraf departed, his eyes rolling, muttering incoherently. "Your kindness is great!" I said, the conventional closing of an interview rather than a comment on the hospitality he was extending to his unwelcome guests. The next day I took off for Birjand with my wife, my Persian secretary, a cook and personal servant, in a vehicle drawn by four horses which had originally been designed for crossing the Alps.

We had the usual difficulties forcing our way through the narrow streets of Torbat, past large caravanserais full of shouting drivers unloading donkey- and camel-loads of wool, past donkeys laden with fire-wood and camel-thorn whose loads all but filled the tortuous passages, through hordes of mewling beggars. After much effort, aided by the imprecations of Mohammad-the-cook alluding to all who blocked our way, donkeys and camelmen alike, as sons of dogs, sons of burnt fathers, and dogs' eggs, we reached the edge of the town and jolted across the watered and cultivated plain to the desert beyond.

Some sixteen miles out we changed relays of horses. In Persian a horse is an *asp*, and the under-nourished, ill-bred and ill-treated stallions of the postal service—they do not geld horses in Persia—behaved as venomously as any serpent. One of the four squealing asps of the new relay fought, bit, kicked and acted in a particularly perverted manner which the cursing driver was quite unable to control since the harnesses were all rotten, with half of the pieces missing and the remainder tied together with goat's-hair rope.

The recalcitrant asp finally bolted on a steepish descent, taking the rest of the team with him over the edge of the road; and for the cumbrous vehicle neither to have overturned nor come apart spoke well for its Alpine design. We cut that asp out and went on with the three others, turning the ungovernable one loose to find its way back across the desert to such forage and shelter as the postal relay station provided. Before it could be freed it had bitten, kicked and thoroughly mauled both the driver and Mohammad-the-cook, whose resumés of the asp's parentage were imaginative and searing.

About a *farsakh* from there—the distance a laden donkey, if prodded, can cover in an hour—we were accosted by a camel driver with a very fine face, who asked if we would take to the village of Mehneh, some five farsakhs away, a young boy of about thirteen, a Seyid—descendant of the Prophet Mohammad—of "a good and noble family" of that village who had run away but whom the camelman had persuaded to go back. We took him, and returned him to his family in Mehneh, who gratefully insisted on giving us strong, heavily sugared tea in small glasses. The boy had little to say for himself except that he was bored with Mehneh. One could sympathize with him.

We spent the night in the open outside a ruined fort that formerly had been one of the strongholds of the Amrani brigands, Afghan Baluchis who usually combined throat-cutting with robbery. Within the crumbling fortress there were myriads of bats, and exceedingly unpleasant ticks called *gerrib-gaz*—"stranger-biters"—whose bite causes a dangerous, sometimes deadly, relapsing fever. It was very cold outside, with a heavy frost, and our

hands and feet were near to freezing while we breakfasted over
a fire of camel-dung and charcoal in the morning. In such fashion
we proceeded towards Birjand, until an automobile sent out by
the Amir Shaukat-ul-Molk, the *grand seigneur* of central eastern
Persia, met us and conveyed us to the hillside town whose
principal reason for existence was because the Amir lived there.

It was nearly three months later when I returned to Birjand,
after having made an inspection trip in Sistan and a rough
survey, by camel, of a possible light railway alignment behind
the eastern ranges of barren, eroded mountains. My wife had
remained in Birjand under the genial hospitality of "B.J."—now
Sir Basil—and Lorraine Gould, the British Consul and his charming wife. I had gone as far as Duzdab, lately renamed Zahidan
because the Persians felt that its original name of "Thieves'
Water," or brigands' watering-hole, was rather too descriptive.

Duzdab was railhead of the Northwestern Railway of India,
just inside the Persian frontier. I went to this curious little jump-
ing-off-place of nine hundred souls, nine-tenths of them British
Indian traders, in the course of my inspection tour; but at the
same time to pick up a new Hupmobile shipped out from the
United States which had been five months on its way from the
factory. The car was there, awaiting my arrival.

When I started back with it over the desert caravan track,
marked only by the bones of dead camels picked clean by vultures, there was little worry about holding the car down to break-
ing-in speed. One's full-out average over the corrugations, stones
and occasional stretches of heavy sand on that nightmare of a
road was eleven miles an hour. We had to carry our water with
us as there was none, save for one well of brackish liquid that
not even a camel could drink, for more than two hundred miles.
I had with me my Persian secretary Hadi Khan, a road engineer
named Hassan Khan, and Mohammad-the-cook, who also served
as my personal servant and man-of-all-work.

At the maximum speed the route then permitted it took the
better part of three days to reach Birjand. All went well during

the first two, though our progress was not uninterrupted. The pick and shovel I carried were put to frequent use, especially in the innumerable dry torrent courses that the road, if one could call it a road, dipped across. Sometimes we had to get out and kick bloated, white-headed and brown-bodied vultures off the track, fifteen to eighteen of them at a time, too gorged on dead camel to hop out of the way, let alone to fly. At night we camped in abandoned barracks of the British East Persia Cordon, built of mud, with their roofs fallen in. On the afternoon of the third day, only about twenty miles short of Birjand, we came to the river Mūd.

The river Mūd is no river, save when it is in spate. The rainfall around Birjand is scant, which was perhaps why the caravan track, euphemistically called the East Persia Road, led through its channel over a normally dry and gravelly bottom for just over a mile. When we came to it there had been some rain in the hills. Turbid water was running down the channel, though it appeared not to be very deep. I didn't much like the look of this, but there was no other way to get through and nowhere to camp with even a modicum of comfort on the south side of that wretched little torrent-course.

I had a lot of rope against possible emergencies. To one end of this I attached Hadi Khan, who volunteered to explore the depth of the water, paying out the rope from the bank as he walked down the channel. If he should be swept off his feet we could pull him out. He reported the bottom as fairly solid and the water about fourteen inches deep.

I left the others on the right bank and drove alone into the torrent-bed, turning down-stream as I came to the middle of the river. It was this turn that had worried me more than anything else. All went well for the first half mile, though it was fairly heavy pulling. My crew followed along the right bank on foot, with some difficulty as it was rough and blocked with a confused tangle of willows and alders. About halfway down the river stretch I heard a shout from the right bank.

The Hupmobile was an open touring-car. Its canvas top

was up. When I heard the shout I looked behind and saw advancing down the course of the river-bed a foaming spate in the form of a series of steps, each a foot or so higher than the one in front, white and sparkling like a mountain waterfall. It came from a sudden and concentrated cloud-burst in the Kuh-i-Baqaran hills above us, as we learned later. There wasn't a Chinaman's chance of getting the car out of the river-bed where it was then. The only hope was to race the spate. This I tried, and lost the race before ever getting started.

I felt the onrush of the foaming steps of water catch the car. The first sensation was of the car's rear end going down, and fast. The descending flood dug out the gravelly bottom from under the driving wheels. The engine coughed once and died. In a matter of seconds the whole car was under water and foundering in the river-bed. I remember rolling out sideways under the edge of the top, over which the surface of the flood was then breaking.

It was impossible to swim in that racing torrent, or even to steer a course. I had learned many years before, canoeing with my father down some pretty wild rivers in the United States, to relax my body completely and let it flow with the current when we upset—which was rare but sometimes happened—in a particularly tricky rapid. This I did instinctively in the spate of the river Mūd, and so escaped external concussion with trees and rocks that beset the way. But there were certain difficulties about breathing under the merging steps of angry water, and when I eventually was swept ashore on the right bank, half a mile or so below the foundered car, I was thoroughly water-logged though still conscious.

My party, of course, had not been able to keep up with me as they struggled through the thickets of willows and alders along the bank. Mohammad-the-cook was the first to arrive. Happily, he was stoutly built. He pulled me onto the bank by my legs after much expenditure of effort, since I was weighed down with a considerable accumulation, inside and out, of water and gravel. For some time I retched gravelly water, while Mo-

hammad-the-cook started a fire of willow twigs and pulled off
my riding-boots. These, though they were well-fashioned riding-
boots fitting closely above the calves, contained an astonishing
amount of water, silt and gravel.

Hadi and Hassan arrived shortly. From a haversack slung
over his shoulder Hassan produced a bottle of arack, the contents of which he poured liberally down my throat. I felt distinctly better. Mohammad's fire was now going, though hardly
equalizing with its external warmth the internal fire from the
arack. Mohammad then removed all my clothes, wrung them
so that the water ran out in streams, and dug handfuls of gravel
and silt out of the pockets. The other two rubbed me down with
arack, and Hassan poured more of the fiery liquid into my un-
protesting mouth.

Well revived by now, I garbed myself in my partly dried
and de-gravelled clothes. Hadi went down to the edge of the
water. It was raining, but the spate had passed by though some
water was still flowing down the channel. He could not see the
car. There was the village called Mūd on the opposite bank, with
a small shrine of some departed saint. People were standing there
watching us, but no one made any move to assist.

"Oh ye asses' sperm!" yelled Hadi. "Oh ye craven catamites;
ye sons of burnt fathers! Get horses and come across the _rūd-
khaneh_"—the river's room, or bed—"to fetch the Chief to shelter!
And there will be money in it!" But none came. Hadi pulled
out a small German pistol and fired several shots in the air to
punctuate his expletives. The villagers simply moved out of
range.

Half an hour late the water in the channel had fallen to
about fourteen inches, the same depth as when I undertook to
try the passage just before the spate descended. Hadi waded
across. He informed the villagers that I was a friend of the Amir
Shaukat-ul-Molk of Birjand, and that their heads would totter
on their shoulders if they did not provide aid. In due course he
returned on a horse, accompanied by three peasants, a donkey
and an ox. I rode the horse back across the river; Mohammad-

the-cook followed on the donkey; Hadi and Hassan tailed up the procession astride the ox. By this time there was no more than six inches of water in the river.

We spent the night in the earthen cottage of the *kadkhoda* —the village headman of Mūd—which he evacuated to put us up. Mohammad-the-cook swept it out, remarking that it was a pity we had lost the flea-powder in the flood as I would probably be needing it that night. A fire was started on the hearth: the smoke from it made one gasp and weep, but its warmth was grateful.

The kadkhoda produced some rice, and killed a sacrificial sheep in my honor (for which I paid later)—slicing its throat in the doorway to avert any possible malevolence on the part of the Evil Eye. Mohammad prepared the mutton and rice in his usual cordon bleu fashion over a charcoal brazier. Long, flat loaves of village bread, part whole wheat and part barley, hot from the pebbles on which they had been baked, served both as platters and as food. The kadkhoda offered a big bowl of excellent curds and whey. Using our hands for tableware, we dined sumptuously on the *ghilim*—an unknotted carpet—spread upon the earthen floor.

Our bedding, of course, was in the car. I was a bit suspicious of the items which the kadkhoda provided, but there was nothing much one could do about it and we were lucky to have any at all. Yet though the floor was hard, and the rugs and blankets undoubtedly verminous, I slept well, and in the morning felt no ill effects. Possibly the arack helped.

We were told in the morning that the car was still where it had been when the flood descended on us. I went out to look the situation over. The *rūd-khaneh* was dry. Not even a trickle of water flowed down the channel, though a few shallow pools lay motionless here and there. The car was just where it had been, as the villagers said. There was no likelihood of its changing place without a considerable amount of external effort. A small patch of dark material, perhaps four feet by three in dimensions, protruded some five inches above the bottom of the torrent-course. This was part of the center section of the Hup's canvas top. The car itself was completely interred in the gravelly bed of the river Mūd.

While I was staring at this melancholy spectacle, horsemen arrived from Birjand. I had sent a mounted man during the night to inform Shaukat-ul-Molk of my predicament. There was a short powwow with the kadkhoda, and then the entire village turned out to disinter the car. When it was freed from its tomb, four oxen were attached to pull it out and onto the bank. It did not look as if it had been new just four days before.

Everything on or in the car, as well as the car itself, was full of gravel. Shaukat-ul-Molk sent out another Hupmobile from Birjand to take us in, with a mechanic who remained behind in Mūd. The mechanic spent two days getting my Hup into such shape that it could be towed by oxen, without risking further abrasion, the twenty miles to Birjand. There it had to be completely taken down and masses of gravel dug out of its crankcase, cylinders, gear-box and all the rest of its insides. Shaukat's two mechanics were a week at this job.

I had a spare German Luger automatic pistol in a holster with a covering flap, that had been in a tightly fitting steel-reinforced suitcase in which I carried my confidential papers. The Luger is a closely machined piece of mechanism, and there was a wad of oiled cotton in its muzzle. When I took it apart I found all the working parts full of fine but highly abrasive sediment. Such was the penetration of the flood-borne gravel.

The remarkable thing was that the car ever ran again. But it did, which testified both to the basic quality of the Hup and the painstaking efforts of Shaukat's mechanics. The electric starter was out for good, the lights were always somewhat temperamental thereafter, the leather upholstery looked as if it had been gone over with emery paper, all the hardware fittings had been divested of their skin, and the attempt at a repaint job left a somewhat mottled exterior. But the car ran, after having been taken apart and completely rebuilt in a primitive town in East Persia, with no major and exceedingly few minor replacements available, by two scarcely literate Persian mechanics in one week. That was the most extraordinary part of it all. It was a lucky chance that Shaukat had two Hupmobiles—even though they were somewhat older than mine had been a few days before it reached Birjand. The latter had aged notably in those few days.

So, what with extraneous adventures and enforced delays, it was more than three months after leaving it when I again passed through Torbat-i-Haideri. The opium bastees were still squatting in refuge in the Telegraf-khaneh, transacting their business, receiving their clients, still launching their telegrams of protest to all and sundry and carrying on a well-set-up housekeeping organization. Their servants, wives or other female solaces brought in and served their evening meals; and it appeared that some of the latter remained on after the meals had been consumed. All in all it was quite a jolly communal arrangement.

Jolly, that is, except for the Rais-i-Telegraf. This unhappy little man had sunk into a state of morbid resignation. I visited the Telegraf-khaneh, announced to the bastees that my attitude toward their basic problem had undergone no radical change during my absence in the south, patted the Rais-i-Telegraf on the shoulder, urging him to bear up. No one seemed particularly cheered by any of this.

I continued on to my headquarters in Meshed. People were not as impressed with the appearance of my new automobile as they had expected to be. In my office I found a great pile of telegrams from or concerning the opium bastees that had accumulated during my absence. These made little advance towards a practicable solution of the problem.

A few weeks later I was transferred to Teheran to be acting Treasurer-General of Persia. The opium bastees were still camping in the Torbat Telegraf-khaneh. I had rather a lot of other matters to take my attention after that, and the prosecution of the smugglers was in the hands of the Internal Revenue Service and Ministry of Justice. I made inquiries from time to time, but failed to get any great enlightenment beyond the fact that the situation in Torbat remained much the same. In the end there was some sort of compromise. I had no hand in this, but I gathered that sit-down strikes pay. Otherwise the bastees, those who had not died off in the course of the years, might still be transacting their affairs in the Telegraf-khaneh of Torbat-i-Haideri.

PORTRAIT OF A GRAND SEIGNEUR

I HAVE YET TO COME UPON a wholly satisfactory definition of civilization. The appliances of modernity for material comfort, such as plumbing and electric washing machines—desirable as these may be—do not constitute a dependable yard-stick. Yet we often take such things as an index.

My friend the Amir Shaukat-ul-Molk of Birjand was one of the most civilized persons I ever met, though he lived in an environment that offered few of the amenities of material civilization other than those that he himself, and his father before him, had created in a primitive and inhospitable area. While the area itself was inhospitable in climate and terrain, his own hospitality was famous throughout the land. He was a *grand seigneur*; and no one I have known of any nationality has surpassed him in charm and unfailing sense of humor.

Shaukat shared none of the anti-foreign complexes, the rabid pseudo-nationalism, that afflicted some Persians (though not the simple villagers and tribesfolk who make up the great bulk of Iran's population) under the stimulus of Reza Shah's concept of Iranian rehabilitation. He liked foreigners and took keen pleasure in entertaining them. Though a devout and sincere Moslem, he had no trace of fanaticism. He was broadly tolerant of all religions. So he was of foreign customs and practices, many of which he adopted in his own life.

As the feudal overlord of central eastern Iran he lived in many respects like an English county nobleman in the days before 1914. There was one notable difference. Shaukat had four wives, as the Koran allowed.

"It is just as well," he remarked to me with a twinkle in his eye, shortly after we first met, "that Moslems do not have to wear wedding rings. With four, I would look a bit over-adorned!"

His four wives never went out in public. They lived in separate quarters. When they did go out, they went veiled, each with her separate retinue of servants. Persian ladies at that time did not accompany their menfolk outside the *anderun*—the inner or female quarters of the house or compound—except perhaps to drive to the house of a close family relation. Shaukat's wives were daughters of important tribal chieftains. The marriages had been arranged by his mother, to strengthen his ties with the families concerned and through them his general situation and influence.

One did not ask about his wives. One inquired as to the state of his *manzil*, his house—or, in such case, his household—and would be told that, by God's grace, his house was enjoying excellent health. When my wife proposed to call on the four ladies, and asked in what order of precedence, she was advised that calls upon them would be unnecessary, but that it would be appropriate to pay her respects to Shaukat's mother.

His mother was the person who counted most with him. She was a remarkable old lady. Shaukat never took an important decision without her advice. In common with most Persian women of her generation, and I think nearly all tribeswomen, she was illiterate. But she was extremely intelligent and surprisingly well informed. She had a keen and an appreciative mind, broad common sense, with the natural dignity of a *grande dame*. Shaukat had the deepest respect for her.

I, too, called and made my obeisance to her, each time that I came to Birjand. I never saw her; for though she was quite an old lady it was not seemly for one of her status and generation to be looked upon even though veiled, in the intimacy of a room, by a man not of her immediate household.

She sat behind a white muslin net, with the light behind her so that she could see me quite clearly, but I could see nothing whatever of her. Nothing, that is, except for one wrinkled but well-shaped hand, a little lace ruffle around the wrist, which she

extended for a moment through a slit in the net to be grasped
or kissed. Across the net we conversed in Persian, with the aid
of an interpreter, who was a retainer of Shaukat's, whenever her
questions became too searching for my limited command of
drawing-room usage of that tongue.

She was dressed, when she received my wife, in the conventional *anderun* costume of a short green jacket, a little flounced
ballet-skirt, baggy Turkish trousers and slippers with pompons—
the garb of the Imperial harem; the original models of which
had been brought complete from the Paris ballet by Nasr-ed-Din
Shah in the latter half of the nineteenth century. (It is said that
the Shah proposed to bring the ballet itself to his *anderun*, or
harem, but encountered French opposition to this idea.) The
indoor costumes of Persian ladies of that generation followed
these models.

Shaukat himself was tall, with a spare, well-knit figure,
closely trimmed black moustache, twinkling brown eyes that had
a slightly greenish tinge, and even, white teeth. His color was a
sun-burnt olive. He usually wore European costume except for
the round black, brimless felt hat, or *kola*, of Persian gentry and
officialdom. In cold weather he favored a heavy double-breasted
overcoat with an attached cape that became him extremely well.
He was very handsome in a virile way, without any trace of self-
consciousness or affectation.

He had an aquiline nose set in a sensitive, oval face, surmounted by a high forehead which bespoke intelligence. It was
a strong face, lighted by a smile that expressed his love of life,
good humor and innate kindliness towards all manner of people.
He looked you straight in the eye. He was not at all buried in the
dead world of tradition. His hands were slim, well shaped and
carefully kept, yet in no wise effeminate. He had the dignity, the
self-poise, of race and breeding in his carriage; unfailing courtesy
in his manner. One felt that his courtesy was completely natural,
that it had the depth of real sincerity. He needed, and showed,
no pretensions.

Shaukat was highly educated in the classic Persian style. His instruction had been partly in the *madressahs* (Moslem colleges) of Meshed and Teheran, but chiefly from mullahs and other private tutors selected by his mother. He had not gone abroad to complete his education in France, Germany or England, as many young upper-class Persians did.

He had a sensitivity for the aesthetic and a strong artistic and literary appreciation. He spoke beautiful, sonorous Persian, Arabic, fair French, a little English, some Russian and some Hindustani. Though a keen sportsman and good shot, he was fond of animals and very gentle with little, young ones.

In his religious observances Shaukat was exceedingly punctilious. He prayed five times a day as his faith required, though many modern Moslems are lax in their devotions. I have often been playing bridge with him (he played an excellent game) when the time came for the sunset prayer. His prayer-rug bearer would glide soundlessly into the room on soft string sandals, place the rug some six feet from the bridge table, its prayer-niche facing southwestward towards Mecca, and silently withdraw. Shaukat would play out his bridge hand, drink up his whisky-and-water, and excuse himself with charming simplicity.

"I am sorry to hold up the game," he would say, "but it is the hour for my prayers. Please help yourselves to the whisky and cocktails. It is not at all necessary to remain silent, you know."

He would then withdraw to the prayer-rug, remove his shoes, and go through the prescribed genuflexions of the Moslem prayer: standing, inclining, kneeling, touching his forehead to the rug three times, rising and repeating it all over again: voicing in humility and quiet fervor his solemn supplications to God, with an absorption that excluded the least consciousness of our presence. It took about ten minutes, while we sipped our whisky-and-water or gin-and-vermouth, nibbled *hors-d'oeuvres*, and conversed in low voices.

When he had concluded his prayers he would replace his shoes and return to the bridge table. The prayer-rug bearer slipped like a white shadow into the room, rolled up the rug and disappeared with it. The procedure would be the same no matter where we might be playing.

"I am sorry for the delay," Shaukat would say, with his engaging smile. "May I replenish your glasses?" And he would do so, along with his own. It was useless to say no, unless one's glass was still full, in which event he would utter courteous reproaches. "And now," he would continue, resuming his seat, "I think it is your deal."

From sundown on Thursdays, when the Moslem Sunday begins, until sundown on Friday, he would not be seen. During this period he fasted as the Koran dictates. He neither drank nor smoked, he did not play bridge or engage in any form of sport. He attended service in the mosque and multiplied his devotions. Precisely as the sun sank below the horizon on Friday he took his first whisky-and-water after his twenty-four-hour fast.

Shaukat loved his alcohol. He indulged this love without undue restraint, in appropriate drinking hours, save only between sunset on Thursday and sunset on Friday. He had a remarkable capacity. I never saw him show more than a controlled exhilaration. He was partial to Scotch whisky, English gin and French vermouth, Russian vodka, Tennant's English beer and Bass's ale, French bordeaux, burgundy and champagne, cognac and liqueurs; all of which he maintained in substantial but not static supply. His stock was replenished weekly from Phipson in Bombay, each shipment coming first to Karachi by boat, thence by train to Quetta, by another train across the Baluchistan desert to Duzdab, and the final two hundred miles by camel.

The only habit Shaukat had that I did not esteem he had learned from the Russians in the first of the World Wars. At particularly well lubricated dinners, when he was the host, he was apt to call, "Chinko!" which meant "Bottoms up," about the second or third time the champagne was passed. He would insist on everyone following him. I do not appreciate drinking champagne bottoms up, but I could never persuade Shaukat that it was an uncivilized practice.

The Koran condemns the use of alcoholic beverages. I was

somewhat surprised, therefore, that one as devout in his religious worship as Shaukat should so enthusiastically disregard this interdiction.

"All religions are good," he explained. "Or, at least, those which teach that there is but one God. But all have to forbid something. Otherwise, perhaps their adherents would feel cheated, as if the word of God were incompletely divulged. Take Kota Singh, for instance, our excellent friend Gould's chauffeur." B. J. Gould was the British Consul at Birjand and at that time my host. "Kota Singh is a Sikh as you know. Sikhs are forbidden by their religion to smoke. You have driven some distance with Kota Singh, have you not?" I had.

"Well, then you know that Kota Singh fills one pocket of his jacket with dried peas and another with cigarettes. He eats his dried peas with one side of his mouth and smokes cigarettes continually with the other, all day long, lighting one cigarette from the last. Yet he is a very good Sikh.

"And Christianity," continued Shaukat. "Christian tenets, I believe, frown upon working on Sundays. Yet you quite often work on Sundays?" I did, from necessity; but perhaps I was not a very good Christian, I said.

"I am more concerned with the positive side of religion than with the negative," said Shaukat. "Of course, there are certain things that should be forbidden. But there are worse practices than the drinking of alcoholic stimulant which the Koran does not even mention, because they were not current vices when Mohammad received his revelations from God." His reference was to the smoking of opium and the use of various other drugs, a serious curse in many districts of modern Persia, as in other parts of the world.

"I drink," said Shaukat, "and enjoy it very much. My drinking affects no one else"—it didn't except when he insisted on others following him in "chinko" with champagne—"and, in spite of it, I feel that I am not a bad Moslem." I would say that he was a very good Moslem, and I have known many Moslems.

He was wholly ingenuous over his repeated lapses from the

Koran's dictate in the matter of alcoholic stimulant. "My mother does not approve, of course." He was then over forty years of age, and it was one of the few things in which he disregarded his mother's wishes. "She doesn't know how much I drink, because no one would dare tell her except the Shahzadeh, and I've promised the Shahzadeh that I will have him boiled in oil if he should tell." The Shahzadeh, a prince of the Kajar blood, was Shaukat's cousin and personal doctor. Shaukat was very fond of the Shahzadeh and had confidence in his professional ministrations, though by no means always following his advice.

"The Shahzadeh, who drinks little, thinks that I drink more than is good for me. Perhaps I do. Every so often the Shahzadeh tells me: 'Jenabali' (Your Excellency) 'you have been drinking too much whisky for your health. You must go and take the baths!' " Shaukat had his own hot sulphur springs up in the hills. He had installed there a sunken bath, in which he could sit on a stone seat, immersed up to his neck in the curative waters. On the right hand, just above the level of the water, was a marble shelf.

"I had that shelf put there," said Shaukat, "for practical reasons. I go to take the baths because the Shahzadeh tells me that I've been drinking too much alcohol and it will be good to sweat it out in the hot sulphur water. Also he makes me drink some of that sulphur water for my kidneys and liver. I do not like the taste of the sulphur water. So I have my servant keep bringing whisky and cool water in tall glasses, which I place on the shelf and sip while I sweat out the too-much whisky-and-water I have drunk before!"

Shaukat's given name was Mohammad Ebrahim, to which he had added the tribal patronymic of Alam when a family name (which comparatively few Persians possessed) was made obligatory for all by Reza Shah's rescript in about 1927. Amir was his hereditary style; Shaukat-ul-Molk—Refulgence, or Grandeur, of the Kingdom—an honorific title conferred by a previous Shah of the Kajar Dynasty.

All Kajar titles were abolished by Reza Shah Pahlevi, after

he had overthrown the Kajar Dynasty, at the same time that he decreed the use of family names. (I had a Kajar prince—there were many Kajar princes, but this one was of high estate—as my senior assistant when I was Financial Administrator of East Persia. He was an unusual type of Persian public official, reliable, honest and efficient. He had also a somewhat cynical sense of humor. When his princely and honorific titles were abolished at one stroke and he was directed, as head of his family, to adopt a patronym, he chose the name of Mahavy, which means "Expunged.")

But those of us who knew Shaukat-ul-Molk well continued to call him by his title. He was not the sort of person whose prestige could be basically affected by an imperial usurper's rescript.

In Sistan—in southeastern Iran—where I went shooting with him, he arranged things in the *grande manière*, as he always did, yet without affectation. I imagine that not many people in modern times, save for the fortunate ones who accompanied Shaukat on his periodic shooting parties, have shot wild duck—of six or eight varieties—and geese and sometimes swan, driven down a considerable section of a hundred-mile-long lake and later back again, by upwards of a hundred and fifty men mounted about equally on horses and on bulrush canoes.

The horsemen kept to the shallows along the gently sloping bank—the "High Skirt" so-called of the Hamūn, the vast lake. The canoemen poled their *tūtin*—chunky little canoes fashioned out of *tūt*, the Sistan bulrush—in deeper water. The ducks and other water-fowl flew past in their myriads over the *kola* made for us in the surface of the lake. These kola, or shooting-blinds, were contrived by building up a cup-shaped atoll, about four feet in diameter at the top, from the bottom of the lake until its rim rose above the surface of the water, then baling it out and camouflaging it with bulrushes. The blinds were called kola after the official Persian brimless hat, in this case inverted and considerably enlarged.

Standing in our kolas, with a huge supply of shells, we

achieved an incredible score when the wind was right and the ducks were flying low. Bulrush-canoemen, their craft camouflaged with upright bulrushes, picked up the kill. There was no limit, save one's supply of shells and accuracy of aim. None of it was wasted. Shaukat always distributed the surplus to the Saiyads, the local tribesfolk of the Hamūn who live by fowling and fishing, and are also the canoemen; who can afford no costlier manner of obtaining their living than by the nets of their own making which they cast with extraordinary skill.

Shaukat was not at all the usual run of Persian overlord. Though his feudal prerogatives included such things as collections on marriages and inheritances, and unpaid labor for the cleaning of his underground irrigation channels, maintenance of his villages, his private roads and other personal and family interests, yet these were customary and traditional practices in Iran. In his relations with the cultivators and tribesfolk he was generous, kindly and unoppressive. He expended liberally from his own income on schools and medical services and other facilities for the people throughout his area, which the central government failed to provide. And, unlike the vast majority of Persian landlords, he paid his due taxes to the central government without evasion or delay.

He was deeply thoughtful of the welfare of his peasants and retainers. In years of bad yield he provided them with sustenance from such stockpiles as he had been able to maintain, little helped by the apathy, the ineptitude and corruption of the government at Teheran and its appointees. Many of the villagers, because of the disastrous system of exploiting the cultivator and producer that passes for government in the Iranian provinces (which under Reza Shah's regime he was powerless to prevent), had scant margin between a pretty stark existence in good years and the borderline of starvation in bad ones. What little was left them when the government-appointed tax-farmers and unsalaried sub-governors got through would be picked clean by Reza Shah's military locusts.

Much of this squeezing of the producers accrued in the end to Reza Shah's personal exchequer when his high-ranking minions had served their purpose, fallen out of favor, been imprisoned, strangled or exiled, and mulcted of their gains.

In the scramble to bleed the unhappy peasantry white, Shaukat attempted to play the part of their protector. He made many sacrifices, but the scales were too heavily weighted against him and he too, along with the rest of the country, was effectively bled by the rapacity of Reza and his predatory cohorts. He was a feudal baron of exceptional character in a country where feudalism—an Asiatic rather than European type of feudalism—still persisted, though not so termed; but without the support of men-at-arms.

A few men-at-arms he had, though far too few to challenge the central authority; nor would that have been in his character. The first time I came to Birjand I started out from Meshed in a fanciful contraption called the "Ark," loaned by a British friend whose brain-child it was. The Ark consisted of an elongated frame with a buckboard-like body mounted on Model-T Ford axles and wheels. It had a canvas hood, and two persons could stretch out and sleep in it, leaving enough space for the baggage behind and for the driver and one's personal bearer, or servant, in front. It was drawn by four underfed stallions, changed at the postal stations every twelve to sixteen miles. The road was not then passable, in numerous sections, by motorcar.

Near the village of Baz-i-Hūr the Ark broke a bearing, not to be replaced in East Persia in that day, and was dragged on an improvised skid to a caravanserai yard where it was deposited amidst solemn circles of squatting camels munching their evening hay. They regarded us with disfavor. We waited there two nights and a day, and then transferred to a diligence—*dilijen* in Persian style—sent out from Meshed by the postal service. This vehicle was of the same type and about the same vintage that had taken me, as a very young tourist with my parents, over the Simplon Pass in the Alps rather more years before than I now care to count.

The dilijen, a painful means of transport over rough going —and it was very rough going—was also drawn by four horses. They were not enough. After many struggles in which we all took part it foundered in the sands of Gounabad, two days out after I had left the opium bastees in Torbat-i-Haideri. After two hours of futile effort and unproductive blasphemy in the empty, wind-swept desert, we gave up. Our four sweating, scrawny stallions had given up before we finally admitted defeat, and took to biting and kicking at anyone who came near. And then five *sowars*—mounted men-at-arms—rode over the horizon, formed in line on one flank, and their leader saluted me.

"Peace be upon you!" he said. "We have been sent by His Excellency the Amir Shaukat-ul-Molk of Birjand to welcome Your Excellency on your way!" Their welcome was put to good effect. In a short while the dilijen was dug and pulled and levered out of its sandy interment. With this modest escort as a start, supplementing our two camel-mounted *sowars*—picturesque but not highly effectual guards provided by the Gendarmerie—we moved ponderously towards the village of Jumend, two farsakhs or about eight miles away.

Half a farsakh farther on there were more sowars, four gaily-caparisoned led-horses of honor, and a large assembly of "no-tables" from the village of Jumend. We drank the strong, heavily sugared tea of welcome in nicked glasses by the edge of a pool where carpets had been spread for the reception, and the surface of the pool was continually broken in concentric rings by fish jumping as if to have a look. Then we drove on with our led horses of honor preceding us, flanked by sowars and followed by a long trail of people mounted on horses, camels, mules, asses and one decrepit droshky; passing groups of salaaming, turbaned peasants in long coats with white sashes about their waists, and groups of veiled women whose smoky-blue silhouettes stood against a background of pale plum-colored sky fading to saffron yellow in the failing light.

At Jumend, where we spent the night, I was informed that Shaukat had sent his Hupmobile from Birjand, 134 miles over an atrociously bad caravan track with many passes of up to 7000 feet altitude, to fetch me down there. At this time I had never met Shaukat-ul-Molk, nor had ever corresponded with him.

We made the trip in one day, though arriving after dark, which was no mean effort at that time considering the state of the road. The Persian Financial Agent of Birjand had arranged accommodations in the town—there was nothing remotely approaching a hotel in Birjand—from which B. J. Gould, the genial British Consul, shortly transferred us to the Consulate: for no short stay, as it turned out. On subsequent visits I was put up in the guest palace that Shaukat's father had built. It was characteristic of Shaukat that he did not arrange for me to stay there the first time, before having ascertained whether this might in any way be embarrassing to me in my official capacity.

He did, however, see that there were servants to greet our arrival—I had left Mohammad-the-cook and Abu Talib, my personal bearer or valet, with Hadi Khan, my secretary, to follow from Jumend in the dilijen—together with partridges and other highly appreciated provender.

At nine-thirty the next morning, having first sent a messenger to ask if that hour would be convenient, Shaukat called. He came with one attendant, whom he left at the door. (The local Governor of Birjand, a man of bovine intellect but a financially astute penny-pincher, would not cross the street with less than three men-at-arms bearing shotguns or Austrian rifles, as a matter of personal prestige.)

We talked in French, with occasional interpolations in Persian, and in a very few minutes, though his French was slightly stilted and my Persian a good deal worse than that, I had the impression that I was chatting with a highly esteemed and cultured friend, and one of infinite charm. That afternoon I returned his call. The impression persisted. He was one of the most *sympathique* (in the French sense of the word) persons I have ever met, that rarity of human being who accords completely with one's own spirit though strongly individualistic in himself. His charm of manner and sense of humor, which was never either slapstick or malicious, were infectious. He never gave me occasion to alter that first impression.

When I left Birjand for the last time, after having made my formal adieu in his guest palace where I had been staying, there was a slight delay in getting started owing to the defection of some servant. It was a planned defection, and during it Shaukat disappeared. We encountered him eight miles out along the corrugated road to Meshed, awaiting us in a tent with two bottles of champagne, foie-gras sandwiches, and four fat partridges nestling on their backs on folds of Persian bread. While we partook of this manna from heaven and toasted one another in champagne, an old and dirty *chavadar*—a donkey driver—rode by on a very small donkey, driving eight others and carrying two pink roses in one hand. The other hand he held cupped behind his ear under his canted turban, to serve as a sounding-board while he sang in quavering falsetto to the blue sky above.

It was a gay and genial *badraka*—the pleasant Persian gesture of seeing the traveller on his way—but as I headed my car for the passes over the encircling ranges of the Ghayenat I felt a heaviness in my heart that even partridges and champagne could not conquer. I was leaving behind as good a friend as anyone could wish to have.

I saw him again in Teheran a year and a half later. He was "celebrating" the coronation of Reza Shah in a tremendous party with champagne and fireworks, which he did, as he did everything, extremely well. It was a desirable gesture (in which his mother doubtless concurred) to gratify Reza's voracious vanity, and it cost him more than ten thousand dollars—not all of this for fireworks and champagne. He managed to live for another twenty years, in itself no small achievement under the highly unbenevolent despotism of Reza Shah.

He died in 1945; an untimely death, undoubtedly hastened by worries in his struggle to preserve something of his individuality, of his properties, his life itself, from the ruthless, predatory hand of the usurper of the throne; to protect his villagers and tribespeople from the ceaseless depredations of Reza's military skinners.

In his death, though I had not seen him for years, I lost a revered friend; the troubled world, a great and chivalrous gentleman. I think of him as he once wrote to me in his cultured, poetical Persian, which the translation does not quite fulfill:

"Your praiseworthy character and high views shine always to me like the sun."

YOU COULD HAVE HAD
MY CAMEL

IN THE COURSE of the first of several trips that I made to Sistan, after having left the opium bastees squatting in the Telegraf-khaneh at Torbat-i-Haideri, I carried out a reconnaissance by camel west of the barren, eroded ranges known as the Kūh-i-Būzan and Palangan Kūh which separate the basin of Sistan from the great central desert called the Dasht-i-Lūt.

The object of the reconnaissance was to ascertain whether it would be feasible to connect Duzdab (now called Zahidan), railhead of the Northwestern Railway of India fifty miles inside the Persian frontier, with Sistan by a light railway passing behind the ranges. Sistan is one of the oldest cereal-producing basins of the world. The more direct way between it and Duzdab, east of the ranges by a camel caravan route, was over terrain of such nature as to make it impracticable for the construction and maintenance of any type of railway without enormous expense.

The proposed line behind the ranges was very far from ideal, but my rough survey showed the route at least to be feasible. It was a rough survey in several respects. Since it was intended only as a preliminary reconnaissance, we carried few and very simple instruments. The country itself was exceedingly rough, without drinkable water; about as inhospitable terrain as any I have ever explored. But the roughest part of it all was my camel.

In mid-January of Oud-il, the "Year of the Bull," I set out from Birjand. We were four: Hassan Khan the road engineer, my secretary, Hadi Khan, Mohammad-the-cook and general factotum, and myself. "B-J" Gould started us off in his car driven by

214

the Sikh chauffeur Kota Singh, who smoked cigarettes without ever stopping though his religion forbade tobacco in any form.

Rugged hills of malachite green, porphyry red and saffron yellow, some topped with the towers of ruined castles, set off the horizon on all sides as we proceeded up the valley of the Rūd-i-Birjand. We stuck first in the gravelly bed of the Rūd-i-Mūd, where I was later to be caught on the way back and have a new car swallowed up in that same gravel; and shovelled our vehicle out while partly veiled women in dirty white or red or blue over-garments watched us from the dark openings of mud hovels.

We stuck in heavy snow at 6000 feet altitude on the Sar-bisheh plateau, and for some distance after digging out could not see the road because of a blinding storm, so we took turns walking ahead of the car in order to keep on the track. Kota Singh never once stopped smoking.

In a narrow pass a shepherd crouched beside a freshly killed sheep with its head cut off. The shepherd said it had been killed by wolves. He held up one severed ear of the sheep as if to certify this. Whenever a sheep dies while out grazing in the hills or plateaux the shepherd cuts off an ear and brings it back to the owner to prove the loss of the sheep. The owner keeps a string of ears as a tally of his losses. Sometimes when a shepherd gets very hungry and has no food he kills a sheep and eats its. Later he brings the ear to the owner and reports that the sheep was killed by wolves, or by a snake or an eagle.

Descending somewhat from the plateau we stuck in slippery wet clay, and again in heavy sand where the track led through low dunes sparsely covered with scrub camel-thorn, its edges marked with the bleaching bones of dead camels. Frequently the route was breached by torrent courses, dry but deeply scoured and pot-holed, and strewn with large, round boulders. In such fashion we came to Shusp, after dark, at a speed of about thirteen miles an hour in a cold, driving rain; to camp in the cheerless earthen rooms of a British barracks built during the 1914–18 war. It had been a tough day. There were others to follow.

In the morning we got off to a late start, Kota Singh having to repair the radiator and a number of other items on the car. We made fair progress as the surface was better though cut by innumerable torrent courses. By the mountain called the Kūh-i-Bid—the "Camel's Neck"—an escort of an officer and thirty-five mounted men met me and led the way to the small village of Khūnik. This involved certain delays, and as there was one good room in the village and nothing beyond we camped there for the night, after a not very impressive run of twenty-six miles that day. Our camels were waiting at Khūnik and were sent out during the night to the point where we would take off from the main track the next day.

Khūnik village, like the other infrequent villages around there, boasted many windmills of a curious type. In their basic conception these mills are at least as old as the Old Testament. They consist of huge stones five feet in diameter, the upper stone driven by a great upright pole perhaps thirty feet high, with seven or eight vertical fins whose surfaces are of reeds. They work during the three months or strong north wind in summer and grind wheat and barley into flour which is sold to caravans and travellers passing along the road. For about nine months of the year they are laid up.

In some places there are ten to fifteen such mills in line abreast. Each one is owned by two or three men. When the wind is very strong (now and then it reaches a hundred miles an hour) it sometimes breaks up the mills, even shattering the great stones, as there is no brake or any way of stopping them when they are revolving.

The wind also ventilates the houses in the terrific heat of summer. Most of the houses have a high, narrow half-section of dome rising above their roofs. The open half faces north and the summer wind rushes down through it, over wetted camel-thorn, to cool the rooms below: probably the earliest, and by no means the least effective, air-conditioning system in the world.

Outside the village were many weather-worn graves, level with the ground. There were also other, temporary ones of mud, built up three feet above the surface, in which reposed bodies

waiting transportation by camel or mule or horse to final sanctuary in the sacred soil beside the Shrine of the Imam Reza at
Meshed. The bodies for which such fortunate interment is in
store usually have to wait nine months to a year or more for
transportation. This may perhaps be just as well, considering the
conditions in which they are transported: in loosely fitting deal
coffins carried by one large, slow-pacing caravan in the blazing
heat of summer. Many of the temporary tombs around Khūnik
were open and empty, showing that their occupants had gone to
rest in the sacred soil which assures their entry into Paradise,
regardless of what they may have done on earth.

We started early from Khūnik and ran south over good
gravelly surface to a crossing of the dry Rūd-i-Janga, where we
met our camels. At 11:30 in the morning we took off by camel
up the Dehaneh Panja pass, a gap through the Kūh-i-Būzan
range. We had ten camels: one for each of the four of us, one
for our Baluchi guide, one to carry our drinking- and washing-
water contained in great Russian oil-drums, one loaded with
chopped straw for the camels themselves, and three to take our
tents, charcoal for our cooking, camp gear and supplies. They
were a mangy looking lot, with their hair in rubbed patches, and
they stank to high heaven. Their mournful regard bespoke complete disillusionment with life.

There were three Baluchi drivers—*shuturban*—in addition to
the guide: a villainous looking crew of brigands in turbans below
which their oiled curls hung to their shoulders, with baggy
trousers and long, loose coats tied around the middle with heavy
cummerbunds. The camels knelt in a semi-circle while the *shuturban* loaded the baggage animals with the packs that had been
off-loaded after their trip from Khūnik the previous night. The
shuturban cursed with wondrous Baluchi oaths; the camels
groaned and grunted and raised their heads towards the sky in
loud-voiced protest. Some of them bubbled as if they were chew-
ing enormous wads of bubble gum, the inventor of which un-

lovely commodity may well have had his inspiration from the camel.

My camel knelt at the head of the line with a morbid expression on her face. It was a she-camel, a *nakéh*. I had been informed that she was a trotting camel, a type highly developed in Arabia but rare in Persia. Perhaps she was, but her trot resembled the kind of punishment that American tire builders inflict with cumbrous machines on specimens of new models of tires to test their endurance. I was the specimen in the case, whenever we trotted.

A British friend of mine with more experience than I in riding camels had advised me to take along two extra pairs of spiral puttees. "Start at your hips," he said, "and wind three individual puttees around your belly and diaphragm up to the breast-bone, just as tightly as you can haul 'em. Get someone else to give you a hand, like a Victorian lady getting herself laced into her corset. That'll help to hold your insides in place. You have to stop at the breast-bone, you know, to allow for the expansion of the chest in breathing. Then if you want to, you can take the fourth puttee and wind that around your forehead like a bandage, as tight as you can make it. That'll help to keep your brains in." This I did, and because of having done so my insides are still in place and so are what pass for my brains. Otherwise things might have been different.

When I was introduced to my female companion of the next five or six days I remarked an absence on her side of what I had hoped would prove to be a mutual understanding and sympathy, growing into a beautiful friendship. I patted her on the nose, whereat she tried to bite my arm and exhaled in my face a breath that would have poisoned a cactus.

It was a pity, I thought, that my lady friend for the next week suffered so noticeably from halitosis; but I was to be the chief sufferer. She permitted me to clamber onto her back. Though I may have done this awkwardly, it was no help to have her try to chew my left knee as I mounted. The wooden saddle on which I perched did not conform to my anatomy. I have ridden horses most of my life, but I was not designed by nature, nor did I start riding camels early enough, to acquire the requisite shape to sit on one with comfort. The beast is too wide for the way my legs are attached to the rest of my body. I was never a hand for doing the splits in a Russian ballet, or any other kind of ballet for that matter.

I received instructions on how to steer my *nakéh* with the single rein of frayed goat's-hair rope attached to her right nostril. She never once understood my signals. Towards the end of the trip I felt that she was maliciously misinterpreting these attempts at guidance. Sometimes she would turn her head around in a 180 degree arc, like a gigantic ostrich or pterodactyl, and glare venomously in my face with her muzzle about eight inches away, wrinkling her lips above her yellow teeth and exhaling a blast that nearly asphyxiated me.

The first day we all kept together. There was no trotting through the rough and stony pass, and the baggage train could keep pace with the more lightly loaded riding camels. The pace was a walk, and the walk of a camel, when one is on its back, is about the most monotonous thing I have experienced. The hapless rider is swayed in a reciprocal motion that never ceases: forward and back, forward and back, hour after hour, until the animal halts. Perhaps it is good for one's liver, but I would prefer to keep fit in other ways.

We did twenty miles by camel that first day, which considering our late take-off and the slow going was not a bad effort; and camped after dark at a place called Chah Shur—Salt Spring— where there was not a single tree nor any other thing but emptiness around it. My *nakéh* refused to understand the signal to kneel. She looked back at me with odorous disapproval. Then she suddenly collapsed in three rough motions, throwing me forward onto her neck, then back onto her rump, then forward again, as she folded herself jack-knife fashion on the ground with her ungainly legs under her. She made another pass to bite me as I slid down her flank.

The Baluchis started a small fire from the wood we had brought along with us, and set up the tents under Mohammad's supervision, while he also prepared our dinner. Mohammad was a most capable and resourceful servant on the road. I felt pretty tired and stiff in my riding muscles and back, which was just the beginning of a stiffness that approached *rigor mortis* on the morning of the third day out. There was a cold, bone-seeking wind. I took a useful slug of whisky-and-water from my two-gallon canteen, and felt better. Hassan and Hadi joined me, though their religion frowned upon alcoholic stimulant, and they also felt better.

In the morning we split the caravan in two. Mohammad and the baggage train took a direct course, as far as the terrain allowed, to our next night's camping ground. Hadi, Hassan and I set off with the Baluchi guide to explore the western side of the ranges. We were all fairly stiff—not, of course, the Baluchis—though the real stiffness of grossly overstretched and overworked muscles had not yet caught up with us. We could still walk, if awkwardly.

The baggage train did about twenty miles, a good day's average for camels moving at two miles an hour. One cannot move a baggage train faster than a walk and hope to find the baggage on the camels at the end of the day, or for long during any part of it should the ungainly beasts break out of their leisurely sway.

We covered close to fifty miles that day exploring the reverse of the ranges, which meant a fair amount of trotting and some galloping wherever the ground permitted. Galloping on those stiff-legged beasts was a sort of medieval torture. I felt as though my spinal cord was being hammered into a solid support for my back, like a steel rod in a reinforced concrete structure, which would never bend again.

Trotting was little less awful. My teeth are reasonably well anchored, or were until then, but I had the sensation that they were being shaken out. As to my insides, I felt that only the spiral puttees wound tightly around my middle kept them in. Whenever we slowed down to study the curious geography of that area, my *nakéh* turned an ungenial regard over her shoulder and expelled fetid odors in my face before being persuaded to start off anew.

We were then cruising not far from the edge of one of the most inhospitable sectors of this globe. The lower slopes of the mountains tailed out to the west into the Dasht-i-Lūt, a vast and fearsome empty waste that supports no form of life. The lower slopes themselves were unfriendly enough. There was no vegetation, and the only living things I saw were a few widely scattered *katá*—sand grouse—a bird of the desert famous for its ingenuity in finding drinkable water, albeit in small quantities, where none appears to exist.

The Dasht-i-Lūt is an absolutely barren, rolling desert covered with a hard layer of black shingle, lacking landmarks of any sort, at an altitude of from 1000 to 1500 feet above sea level. It is waterless except for a very few shallow holes where the water is saltier than the sea. In summer it is impossible for man or beast to exist on its black surface owing to the withering heat and lethal winds. In some parts of it there are zones of *kavir*: soft, salty clay surfaces, risen in bubbles as if by the action of baking powder and set in a hard crust. The central part is unexplored. That its outer edges are occasionally crossed by caravans is a testimony to the hardihood and gambling instinct of man.

No animal would venture across any part of it unless driven. To by-pass it, however, is a very long way around, since it covers an area nearly 300 miles north and south and 135 miles east and west at its widest part. So in winter caravans occasionally cut across moderately short sections of it. They run the risk of being caught and frozen to death in a sudden icy blizzard, against which no man or camel can stand, driven by the same north wind that brings the shrivelling heat of summer. If someone strays at night a short distance from the rarely used track he will probably never find it again.

Caravans that attempt this unalluring passage march from ten o'clock in the morning until five o'clock in the afternoon, halt to rest and feed until nine o'clock at night and then march till eight o'clock the next morning; and so on until the desert has been crossed. The drivers, who usually ride donkeys, become so exhausted that they sometimes roll off to the ground while asleep and never even wake up from the shock. All in all it is a traject to make even the most rugged cameleer quail at the prospect.

That fifty-mile jaunt the second day out really fixed us as far as stiffness was concerned. On the morning of the third day we were barely able to move. Mohammad-the-cook, who was fairly stiff himself though he had done no trotting or galloping, helped heave us onto our camels. The first hour or so was sheer agony. Every muscle of my body had been stretched to the breaking point, pounded, bruised and battered. Yet we did a good thirty-five miles during the day, much of it over rough going, and by late afternoon we could bend a little without breaking. When we came to the already prepared camp just before the winter sun sank indistinctly beyond the Dasht-i-Lūt, I was able to dismount from my camel unaided, though ungracefully.

Our camp that night lay to the west of the Mountain of the Forty Maidens, on an eroded slope where there was a little camel-thorn. The camels were turned out to graze. I was tired and slept heavily. During the course of the night I had a vivid sensation of being pitched off a camel over the side of the mountain and of bouncing down the hard, steep slope with the camel on top of me.

I woke suddenly to find that I was on the ground, with my camp cot upset and half the tent collapsed over me, and that there was a camel mixed up in it. The camel was my *nakéh*. She had strolled aimlessly into my camp when everyone was asleep. With infallible instinct she had fouled my tent ropes, pulled down the tent, overturned my cot and my lame and weary body with it, and managed to entangle her ungainly legs in the ropes in such a way as to throw herself into the midst of the shambles she had created.

She lay there on top of and ensnarled in it all, thrashing

around with her great padded feet, emitting loud grunts and hideous belches. She kicked my neatly set up camp gear hither and yon; she kicked me with seemingly deliberate and malicious intent, and I sensed that she was searching for some part of my anatomy on which to commit mayhem with her slobbering yellow teeth.

I extricated myself with difficulty from the mêlée, breathless and angry, in flannel pyjamas and bare-footed. By this time the whole of the tent was down. I could hear the rending of canvas as that devil's handmaiden kept on thrashing about in the wreckage. The night was dark and extremely cold. I could not find my electric flashlight. After some effort I succeeded in awakening the Baluchis, snoring sonorously around the dying embers of the camp fire. There followed a terrific commotion as they tried to disentangle the fulminating *nakéh* from the debris of my tent.

They finally extricated her, but even with Mohammad's capable hand—he was the last to be aroused, being in no sense a light sleeper—we were more than an hour re-erecting the torn fragments of the tent and retrieving the scattered pieces of my camp gear and clothes. There were many things that could not be found in the dark. Some were recovered in the morning, no longer in their original shape or likely to function again in the manner for which they had been designed.

I was half frozen all over, well more than half as to my feet, before I was able to locate any extra clothing or even pull out a blanket from the mess to throw over my shivering body. Hadi produced a pair of heavy socks which saved my feet from completely congealing. It was a long time before I could find my canteen of whisky-and-water. I recall few occasions when I needed it more.

When I finally got to bed again I was short a blanket. It had been quite unpleasantly sullied by my *nakéh*. By then, had it not been for the matter of transportation over a still considerable distance of mountainous wastes, anyone could have had my camel.

After a not wholly successful attempt to repair the damage of the night before, we continued next day over the undulating foot-hills of the Mountain of the Forty Maidens. I was not in very good temper. Between my *nakéh* and me there was a kind of armed truce. From time to time she bared her yellow fangs and belched noxious fumes in my face. I fingered the muzzle of my pistol, repressing an acute desire to crack her over the skull with its butt. Each time she turned her great, misshapen head backwards like a four-legged ostrich we glared at one another with acrid mutual distaste.

But she had done her worst. She had taken her revenge, and for the time being was moderately satisfied. The next few nights I had her double-hobbled, and slept in peace. I was also getting hardened to the daily jolting. Not that I had grown to like this, but I could now take it without wondering, hour after hour, how much longer I would be able to stand the punishment.

We came eventually to Garageh or Gharagoh ("Crows' Water"), a spring whose water is not too brackish to drink, located on the caravan track from Kirman to Sistan. There was another camp established there, a smallish camp of two tents with a road-weary *kaleska*—a Russian-built carriage something like a victoria—parked in front of one of them, and four scrawny stallions tethered alongside. Shortly after I slid from the back of my *nakéh* I received the call of the earlier arrival, in accordance with Persian custom.

He was a Polish engineer in the employ of the Persian government. We partook of strong tea in small glasses, brewed by Mohammad-the-cook, and then I offered him whisky-and-water from my two-gallon canteen which, with the help of Hadi and Hassan, was beginning to run a bit low. He downed it without expression and shortly returned to his own tent. About twenty minutes later, as custom requires, I returned his call.

He offered me the prescribed two glasses of strong tea, which I did not particularly want. We discussed at length the engineering work that would be necessary to make the Kirman-Sistan caravan route, which crosses a considerable expanse of desert, practicable for motor transportation. I noticed that his tent was quite well equipped and that at the end of it stood a tall and wide, though not very deep, brass-bound mahogany chest. It was surprising to find such an item of equipment in a camp on a Persian desert caravan route. The Polish engineer remarked my interest in this piece of the furniture of his tent.

"Ah that!" he said. "That is my case of technical instruments. It belonged to one of the principal engineers of Tzarist Russia. After the revolution I happened to acquire it. I brought it into Persia with me when I came. I never travel without my technical instruments."

He extracted a bottle of Circassian brandy from behind his cot and poured out two glasses. The bottle was rather less than half full, but we did well with it and, perhaps on the strength of this, he insisted that I remain to dine with him. I accepted, after he assured me that he had a very good cook and more gazelle steak than he could possibly eat himself.

The gazelle steak, with beautifully prepared rice, was excellent. We also had goat's cheese and very good bread that he had brought from Nasratabad Sipi. We discussed many things, ranging from his experiences during and after the Russian revolution, to the fauna and geology of Iran and some of the complications of working for the Persian government.

The partly filled bottle of brandy having run out, he looked for another. Not finding one, he went to the brass-bound mahogany chest, unlocked it and swung back the doors. I thought that perhaps he had a spare bottle tucked away among his technical instruments. There wasn't a single instrument in the chest. It was completely filled with bottles of brandy, arack and whisky, all neatly packed against possible breakage from jolting over the caravan track.

"Unhappily," said the Polish engineer, "when I acquired this chest which had belonged to one of the chief Russian engineers, after the revolution, I was unable to get the instruments that went with it. They had disappeared." It turned out to be an entertaining evening.

In the morning a car came to fetch me down the corrugated track to Duzdab. I said good-bye to my *nakéh* without deep regret. She spat at me and exhaled a poisonous odor. Hadi, Hassan and Mohammad were little more distressed than I at leaving their camels. I tried to think generously of how my *nakéh* had carried me over that blasted, waterless expanse of eroded foothills, but could not work up much sentiment. Though I had been shaken and battered into about as tough physical condition as I have ever had, and felt as hard as nails, you could still have had my camel.

V

EACH CONSCIOUS SHADE

"With pleas'd reflection I survey'd
Each secret grott, each conscious shade"

ARABY THE BLEST

IT IS EARLY SUMMER on my hillside. The fields are variegated strips of green in many shades, interspersed with the yellows of ripened grain and of mustard, and the brown of ploughed earth. The harvest has begun. Orderly stacks of mown wheat dot some of the fields, sharply etched in highlights and shadows under the July sun. The hay is rolling in from the meadows piled high in long, creaking two-wheeled carts, some drawn by strawberry roan horses with blond manes, hitched tandem, some by yoked pairs of cream-colored Charollais oxen.

Hunters of the wily snail stalk slowly through the fields and along the edges of the roads and walls, each armed with a stick and a sack or pail. They go poking about with their sticks, peering intently at the ground or walls. Their captures, after being purged of grit and other foreign matter by a fortnight's enforced fast in a pail or a box, covered over against their escape, will be plumped into the pot and served with a rich Burgundian sauce.

Père Olart catches his snails in my garden and purges them in a large, upturned bucket where they leave horrid, sticky trails trying to find a way out. They then look extremely unappetizing. But well purged and properly cooked in Burgundian style they serve as an excellent medium for eating the sauce, redolent of garlic and of wine, which to my thinking is the primary reason for eating snails at all.

Cuckoos are still calling back and forth from the hedges but they will not be heard, so local wisdom has it, after the 14th of July. Quantities of bees are dipping into the honeysuckle and the roses. Every now and then one gets in the drain-pipe by mistake: its infuriated buzzing against the metallic sides of the pipe sounds like boogie-woogie.

The grapevines are coming along. It will be an abundant wine year if there is no hail—the curse of the viniculturist that at the very last moment may destroy the greater part of a promising crop. Wine means much to Burgundians, who had but feeble rations—and astronomically priced compared with before the war—during recent years of war and shortage in this fertile region whose produce includes some of the most excellent wines on earth. In 1937 one could have six liters of wine for twenty francs. Now it costs that for a glass at a café.

"Yes," say the people of the hillside, "barring calamities of season it should be a good year for the grapes. But think you that will bring down the price of wine?" They are frankly sceptical, and criticize their government with hearty disdain.

"And the bread, what of that? Ah, those camels of politicians! How is it that one works without bread or wine?" Bread and wine, the basic requirements of a Burgundian. There has been no flour and consequently no bread in Vézelay for the past fifteen days. None but a Frenchman, or someone who has lived in rural France, can appreciate what that means to a French peasant who has been accustomed in the past to eat his two pounds of good bread daily as his staple diet, and is now reduced to a quarter of that amount, of inferior quality, if he can get it at all. This is the most serious privation that the Frenchman and Frenchwoman of the countryside and of the towns have to face, and they are by no means inarticulate in expressing their discontent.

Like the weather, everyone talks of the government but no one seems in a way to do anything constructive about it. Yet the government, whatever its shortcomings, is not entirely to blame.

Underlying my terrace is a long field planted in potatoes. The farmer is cultivating between the rows with a hand plough pulled by a donkey, the latter in turn pulled by the farmer's young son. The farmer talks loudly and continuously to his donkey, while the solemn-faced animal carries out its task with an expression of sad resignation. The conversation, maintained for the whole of the morning, embraces cajolement, advice, flattery and curses, and every now and then the donkey answers back.

"*Gee*, Coco! Oh la!"—it goes. "Name of God! What's holding you back? But you've eaten well; let's go! Whoa! Gently, quite gently there! Will you get on with it? Hold, my pretty! Here we go!" The donkey brays lustily. "Oh name of a name of God! Who sired you, you kind of toad? Oh la la! Gently my pretty! Oh, not like that! Let's go! Get on with it! Oh la la! Oh pretty one!" This keeps up for five hours without cease.

With infinite labor the farmer has ploughed that field with his cream-colored oxen, harrowed it, ploughed it again into rows for the planting, placed his seed potatoes by hand and then turned them into the rows, cultivated it four times against the devouring weeds. In the strip of field alongside he planted oats, in which the crows descended in their hundreds to snatch the seed. I have seen him working on the land, as I have seen others on the hillside, from five-thirty in the morning to seven-thirty at night. That is a long day for anyone, particularly for one no longer young, steering a plough under a hot sun without a sufficiency of bread. And yet if it should not rain within the next few days—for the early summer has been very dry—his labors will have been of little avail.

In another strip alongside my walled garden, this one being in pasture, Madame Hen-parrot (Perruche) of Asquins village brings her three cows each morning to graze. One of them has red and white markings, one grey and white, one mauve and white. Madame Hen-parrot is more than threescore years from the early flush of youth. She walks slowly up the hill in her wooden shoes at a cow's pace, with her knitting, a folding milking stool with four slats for seat, a long stick and an umbrella. She has a blue or sometimes a white kerchief over her head, and wears a faded and much patched blue apron upon I know not how many faded and patched skirts and petticoats. A black dog with a simple strap muzzle—lest he nip the cows' behinds too hard—accompanies the procession.

Madame Hen-parrot unfolds her milking stool, unfurls her umbrella if there is rain or strong wind, takes to her knitting and talks continually in a shrill-pitched voice to the cows and the dog. Her admonitions and imprecations reflect on the ancestry as well as the judgment of her beasts. They are impervious to her invective, though clearly not unaware of the tenor of her commands. Unlike the farmer talking to his oxen or his donkey there is no cajolement in her directives, but she gives the reasons underlying them.

"Now chase that completely idiotic animal out of that corner"—this to the dog—"because she has been there too long and should know that the grass is better below!" The dog makes a swift pass at the nose of the mauve-and-white cow, which snorts defiance but saunters reluctantly down the field. The dog barks and goes for the cow's hindquarters, and the cow breaks into a trot. "Not so fast, not so fast, name of God!" cries Madame Hen-parrot. "On account of the milk!"

My hillside is quiet; save for the nightingales in the springtime and the voices of the cultivators and cattle tenders conversing with their beasts.

Within my house M'sieur Buddha looks with his slightly enigmatic smile through half-closed lids, over the roses in the little Persian bowl below his folded legs, across the living-room at a Druse chest. The chest is the work of some craftsman who knew not the Way of Gautama, but M'sieur Buddha is tolerant of all religions. The deep carvings on its face portray the cedars of Lebanon along with stylized designs that show both Byzantine Christian and Arabic influence.

This was the hope-chest of some unrecorded damsel of the Jebel Druse, in which she stored a trousseau fashioned patiently by hand in anticipation of a hoped-for marriage. She must have been of good family and therefore well educated, for the chest is of excellent design and workmanship. She wore a black dress, red slippers and a head-horn to hold the veil she carried over her face outdoors, and she may well have been good looking, for many of the Druse women are quite beautiful. She believed firmly in reincarnation and held that wicked human beings would reappear in the next life as dogs or camels. She has gone to her forebears these many years: the chest is old. May she have had a multitude of sons and ten thousand grandchildren, as the wish for fecundity goes in the Middle East!

Atop the Druse chest are more flowers, which M'sieur Buddha likes to behold wherever his glance falls, and behind these stands a very large Persian brass tray, deeply incised with verses from the Koran, a lion biting a snake-like dragon through the back, and Persian legendary heroes on curvetting horses. Within the chest are kept certain items of provender—jams, honey and the like—and alcoholic liquids, which from experience I have found it better not to parade before the gaze of Père Olart.

The chest was broken open by the Germans during the occupation, but unlike their impact on certain other locked pieces of furniture, trunks, cupboards and closets, they broke only the lock, which was reparable. What they found inside I do not recall, having kept no list of its contents. In any case, the chest was empty when I returned from the war.

It was in early summer, twenty years ago, when I departed from Persia and headed westward across the Arabian desert towards the Lebanon, where the Druse chest first saw the light of day many years before. My five-year contract with the Persian government as a Director of Finances in the first American "Mission" led by Dr. Arthur C. Millspaugh, had terminated, and I was driving back by automobile to Le Havre in France; there to ship across the intervening ocean to the United States.

I left Shiraz, in South Persia, in mid-June with my wife, my Persian cook and a formidable amount of baggage, in an eight-cylinder Hupmobile "touring car"—a type of vehicle both as to body and manufacture that has now, save for rare relics, disappeared. I had installed extra spring-leaves all around, a 40-gallon auxiliary tank clamped on one running-board and a large folding camp bed complete with tent and mosquito-curtains on the other. The cook perched unsteadily atop the luggage that all but filled the "tonneau"—the rear section.

Our setting forth was launched on a wave of good wishes from many Persian friends and members of my staff who had gathered for the *badraka*—the ceremony of setting the traveller on his way—under five tents pitched by the roadside eight miles out from our house in Shiraz. We spent the first night with my genial friend Bristow, British Consul General in Isfahan, and a few days with Tom Pearson in Teheran; then took off for Baghdad.

As we zigzagged down from the Iranian plateau towards the plains of Iraq, over the last of the mountain passes, it was like descending into the maw of a limitless furnace. Successive waves of heat rolled up, each one hotter than before, until the thermometer on the radiator cap—one had none on the instrument panel then—showed "danger" even while I coasted the car down the tortuous slopes.

Blinding flights of locusts twice darkened the sky and forced me to halt the car. They got in our hair, in our eyes, in our mouths and down our necks as we fought them off with pawings like bears after a wild-honey comb. The well of the car was full of them. Near some of the villages people were collecting locusts, a highly esteemed delicacy in the East, to fry and eat.

Thus we came to Baghdad, hot, dirty and exceedingly tired.

"It is unusually warm here for June, you know," they said in Baghdad. That old, old story. It certainly was not what one would call cool during the week we stopped off there. The temperature in the daytime ran to around 119°, though it dropped a good bit at night. Yet my memories of that city of disillusion, a disillusion undiminished in recurrent visits since I first passed through it in 1922, are far from unpleasant.

Air Vice-Marshal Sir Edward Ellington, with whom we stayed, I had known while I was Attaché for Aviation at the

Embassy in London seven or so years before. He now held the post of Air Officer Commanding the forces in Iraq. I believe this was the first time that an Air Officer had been placed in command of all arms in the defense organization of an important area. Because of this his command was of particular interest to me. It was one that appeared to function admirably.

Sir Edward was a bachelor, handsome, with a face that seemed almost boyish, a shy manner and a great deal of charm. "Shy as a wild pigeon with ladies," Colonel Robinson, his chief of staff, informed me. "Apt to take flight any minute." But of this I saw no concrete evidence.

In the rambling, high-ceilinged, comfortable old palace on the banks of the Tigris that was the Royal Air Force headquarters we stopped for seven days, because the Syrian desert was at the moment infested by raiding tribesmen and Sir Edward refused to let me proceed until the situation had cleared. We went to the races (a young R.A.F. Flight Lieutenant won consistently against the best that Iraq and Egypt could offer with a horse he had bought straight out of a Baghdad watering-cart); we drove out to admire Ctesiphon's stupendous sixth-century arch, and each evening slipped up the Tigris in the R.A.F. motor-launch for a swim.

The young Baghdadis had the same idea for cooling off, but they slipped down the river. All the long, hot day troops of them paraded up to the Maude bridge, garbed in gee-strings around their middles, with water-wings fashioned from the bases of palm-leaves hung around their necks. They would drop off the bridge in platoons into the turbid current, float two miles or so down-river, and stroll back afoot to repeat the performance over and over again. In the evenings the river was alive with them. Until we passed up-river of the bridge we had to pick our way carefully, with the launch at quarter speed, amidst hundreds of bobbing heads, some chanting together in high-pitched quavers, some bouncing inflated rubber balls back and forth, some just relaxed in cheating a nature over-generous in her dispensation of warmth.

Often we went out after dinner in the launch to cool off again, when Baghdad, under the moonlight, looked really romantic.

The R.A.F. headquarters and mess, as also the Alwiyah Club, were equipped with overhead fans, their two large, propeller-like wooden blades quietly revolving at slow speed. This type of fan, usual in most areas of the East where the British have installed their comforts, is far more agreeable and less likely to cause pleurisy and other disabilities to a perspiring body than the more modern, high-speed electric fan. But the blades of some of the older ones often wobble in what seems to the uninitiated a highly precarious fashion.

One young R.A.F. officer had a peculiarly unsympathetic manner of amusing himself at the expense of his elders at the Alwiyah Club—those who had not been long enough in the country to know the ropes. He would approach some gentleman or lady sitting under one of the fans, enjoying its gentle breeze, and with a courteous manner say: "Pardon me, sir"—or "madame," according to his victim's sex—"but do you think it wise to sit here under that wobbly piece of mechanism?" pointing to the fan. "Those blades quite often come off, you know!" The grateful recipient of the advice would thank him and move hastily out of the trajectory of the blades, to swelter in the dead heat while the young officer, with a pleased expression, went to get himself a drink. The blades, as far as my knowledge goes, never did come off.

During the stay in Baghdad I made a trip to the sacred cities of the Shiahs; the "Holy Thresholds" of Najaf and Karbala, whose golden shrines all good Persians of the Shiah persuasion, which is the official faith of their land, hope to visit in pilgrimage before they die. Very many, after death, subsequently repose in the hallowed ground where lie the earthly remains of their martyred saints, Ali and Hossein, the son-in-law and grandson of the Prophet Mohammad. At Najaf we stayed with Agha Hamid Khan, a high official of the Shrine, whom we had met in Meshed when he came there on a pilgrimage with the Lady Elishah of Bombay, his aunt and the mother of the Agha Khan.

Najaf is a city of graveyards without a single spot of green, though there are gardens outside. It spreads around the splendid dome, twin minarets and clock-tower—all covered over in finely beaten gold—of the Shrine of Ali. It is located in a deep depression that used to be a sea, and great fields of tombs and graves stretch outside the walls over the desert plateau.

There is a constant influx of pilgrims, some carrying the bones of their relatives in sacks, and of corpses in all stages of decomposition—for whoever is buried here will surely enter Paradise. The sick and aged hobble in to die in the sanctity of the Holy Threshold. From all this the Shrine and the town have in the course of time become extremely wealthy; what through the donations of the pilgrims, the taxes and tolls upon them, their expenditures for lodging and sustenance, and the fees for burial within the sacred limits.

The town and the gardens outside are watered by an underground aqueduct from the Hindiya canal. Otherwise it has not a drop of moisture.

Najaf is a city of departed spirits. One feels them to be floating in the torpid air amidst the storks that flap slowly back and forth. Karbala, too, is full of the dead. The golden dome, minarets and clock-tower of the Shrine of Hossein are similarly surrounded by graveyards but with immense palms and beautifully green Persian gardens to relieve it of the grim mortuary aspect of Najaf.

Conducted by Hamid Khan we were able to approach the doors of the Shrine of Ali, that are guarded by chains and silken draperies beyond which no unbeliever may tread, without our passage through the tall, arcaded bazaars acting as an expectorant on the population. From the roof of Hamid Khan's house, which gave upon the sanctuary, we watched the sunset turn the dome and minarets into a reddish-gold miracle, with mauve-tinted storks flying in solemn parabolas round and round about. Very honored storks they are, these denizens of the Holy Places: *Haji* storks that have made the pilgrimage to Mecca, and which perhaps lend their wings to transport the spirits of departed Shiahs who would revisit the Shrines of Martyrdom. The sun's flaming rim sank into the desert and the tremulous voice of the muezzin called the faithful to prayer—all the souls and spirits of that strange, unrealistic city save only us; for no unbeliever may live within its limits.

On the roof of Hamid Khan's house we also slept, or tried to. The unholy cats of the Holy Threshold congregated there in incredible numbers, fought, screamed and hideously misbehaved in phalanxes under and over and about our camp beds until the hour before dawn brought, as always in the East, its brief respite of silence. All too soon the sun rose again to torture the world of the living, and we stumbled down the precipitous flights of steps to the *sardab*, the deep underground chambers that are a feature of all Arabian houses.

"We spend the best part of our days here throughout the summer," said Hamid Khan. "It is from fifteen to twenty degrees cooler down here than above." It was also somewhat dank; but even the most devout of the Shiah faithful would be hard put to support a Najaf summer were it not for these dug-out retreats. In Hamid Khan's elaborately furnished *sardab* I dropped for the moment a decade in time. It reminded me in a way—though the furnishings of my recollection were distinctly less luxurious, save for certain items "rescued" from burning houses—of the war-time cellars in Ypres in 1915–17.

We returned to Baghdad by the green and gold of Karbala, the turquoise-blue dome of Kūfa where Ali was done to death, and Birs Nimrūd's brick mound which is reputed to be the Tower of Babel. I then made ready for the crossing of the Syrian desert, the practically waterless waste of northern Arabia between the Euphrates and the folded mountain ranges of the Anti-Lebanon.

The trip of 520 miles to Damascus was not then one to be undertaken casually in any season. In the terrific heat of summer, with my wife and a heavily loaded car, I had no wish to start off at haphazard. I had sent my cook and general handy-man back to Persia, as he spoke no Arabic. By a stroke of luck, for he was usually in Beirut, I ran across Norman Nairn, one of the two

Australian brothers who had started a regular motor convoy service between Beirut and Baghdad. He happened to have with him the Badawi guide of the first motor convoy in history to cross those waterless wastes. Norman Nairn was very helpful.

"You had better take my Badawi with you," he said. "He has to go back to Beirut anyway. He's a good Badawi, and knows the desert like a book. Also, he might save you some unpleasantness should you run into raiders."

I paid five pounds as a sort of insurance, against a guaranty that if I kept ahead of the west-bound convoy the latter would pick me up and bring me through should my car break down. "They'll take you along if they find you in trouble," promised Norman Nairn. "But only if they find you, of course. That's another reason why I suggest you take my Badawi. There are a lot more tracks than you would expect, especially where the going is soft. The convoy drivers keep shifting 'em you know, avoiding those that get too deeply rutted. You can't always tell which is the right one, and unless you know the desert damn well you don't know when you're lost.

"Every now and then some bunch of Baghdadis or Syrians try to do the passage on the cheap," continued Norman Nairn. "They hire an old Ford and strike off by themselves. Like as not they get lost, and go hareing off on the wrong course. They leave a track that may look pretty sharp, particularly at night under your headlights, where a number of tracks may be diverging. But if you follow the wrong one you're apt to come eventually on a car just rusting out there in the desert, without petrol or water, with a bunch of skeletons in or around it. That's happened to me. It's kind of a depressing sight, when you don't know where you are."

But when I was all set to go, there came a great party of Badawi raiders from the west who spread across our way, shot up and plundered an irregular convoy, looting two thousand or so camels from the caravan route and the various tribes along the river.

"Can't let you go just yet," announced Sir Edward. "These

fellows are out for business and they'd take you as fair game. I'm concentrating the Air Force and a detachment of armored cars to argue the point with them. I hope we'll have the way clear for you in a few days."

We waited in Baghdad without lament: running up and down the Tigris in the R.A.F. launch amidst the bobbing heads and *guffas*—the round, bitumen-covered coracles that are the world's most ludicrous appearing craft; taking our evening swims up river; spending much of the day in the little museum with its amiable curator Captain Cooke as our cicerone. What exquisite things were harbored in that dingy little building! There were magnificently wrought gold ornaments dug out from Ur of the Chaldees, from Kish and other Sumerian ruins. There were royal trappings elaborately decorated in colors as brilliant now as the day when they first were applied three millennia before Christ; and simple, utilitarian articles of extraordinary interest such as safety-pins of annealed copper (a forgotten art, I believe) with the spring still in them after more than five thousand years. These objects, entrancing in themselves, were made to live again under the fond hands, the intimate descriptions of all that was known or surmised about their history, of Captain Cooke.

There turned out to be a humorous and quite human side to the particular raid that was holding us up. The British had long been trying to get the important Badawi chieftains together for a conference, whose objective was to call a halt on tribal raiding in north Arabia. To this the tribes had finally agreed. The date of the conference was set; the chieftains were shortly to forgather. Two of them, at least, felt that this move was destined to restrict their fun in future. So they sallied forth on one last, grand fling before it might be too late: two merry gentlemen of the desert, accompanied by their tribes, indulging heartily in their favorite sport on the eve of prohibition.

They made it quite a party while it lasted. That was the biggest tribal raid which had hit Iraq in a long while. After a few days Sir Edward gave me clearance to proceed. "We've driven them off the convoy route," he said, "and are patrolling this with armored cars. But they're still on the loose, so watch out for them. God-speed!"

We left H.Q., R.A.F., at 3:30 in the afternoon, with Colonel Robinson's parting cry: "Now don't be led astray by a mirage: and remember to give my compliments to Frau Sacher in Vienna!" The Nairn convoy was due to leave at dawn the next morning. That night we spent on the hospitable roof of Colonel Stafford, British Political Officer, in Ramadi on the Euphrates, after dining most pleasantly with him there; and before dawn broke headed due west into the empty spaces.

The sun brought strange and distorted images. It was ghastly hot. In some parts the track wound through slow and heavy going; in others it ran over sun-baked clay as smooth and hard as a billiard-table, the only limit on one's speed that of the car itself. For perhaps two hours we drove straight into a blue lake at fifty-five miles an hour, without ever quite reaching its edge that kept receding a stone's throw ahead of our wheels. Towns loomed up before us: walled towns with blue-domed mosques and slim minarets, with gardens of tall trees, cool and inviting, where there was no tree, no habitation, no drop of water, nearer than Rutbar Wells, 191 miles from Ramadi.

My wife was not convinced by my maps of the empty spaces. "Those may be phantom towns," she said, "but that *must* be water!" Out of the phantom lake there emerged a shadowy line of brontosauri. As we drew nearer they shrank in size, turning at close range into armored cars with very hot Tommies grinning from their open turrets.

"Seen any raiders?" I called.

"Ain't seen no blarsted thing in all this blarsted Paradise!" one of them cried back.

We rolled up to Rutbar Wells at two in the afternoon. The thermometer showed 123° in the shade of the fortress rest-house —the only shade in all that desert waste. It was much too hot to keep the wind-shield open as we drove; too hot to sleep as we lay outstretched on the rest-house cots. We remained at Rutbar Wells, turning restlessly on the sheets of the iron cots, whose metal parts were unpleasantly hot to touch, until the comparative cool of late evening. The Kawattly motor caravan—a Syrian competitor of Nairn—came in from Baghdad, halted for supper, and set out for Damascus in the starlight. Then the Nairn convoy arrived, and while they were supping we pulled out. It was eleven o'clock. The desert was a ghostly silver sea.

About two in the morning we overtook the Kawattly convoy on a fine, smooth stretch. This gave great elation to our Badawi guide, who as a loyal Nairn man looked upon the rival and less well-organized outfit with hearty contempt. There was a touch of the fantastic in that race across the desert by moonlight at better than sixty miles an hour, the Badawi squatting cross-legged on the luggage, shrieking encouragement in Arabic at the back of my head.

"Go to it, Big One!" he yelled—one did not have to know much Arabic to get the general effect of his exhortations. "Let's go! Step on it! What's holding you back? Show your stuff! Show those lousy Kawattly dogs where they belong!"

The Kawattlys were full out, their drivers leaning over their wheels with tense faces, the passengers bellowing from the sides. My speedometer was now showing 75 as we tore across the hard surface of the moonlit desert, of whose possible pitfalls ahead in the way of *wadis*—dry river courses—I had no knowledge. Tahar the Badawi, my guide, urged me on with louder and louder cries.

"Hi-yi-yah!" he shrieked as we drew past the eight cars of the Kawattly convoy, one by one. "Oh ye sods! Oh ye craven catamites! Go back to your burrows: we be Nairn! Hi-yi-yah!"

It was a silly business, undoubtedly; yet in its odd setting it had something of the blood-stirring effect of an intercollegiate boatrace. Over the silvered desert we tore into the night, dropped the lights and the howls of the Kawattlys behind; and Tahar the Badawi then burst into a loud paean of victory. There was, I think, no happier Badawi that night in all Arabia.

The excitement past, I took a more sensible pace. Tahar knew his desert, and where we were hitting 75 the going was remarkably good. But not far beyond this stretch the smooth surface faded out; it was cut by many dry *wadis* that took careful negotiating at five miles an hour, and the gravelly floor became heavy. So did my eyelids. Two or three times I had to stop and run round and round the car to keep awake. Tahar was happily asleep on his perch atop the luggage.

In the early morning we met a patrol of French armored cars, almost on the spot where Dr. Millspaugh and Tom Pearson had been ambushed two years before and several in their convoy killed and wounded. At the last moment, when Tahar was sound asleep, I lost the track. By this time it did not matter greatly. We found ourselves in a Druse village that was not on our route. The villagers were amazed—they were not used to motorcars coming their way; Tahar looked very sheepish when he awoke; and I was refreshed by a gorgeous view of the fertile Damascus valley, with its orchards and gardens and vineyards contrasting with the emptiness over which we had passed, below Mount Hermon whose crest was still capped in snow. A little before noon we rolled into Damascus, the Syro-Arabian desert behind us.

Damacus's recently bombed bazaars stood gaunt and shell-torn. Armed French patrols roamed back and forth in an atmosphere of unrest. Whatever the underlying causes, the lot of a mandatory power is rarely a tranquil or a grateful one. But the French method of calming that unrest, their reprisals against the town for political disturbances on the part of certain elements, seemed to be excessively rugged. The Damascenes were bitter, and with reason, over the bombing of probably the oldest presently inhabited city in the world, an important religious center with its widely venerated Great Mosque, along with some two hundred others of less renown; with its Moslem, Christian and Jewish quarters, and world-famed bazaars. The damage to property and the casualties caused by the bombing and shelling had been extensive, the damage to French prestige irreparable. I met not a few French in Syria and the Lebanon who felt the bombing to have been a grievous error.

The rough earthen walls of many of Damascus's private houses conceal considerable splendor within. In the vast bazaars there was formerly exposed for sale—after appropriate haggling over the price—much that was beautifully wrought in silver and steel, brass and copper and ornamental woodwork, carpets from Persia and Afghanistan and Turkey, and fine silks and cloth shot with threads of precious metal. But fires and looting had, as usual, followed the bombing, and what remained in the hands of the original owners was now mostly hidden from view. The bazaars were full of holes, and of little else. Yet it was here, in an antiquarian's storehouse, that I found the Druse chest.

We slept like two logs for twelve hours in the Hotel Victoria, and the next day set off across the ranges of the Anti-Lebanon and Lebanon Mountains to Beirut, 120 miles farther on. Here we stayed with Bayard and Mary Dodge at the American University, charmingly situated on an escarpment overlooking the sea. I had attended school and Princeton University a class behind Bayard Dodge, and have long held the greatest admiration for the way he, cultured scion of a wealthy American family, threw his energies and spirit into the spread of learning and of racial accord in the Near and Middle East. As in medieval days following the Dark Ages, when men seeking knowledge travelled immense distances in fearful discomfort to acquire wisdom at the feet of a famous master, so came, from far and wide, the youth of some twoscore nationalities, of many different races and creeds, in search of enlightenment under the guidance of Bayard Dodge and his associates.

Bayard was then President of the University to which he had dedicated his life's work. There are few persons, of whatsoever nationality or persuasion, who understand so well the problems of the conflicting racial and religious elements of the Near East; few, if any, who have inspired such respect and confidence among all those factious elements; none, I think, who has contributed more towards racial accord.

I have met, in many parts of the world, a large number of graduates of the American University of Beirut: Persians and

Arabs, Turks, Bulgarians, Greeks, Egyptians, Romanians and many others, of all the multiple cults of the Levant. Those former students of wide divergence in outlook have a stamp, a pattern of mind, that reflects the tolerant genius of Bayard Dodge. The cancer of racial and sectarian hatreds, the cultivated suspicions of our times, if not completely cured are at least assuaged in the atmosphere of mutual respect and interdependence of the American University. I know of no establishment with a finer record or more concrete accomplishment in attempting to further the brotherhood of man.

We ran down to Palestine, stopping in Jerusalem in the old Austrian hospice, and toured around the country for a fortnight under the genial guidance of Edward Blatchford. Jews and Arabs were potting at each other, Arabs ambushing the British police and isolated military patrols striving manfully to keep order. The British were damned by both sides for every show of impartiality. Even the stoutest hearts among the executors of the mandate were appalled—privately they admitted it—at the hopelessness of the task of reconciling those two contentious claimants to the Holy Land.

The Jews had already made an impressive effort in rendering fruitful considerable areas of their homeland of some two thousand years before. The Arabs, whose promised independence after the war of 1914–18 had not been fulfilled, viewed with little serenity the rampant Jewish nationalism manifesting itself in the homeland that the Arabs had regarded as *theirs* for longer than most countries have existed.

I tried swimming in the Dead Sea—1300 feet below the level of the Mediterranean. This was not very successful, though the setting was splendid, beneath rugged precipices in a constantly changing play of color and of light and shade. In the extreme saltiness of the water one floats like an inflated rubber ball high on the surface, and churns this with little effect in futile thrashing strokes when one attempts to swim. There may be a way of getting down into that over-seasoned soup, which is twenty-five per cent salt, but I did not discover it.

I had hoped to go to Soueida, up on the Jebel Druse, but the French were then in punitive battle with the semi-independent Druses and the way was cut. We did, however, despite some difficulties, run out via Baalbek to Palmyra's fantastic skeleton on the desert cross-roads, and this at the full of the moon. Baalbek's wondrous columns of marble and rose-white limestone were edged with silver against the star-spattered nightshade of the sky. Palmyra's gleaming colonnades, that marked long-deserted streets, were peopled with ghosts: third-century ghosts on their appropriate occasions, for the moon was blue. At such times the shades of the departed ones return to the scene of their earthly endeavors.

To see them one must first drive across the desert in the full heat of a summer day; then sit for hour after blue moon-swept hour on a fallen Corinthian capital while the colonnaded shadows creep slowly over the desert floor. This I did, and so I know. But before doing so I drank seventeen little quarter-bottles of cold Perrier water, for I was remarkably dehydrated and the unpretentious French resthouse boasted—a most welcome surprise, out there in the desert—a Frigidaire of sorts. The last three or four glasses were pleasingly colored with cognac, which helped no little in reviving my wilted state. The cost was about the equivalent of the same amount of Paris night-club champagne, but the relief was worth it. Only once before, in Persian Baluchistan, have I felt such an overpowering thirst.

Then I went out and sat on a Corinthian capital that was warm from the long July sun, while the moon rose round and blue. And as I sat there, gostly third-century caravans wound past the triple archway and down the arcaded main street. Caravans from all of Araby the Blest, laden with frankincense and gold and myrrh; caravans from Phoenician ports with the produce of the Mediterranean littoral, and sacks of Tyrrhian purple to dye the robes of Kings and their horses' tails.

I saw Odenathus's inspectors with their armed guards halt

the caravans beside the graven stone schedule of customs and transit duties, collecting the tolls that made the Palmyrenes rich, their city one of the wonders of the world. With much waving of arms, of pikes and sabers, they carried out their inspections; but with no sound save the whisper of the breeze through the roofless colonnades. I saw Queen Zenobia, imperious and beautiful, return in her chariot from a visit to the Temple of the Sun, the shadowy populace salaaming low as she passed.

All this I saw in the light of a moon that was blue, after driving across the desert under the summer sun. By morning they all had gone, and only lizards crept about the deserted emptiness of sixteen hundred years beneath columns of golden-ivory against a burning blue sky.

THE CONQUERORS' WAY

FROM ARABY THE BLEST we struck out across Anatolia, after having been warned that the route, though it was possible to get over it, would prove a major test of the stamina of car, driver and passengers. In Aleppo I was lucky to find a pleasant and cultured young Turk, son of an affable Pasha who was Turkish Consul General there, who wanted to return to Istanbul. Ferid Sherif Bey was his name. He was in Aleppo on short leave, after having passed his examinations for the Turkish diplomatic service.

"Ferid will be most happy to go with you," said the Pasha, "and I think you will find him helpful." It was an arrangement of mutual advantage, and we found Ferid both a helpful and an agreeable companion.

Ferid Sherif Bey was a product of the new Turkey. The evening before we set off I danced with his sister in the *Cercle*—the club—of Aleppo below the massive citadel that defied the Crusaders, though it later fell to Tamerlane. She was a charming girl of nineteen who, but for Mustafa Kemal's Westernization of his country, would have been veiled and secluded in the *haremlik* away from the eyes, still more the touch, of any male not of her own family.

We passed through Alexandretta, and had a view of Musa Dagh of the "Forty Days." At Durtyol the Turkish customs officials held us up for seven hours while they figured the amount of the cash deposit I would have to put up against the transit of the car. There were three of them, amiable but bewildered under a responsibility for which they had no precedent.

The newly established Turkish customs regulations would

have bewildered anyone. They were also tied up with an import quota system which limited the weights of certains items that could be brought into the country monthly, and pro-rated these over the various ports of entry. This resulted in such absurdities as, in one important port, a quota of three-quarters of one Ford car and one-half of a live water buffalo per month. Fortunately my car in transit did not fall under these restrictions.

As far as I could follow the customs officials took sixteen per cent of the value of the car and added this to the weight; then took eighteen per cent of that total and multiplied it by ten; dividing this outcome by some abstruse fractional coefficient they then multiplied the proceeds again by eight; and after doing it all over five times, with a different result each time, relieved me of a large block of Turkish notes I had purchased in Aleppo. (To the credit of the Turkish customs service, be it said, the amount was returned in full on my exit from the country, though it took approximately the same length of time.) I had, fourteen years earlier, gone through a similar procedure on the Finnish border, but the deposit then was very much less.

When I suggested to Ferid Bey that an appropriate present to the inspectors might expedite matters, he did not concur. "But no!" he cried. "It was unhappily like that in former days; now the Gazi is changing such things! In our new Turkey there must be no bribery, nor presents for the performance of official duties! Most of our administrations have already been reconstituted on that basis. In the customs service I admit that there still remains a good deal to be done, but we must all help do it." I thought his attitude, at the age of twenty-two, a very encouraging sign.

In the end we had to camp for the night at Durtyol. I would not voluntarily have chosen it as a stopping place. It was a "dirty 'ole" in fact as well as in name, and a very smelly one: hot, feverous, and teeming with man-eating mosquitoes. Driven by those mosquitoes, I pitched the shelter-tent and netting over the collapsible camp bed affixed to the running-board in record time.

In this fashion we camped each night through Anatolia, though most of the locations were considerably better selected. Ferid slept sometimes in the house of a village "notable," sometimes on the cushions of the car with an improvised mosquito-net over his face. Several of our camping sites, once we escaped from Durtyol, were superb.

One was at the edge of the Cilician Gates through the Taurus Mountains, the defile known as "The Conquerors' Way." Up this we crawled at an average of three miles an hour, over irregular flights of rocky steps, where the whole surface of the road had disappeared. Through that pass have surged the long columns of the invaders in each direction—as conquerors, or on ill-omened raids or dispirited retreats. Alexander the Great followed it. Greeks and Persians, Romans and Mongols, wound through the narrow gorge. So did the armed mobs of the First Crusade, and countless others. By tunnel under it the Germans launched their commercial attack on the Central East—the *Drang nach Osten*—with the Berlin-Baghdad railway, whose gap between Nisibin and Mosul the British were then in process of completing.

On the lavender-scented uplands we camped by the edge of gorges fringed with magnificent pines. In cool and tranquil comfort we slept where brigands held sway a brief while before, until Mustafa Kemal broke their power and hanged their leaders. Nomadic herders now pitched their black wool tents on the grassy slopes below us. Their sheep browsed unmolested; their goats were busily eating up every growing thing within their reach. The crumbling fortresses atop of isolated crags, many of which the brigands had used as their strongholds, stood stark and empty, etched in picturesque outline in the clear air.

On the road, or in rutted tracks alongside it—for the "paved" highway itself was often impassable—we encountered numerous four-wheeled wooden carts with long, shallow bodies, unsprung and as gaily painted as the carts of Sicily. They were all jam-packed with passengers, who appeared not especially to mind the bone-shattering jolts and incessant rattling.

There were many other, two-wheeled carts of very ancient form drawn by two small oxen or large buffaloes under yoke, mostly transporting grain. These are made of two massive beams joined in a narrow V in front, extended upwards to the rear, with wide-sloping, slatted sides; mounted on a heavy crosspiece above a square wooden axle and solid wood disk wheels, sometimes with iron strap rims. They formed the basis of Turkish army transport during the war of 1914–18 and in 1921–22 against the Greeks. It is interesting that they very closely resemble the primitive carts used in the Morvan in Burgundy until about the middle of the last century, though the latter now have disappeared. The same type is still found in Sardinia. Probably they all had a common ancestor in the carts brought from Italy in the days of Imperial Rome. It may be, however, that the crusaders reintroduced the model into Burgundy on their return from their ventures in the Near East.

The Anatolian peasant is a sturdy and withal a likeable type. Sober, dependable, courageous, he is innately peaceable and has a fine sense of hospitality. One day we were stoned in the open country by a small boy and a girl. They thought it huge sport but nearly broke our windshield, so we chased them. They fled like hares, and the girl by ill luck ran straight into the arms of her father who was working out of view over the brow of a low hill. Ferid explained the matter to the farmer, whereat the latter belabored the girl with resounding thwacks. When the punishment seemed to fit the crime we interceded. "They only did it in fun!" we assured him through Ferid. "Please don't beat her any more!"

"Nay," said the farmer, "but my face has been blackened by a lasting shame!"—*whack! whack! whack!* "For children of mine to behave thus to honorable strangers in my land . . . !" —*whack! whack!* Not in every land would parental reaction take quite that line towards one's children fleeing from foreigners who chased them from a motorcar.

There was an evening on the plateau near Afium Karahissar when my wife was laid out with a touch of fever. Ferid asked for milk in the village nearby, but the one man who kept a flock of goats and might have furnished it said that all his supply had been sold.

"The lady is unwell and needs warm milk," Ferid explained.

"She shall have then what she needs," replied the flock-owner promptly. "For, by the grace of God, my own family is well and can do without!"

The Anatolian peasant asks only to cultivate his land and to herd in peace, to suffer not too grievously at the hands of the tax-collector, and dispose of a little surplus so that he may buy the few necessities of life which he does not produce. Fatalistic, self-respecting, he is yet readily amenable to discipline by those in authority. Inducted into the army, which he views as one of the inevitable tribulations of life but does not attempt to avoid, he obeys stolidly whatever order is given him. And this, in large part, explains the anomaly of his behavior on certain occasions.

In the open square of Eskishehir I heard my first radio broadcast, this method of public communication having been developed while I was in Persia where it had not yet hit. It was quite a broadcast while it lasted, though I admit I did not listen to the harsh-toned amplifiers through any great part of it. It was Mustafa Kemal Pasha's speech outlining his accomplishments to date in the rebuilding of his country; and it kept up for four days.

Eskishehir—"Old Town"—is the junction of the railway to Ankara and of the German-built "Berlin-Baghdad" line. The remains of burnt-out houses, the trenches on the low surrounding hills, offered evidence of the desperate struggle for existence that Mustafa Kemal had waged with the Greeks in 1921–22. Against the Eskishehir line, a little farther south at Dumlar Punar, the founder of modern Turkey launched the attack of the 26th August 1922 which within ten days swept into the Mediterranean Sea, some two hundred miles away, the entire Greek army, numerically superior, better equipped, and supported by the authority of the victorious Allied Powers then ensconced in Constantinople, at that time the capital of what was left of Turkey.

The recount of his achievements in the five years from that date, considering what he had to work with, was one of the most amazing stories of modern times.

Eskishehir is not in itself an inspiring place. One glimpse of its hotel as it was then (it has improved considerably since) confirmed my inclination to camp outside. I fought a last, and it seemed for the moment a losing, battle with the cannibal mosquitoes in setting up the tent and netting. Once inside its protection the night was tolerable, though very far from among our best. I departed from Eskishehir in the morning without regret, unsuspecting how often I was destined to return there a few years later.

We spent our last night in Anatolia in an olive-grove on a cliff overlooking the Sea of Marmara. It was a marvellous evening; and in the morning we swam in a cove whose water was as blue as the grotto of Capri. The quavering songs of fishermen casting their nets from row boats in the mid-distance floated over the calm sea, and on the hillside a young Pan was tootling on a reed pipe to his goats.

The Turkish General Staff would permit no foreign nationals to travel over the Ismet peninsula except by train. We therefore had to take the doddering ferry from Mudania to Istanbul, the former Constantinople, across the Sea of Marmara. Full out, it did about six knots. Off to the port side lay the small, barren islet on which the entire canine population of Constantinople once was impounded and left to carry a highly desirable thinning-out process to its logical conclusion. To starboard rose the Isles of the Princes, summer playground of the residents of the former capital, where the British General Townshend was interned following his capture by the Turks at Kut-al-Amarah, and the exiled Trotsky came to seek refuge after Stalin's first purge.

In the late afternoon we chugged slowly past the Byzantine walls that encircle the clustered domes and minarets of the Sublime Porte, around the Old Seraglio of the Sultans on the cypress-studded point, into the Golden Horn. The significance of the latter name showed clearly in the light of fading day: a watery horn of burnished gold glowing in the sunset, all dotted with little boats, curving inland to where the "Sweet Waters of Europe" are fed by three small streams. There we debarked once again on the European continent, after three months short of five years in Central Asia.

In the course of a ten day stop-over in Istanbul, a city I was destined to revisit very often in ensuing years, I saw for the first time the Gazi—"Conqueror"—Mustafa Kemal Pasha during his first visit to the demoted capital since his overthrow of the Sultanate. This was at Therapia, some twelve miles up the Bosporus, where he was attending a reception given in his honor at Tokatlian's summer hotel, facing across the narrow strait that divides Europe and Asia. The Gazi, a blond and smallish man dressed in a European morning-coat, swayed a little on his feet as he left the reception and returned by launch to Dolmar Bahçe palace down the Bosporus, for he was an enthusiastic tippler of arack. One's first impression of him was not remarkable—save for his strange, unfathomable grey-green eyes. Those eyes, one felt, would shine in the dark, greenly, like wolves' eyes, when a light was thrown on them.

Later he renounced his honorific titles of Gazi and Pasha and took the name of Atatürk, "Father of the Turks," when he was the first President—the George Washington—of the new Turkey he had created. Whether or not one's early impression of him was particularly favorable, and though he habitually drank more arack than was good for his coordination or his liver, he was one of the few great figures of the post 1914–18 war period and his achievements were prodigious.

In Istanbul I was required to take a driving test, as after nearly five years in Persia my licenses had expired and the only current document I could produce was the Persian registration of the car which the Turkish authorities were unable to decipher. That I had just driven well over two thousand miles from Shiraz, across the Syro-Arabian desert and Anatolia, was no proof that I knew how to drive.

That was the quaintest driving test I ever hope to take. It

consisted of my backing the car up the steep and tortuous hill
of the main street between Galata and Pera in Istanbul, down
which a lot of vehicles of indeterminate age came slithering with
worn-out brakes and dubious control, and semi-blind porters
staggered under heavy loads on their backs. I passed the test, but
suffered from acute stiffness of the neck for several days afterwards. The reward was a license which few outside of Turkey,
and by no means everyone in it, could read.

Supported by this attestation of my abilities as a chauffeur,
and subsequently with a Romanian registration to supplement
the car's Persian license-plate inscribed in Arabic numerals, I
drove across the continent of Europe from east to west without
hindrance or discomfiture, which would be a highly speculative
undertaking in the present day of enlightenment.

THE MINISTER AND THE CANARY

IT WAS ON A LATER TRIP out of Turkey—
this time an air junket with four flying companions of whom the
wildest was Jimmie Doolittle—that I ran into Dr. John Dyneley
Prince. He was then the American Minister to Yugoslavia. I had
known John Dyneley Prince for many years, having first met him
in Winter Harbor, Maine, where he spent the summer holidays
and where my parents took me, as a young boy, to the same end.

Anglo-Saxons, on the whole, are weak in their ability to
grasp foreign tongues. This was not the case with John Dyneley
Prince. He was the most astonishing linguist I ever met, and I
imagine that few such polyglots have existed of any nationality.
When I first knew him he was Professor of Semitic languages
at Columbia University. He had then the reputation, if my
memory holds, of knowing some twenty-five languages and dia-
lects, including a number of North American Indian tongues. I
recall rather immature young ladies from Philadelphia asking
him how to say "I love you" in all of them. Subsequently he
acquired a number of others.

His command of certain of the less familiar ones was better
than that of most of the more erudite nationals of the countries
where these were spoken. He wrote, among other works, a grammar of the Lettish language, a grammar of the Serbo-Croatian
language, an Assyrian primer and a Sumerian lexicon.

I ran into him on and off through the years, always in different places. In the course of the European air junket in 1930 I
dined with him at the American Legation in Belgrade.

I arrived at the Legation promptly at the appointed hour of
seven forty-five. A solemn Serbian butler ushered me into a dimly

lighted reception room in which at first view there appeared to be no other person. But from a grand piano in one corner, whose sounding-board concealed the player, came soft strains of music, the chords searchingly repeated over and over again with minor variations.

From a staircase on the other side of the room arrived my hostess, Mrs. Prince, affectionately known to younger Foreign Service officers of the time as "Aunt Addie." She greeted me with a brief apology that no one had been present to welcome me, excused herself for a moment and went to the piano. From behind the raised sounding-board that had hidden him she extracted John Dyneley Prince. Gently she said: "John Dyneley, please go upstairs right away and do all the things I've told you to do, and then come back at once. The guests are already here."

The Minister disappeared up the stairs. Aunt Addie returned and explained quietly: "He has not a very exact sense of timing, you know. Musical time, yes, but dinner time, no. He has been working on a new marching anthem for the Yugoslav Army"—I think that is what she said it was—"for which he's composing both the words and the music. He sometimes forgets about such things as dinner."

"The Minister is an extraordinary person," I said. "There are not very many American Chiefs of Mission who would undertake to write the words and music of a marching song for the country to which they are accredited."

"Yes, he's an unusual person in a number of ways," Aunt Addie responded. "His few minor eccentricities, in time and occasionally dress, for instance, are understandable. Perhaps you overheard me say to him to go upstairs and do what I have told him—told him before, you know, and more than once—and to return without delay. Well, what I've told him is something like this: 'John Dyneley, you go up to your room, and when you get there you take off every single thing you have on and throw it all on the chair. Then you go to your bath and get into it—the water is all drawn. Don't dawdle in it; get out, quickly, dry yourself with a towel and go back to your room. On the bed you will find clothes. Put on *every single thing* you find there, and nothing else!'

"He's not really quite as vague as that," concluded Aunt Addie, "but his mind runs to less mundane things—you know—like languages and music. If he follows my directions, he will come to dinner properly dressed and approximately on time. Otherwise he's apt to show up late, clutching an open language book he has been consulting, in a dinner suit with brown shoes, yellow socks and a green tie; or perhaps not show up at all."

Other dinner guests arrived and were ushered in. Aunt Addie greeted them in her kindly manner. Not too long afterward John Dyneley Prince descended from his chambers, smiling genially and impeccably clad.

The story of Clarence the Canary is really Phil Cable's, but unhappily Phil is no longer here to tell it. It occurred several years before I saw John Dyneley Prince in Belgrade; shortly after the death of President Harding, when Dr. Prince responded to the notes of condolence from the Danish Court and the entire Diplomatic and Consular Corps at Copenhagen in the languages of the countries concerned, including the Japanese, all penned in his own hand.

John Dyneley Prince was then Minister Plenipotentiary to Denmark. The First Secretary of Legation was John Wylie; the Second Secretary was Phil Cable. The Legation occupied a large palace in Copenhagen, spacious enough to house, on several floors with several wings, the Chancellery, the Minister's living quarters, and quarters for the First and Second Secretaries as well.

John Wylie was a young man who entered with commendable zeal into the sports of the country in which he happened to be located. The favored summer sport of Copenhagen was racing small sailboats over a triangular course that led around a number of little islands. John Wylie had acquired one of these small sailboats and had entered it, with himself as skipper, in a race for a large silver cup.

Many of the Diplomatic Corps went out to watch the race. John Wylie, on his first venture in this field, tacked up to the starting line in his newly acquired craft and in the excess of his zeal crossed the line a little before the starting gun was fired (so Phil Cable told the story). The starting gun was not fired, but this failed to deter John Wylie. Undaunted, he beat along the first leg of the course, tacked around the islands and ran free on the homeward leg, looking back happily from time to time to see no one following him within such distance as would constitute a serious challenge. In point of fact no one was following him at all, because the race had never been started. But John Wylie, sure of his predominant lead, was unaware of this minor detail.

As he ran free down the final leg of the course, without competitors, his diplomatic colleagues watching the event felt a pang of regret over the disappointment that was facing John Wylie when he would be told that the race had not been started. So a number of them jumped into motorcars and drove hastily to the bazaars of Copenhagen in search of a suitable award for persistence and stout effort. They decided unanimously upon a handsome yellow canary in a gilded cage.

This was presented with due formality to John Wylie after he crossed the finish line to win the race that had never been started. John Wylie accepted the trophy in good spirit. He bore it off in mock triumph to the American Legation, and deposited cage and canary on a table in the outer reception room. The canary was given the name of Clarence, though I doubt if anyone knew its sex.

Clarence did not immediately respond to his new environment with song. In fact, he did not respond at all. He clung to his perch and stared stonily out. The summer days of Copenhagen are long, so a cover was put over the cage that Clarence might sleep off the emotion of his sudden displacement.

In the morning the cover was lifted. Clarence still remained glum and uncommunicative. He took food and water, but showed no signs of gaiety.

"He was a dumb looking bird," said Phil Cable. "He just didn't have song in him."

The reception room headed the entrance stairway, and from it the stairway mounted to the Minister's quarters above. Each morning John Dyneley Prince descended at a conventional diplomatic hour and passed through the room to his office in the Chancellery. On this morning he noticed the canary as he descended. Some member of the Legation staff explained to him the manner in which the trophy had been acquired. The Minister walked slowly over to the table where the cage was placed.

"Good morning, Clarence!" he said in Danish. "Will you sing for me?" Clarence clung to his perch and stared stolidly. The Minister repeated his request in German, English, Spanish and several other tongues, whistling a few bars of appropriate tunes. Clarence maintained a bored silence.

"H'm," said the Minister. "He doesn't yet feel at home here. But I'll get him to sing," and passed into the Chancellery.

This procedure was repeated four times a day for several days, the Minister stopping at Clarence's cage for five or six minutes each time, talking, whistling and humming snatches of song in half a dozen languages and intonations, to which Clarence responded not at all. The Minister took an increasing personal interest in the problem.

"Gentlemen," he announced to his staff, "that bird doesn't know *how* to sing. But I am going to teach him!"

On the second or third day the Minister decided that Clarence needed exercise. The order was given that the canary should be allowed free access to the room, the door to his cage to be left open. Clarence took advantage of the opportunity and flitted about from the back of one tapestried chair to another, from each veloured sofa to the next. Methodically the canary made his rounds, leaving a little visiting card at each stop, and returned to the protection of the cage where pure water, a variety of seeds, and certain special powders assured to make tuneless canaries trill merrily in song were provided in generous supply. But Clarence would not sing, though the Minister daily cajoled the bird with whistled bits of folksong from a wide range of countries. John Dyneley Prince was not to be put off from his objective. He had set himself up as a serinette.

"Gentlemen," he repeated, "I shall teach that bird to sing!"

It was not long before the daily exercising of Clarence in the reception room began to show its effect on the furniture.

"I suggested to the Minister," Phil Cable said, "that we couldn't very well invite high Danish government officials and the plenipotentiaries of other countries to a room that looked like the inside of a *pigeonnier*. I offered to have the chairs and sofas re-covered if he would have Clarence exercised in the dining-room. There the furniture was all wood, and Clarence's traces could be removed more easily." The Minister agreed and Clarence thereafter took his exercise in the dining-room, where the Minister continued the canary's daily vocal training as before.

At about this time John Wylie was transferred to Warsaw. Clarence remained behind, now firmly ensconced in the Legation at Copenhagen. John Wylie's successor, Oliver Harriman, brought with him a very large dog, a wolfhound or some breed of equivalent stature. The dog had the run of the grounds and moved freely about the Legation, but it was stipulated that under no circumstances was he to have access to the dining-room where Clarence exercised.

Shortly after this the Minister left for what Phil Cable described as "one of those entertainments in someone's feudal castle or country estate, that they call a Danish teaparty and which usually lasts for about three days." On the afternoon of the day the Minister was due back, Phil Cable went into the Legation dining-room during Clarence's exercise period. The cage, open and empty, stood on the table. Clarence was nowhere to be seen, but Oliver Harriman's dog was conspicuously present. Phil discovered one yellow feather on the floor. This was all that remained of Clarence. The dog was circulating amiably about, looking for more canaries. Phil Cable went to the Chancellery to inform the Legation staff.

"My God!" he said. "This has the makings of a major

catastrophe for all concerned. The Minister has set his heart on teaching that bird to sing. He has made it a sort of life work, you know, along with learning all the languages in the world. And he's coming back this evening—we don't know how early. We've got to do something about it, and *pronto!*"

Under Phil's guidance a considerable part of the staff of the American Legation, armed with one yellow feather as a sample, piled with serious faces into two automobiles. Swiftly, since it was already late afternoon, they drove to the markets of Copenhagen, to the bird-and-exotic-fish shop where Clarence had been purchased. With Phil in the lead, waving the yellow feather, they stormed the shop.

"We must have a canary, at once," Phil explained, "to match this feather. He must be all yellow, about so big, and must sit on his perch in a sort of hunched-up way and look stupid— like this. It's very important that he should look just *so*." Phil gave a creditable representation of Clarence clinging to his perch and looking glumly with outthrust head.

The bird-and-exotic-fish merchant, expressionless as one of his own fish, produced from his shelves half a dozen little wooden cages housing yellow canaries which he thought might bear a resemblance to Phil Cable's interpretation of the defunct Clarence. The Legation staff solemnly inspected each canary in turn, holding up the yellow feather for color check. At length a rather morose-appearing bird was submitted for examination. He clung to his perch and thrust his head forward with a dumb look. His plumage matched the yellow feather perfectly. The conspirators gathered around him.

"There's the one!" cried Phil Cable. "He's the spitting image of Clarence!"

The staff agreed. Hastily they paid for the canary, rushed him back to the Legation and transferred him to Clarence's gilded cage. It then being nearly dinner-time, though not nearly sunset, they covered the cage for the night. After reporting their results to those of the Legation personnel who had not accompanied the expedition, they repaired for a well-earned drink.

The Minister returned late and went directly to his room. When he descended to the Chancellery in the morning he stopped at Clarence's cage, as was his wont.

"Good morning, Clarence!" said the Minister in Danish. Leaning closer over the cage he whistled a few bars from some obscure folksong. The canary looked inquiringly at the Minister. Then, raising his head, he burst into a full-throated trill.

The Minister stepped back. He rushed to the Chancellery and threw open the doors.

"Gentlemen!" he called out happily. "I always told you I would teach that bird to sing!"

"SMELLS ARE SURER THAN SOUNDS OR SIGHTS"

THE SEASONAL FRAGRANCES on my hillside are reminiscent of a multitude of things that carry beyond the horizon to other climes; sometimes to other manners of living, no few of which have changed immeasurably even in my span. The association of places and odors—the power of smells, pleasant or otherwise, to transport one to some far-off spot or recall a distant episode—is greater than that afforded by any other sense.

Perhaps the scent of wood smoke is the most abiding. Where this may carry me depends on the type of wood being consumed. The burning of autumn brushwood and dead leaves in the Vermont hills sloping down to the Connecticut River valley where I was born is my earliest recollection of odor, and the one that still retains the greatest nostalgic appeal.

I get this autumn scent on my Burgundian hillside when the cultivators burn the brushwood on the slopes above Asquins village, and Père Olart does likewise in my garden. The blue-grey smoke drifts across the valley, over the red-tiled roofs and the yellow leaves of the poplars. The skies and the fields are full of ravens, marshalling in large formations before taking off to pass the winter in the fir forests of the Vosges. From the strips of furrowed earth come the voices of men calling loudly to their plough animals.

In the late afternoon the harvest moon rises round and yellow over La Cordelle, where the Protestants once bowled with the severed heads of monks against the heads of still living monks buried to their necks.

The hedges have turned a rich russet, contrasting with the yellowed poplars and deep greens of the conifers farther up the slopes, together with the tender green of winter rye just appearing and the chocolate brown of the freshly ploughed fields. The autumn coloration in Burgundy is splendid; though nowhere else in the world have I found any combinations of colors like those of the Green Mountains of Vermont.

Another wood-smoke odor of my first recollections is that of spruce. This traces back to the ritual burning of the spruce Christmas tree which my father and I, each year in my early youth, went into the Vermont hills to chop down. We drove some distance by sleigh, the pair of sleek horses flinging lumps of frozen snow from their calked shoes against the wire screen above the curved dashboard, their harnesses studded with tinkling metal bells. We would leave the sleigh at some hillside farm and tramp into the woods on snowshoes.

Choosing a good-sized tree, since the living-room of my family's house was two stories high, we would fell it with axes—my father wielding a big axe and I a smaller one—and then drag it over the snow through the woods to the sleigh. With the tree tied behind the sleigh we would drive home in triumph, I grasping the ends of the reins in a sort of dual control, vastly elated over the whole procedure.

We mounted the base of the tree on a wooden cross-piece in the living-room and stayed the top with wires to the balustrade of the oval balcony. Decorating it was a process that occupied several days, with much use of a wobbly step-ladder which I would steady while my mother, and my father in the evenings, hung the ornaments and fixed the candles overhead. These preliminaries enchanted me even more than the climax on Christmas Day, when everything was set and the candles were all lighted, for the wrapped presents on the moss-covered floor by the base of the tree then absorbed my attention.

When the time came for dismantling the tree on Twelfth-night, I was sad. We took it down and sawed it into sections, branches and all, and burned the sections in the big fireplace.

This lasted several days. The wood, of course, was green, and burned slowly with much spluttering, but the needles on the branches were fairly dry by that time and snapped merrily with golden sparks, while I sat cross-legged in front of the fireplace munching popcorn balls molded with maple syrup, molasses and honey.

On my Burgundian hillside, a good many years later, Père Olart brings in the *Bûches de Noël*—the Yule logs—sizeable splittings of the trunks and roots of aged cherry trees that have died and been dismembered in my garden. They burn well with a lovely mauve flame; but they are not spruce, and I do not get the same sensation of Christmas. But if I smell spruce logs aflame, especially when the dried needles of their branches snap with golden sparks, I am taken back to the Christmas trees of my youth in Vermont.

There is the mellow smell of drift-wood burning, with blue and orange and violet flames, which carries my memories to a camp on the Great Ossippee during one of many canoe trips taken with my father. We pitched our balloon-silk Baker tent on the gently sloping bank late in the afternoon, and by the time I collected the drift-wood and we had made the fire, the full moon was rising over the water.

By its light we broiled the trout we had caught; and though it is probably a figment of imagination to think that trout broiled over a drift-wood fire in the open taste better than when done in any other manner, yet that thought is none the less firmly embedded in my sensibilities. After supper we sat in the moonlight, whiffing the smoke of the drift-wood blaze until it died down into still fragrant embers. The silence of the night, when the fire ceased to splutter, was broken only by the calls of a few birds keeping late hours under the moon.

In the morning I awoke early. We had left the front fly of the tent up, supported on a couple of bamboo poles, since the night was splendid. I looked out, and for perhaps half an hour watched a mother loon—Great Northern Diver to the ornithologists—with four baby loons paddling gently in the early-morning mist within the fringe of reeds that rose above the glassy-calm surface of the water, perhaps twenty feet from the bank. This was before I had been to Japan and developed an interest in Japanese prints. Otherwise I would have remarked the extraordinary likeness of the setting to an Okyo drawing.

Other fragrances of wood smoke carry farther afield than the early recollections of New England childhood. Among many is the odor of resin-fat pine logs cooked under a cover of turf and charcoal on open tar kilns in Lappland, just beyond the Arctic Circle. Another is the aroma of cryptomeria wood burning in the courtyards of Buddhist temples in Japan, with joy-fires on the surrounding hillsides making a play on words in Japanese characters. And another of enduring memory: the pungent scent of camel thorn, brought in from the desert on the backs of little donkeys, flaming under the curiously shaped ovens producing five-foot-long slabs of bread about an inch thick—marvellous bread, baked on hot pebbles—in any Persian town or village. With this aroma is associated the tale of the baker who cheated the people both in the quality and the price of his bread, until they rose in their wrath and baked him in his own oven.

There is no end to the recollections revived in the fragrance of wood smoke blended with other odors. The smoke of white birch along with the sweetness of maple sap recalls again my childhood in Vermont, for white birch was what the farmers burned under the big pans in the sap-houses to boil down the sap into syrup and maple sugar. But white birch smoke blended with the smoke of Russian cigarettes brings a different memory.

I do not especially care for Russian cigarettes. Yet now and then a Russian friend gives me a package of the cardboard-tipped weeds and I smoke them as a gesture of appreciation. If it should happen that I have white birch logs on my fire, even lacking the added stimulus of a glass of vodka, I am conveyed without conscious effort to the Trans-Siberian Railway, when the trip across northern Asia was something of a venture.

I boarded the weekly trans-Asian "express" at Moscow, after gorging for a week on fresh caviar, along with other delicacies provided by the Russian cuisine, then unsurpassed anywhere in the world. One evening during that week of gormandizing I had caviar that was *really* fresh. I think no other experience at the table has ever made quite the same impression on me. The west-bound express had arrived in Moscow a few hours before my usual late dinner at the Hôtel Métropole. The *maître d'hôtel*, who by then had learned how greatly I appreciated caviar, came to me with a pleased smile on his face.

"Tonight," he said, "the caviar is quite special. I am sure you will like it very much. Shall I serve you as usual?"

"As usual" meant an enormous portion nearly filling a glass dish the size of a finger-bowl, set in a larger china bowl packed with cracked ice. With it was served twisted, unleavened sticks of bread and slices of lemon. The knives as well as the spoons were silvered: one should not touch fresh caviar with a steel knife. This huge serving, at what was then the best hotel in Moscow, cost two rubles, the equivalent of a dollar. It was, for those days, an expensive luxury, but I wish I could get such a portion at that price now.

The "special" caviar, the *maître d'hôtel* told me, had been brought on the Trans-Siberian express in the still living fish, mother sturgeons netted on the Volga River and transported alive in Volga water in large containers. The train arrived at the Moscow central station in the morning; the eggs were squeezed out of the sturgeons and rushed to the Hôtel Métropole ice-box. The chilled caviar was served the same evening, eight or nine hours after it had left the fish. I recall few gastronomic adventures so wholly satisfying.

A day or so later I took the eastward-bound express for Harbin and Pekin. I shared a narrow, two-berthed compartment with a very large and luxuriantly bearded Russian who spoke no word of any language but his own. My knowledge of Russian was confined to a score or so of words, most of them having to do with food, drink, and the means of obtaining these commodities. Our exchange of thoughts was therefore limited, but I very soon gathered that his ideas on how to spend ten days in the cramped space of a Trans-Siberian sleeping compartment were in fundamental disaccord with mine.

I wished the window partly open at night, to counteract somewhat the effect of his continual cigarette smoking. He objected volubly to this, and would spring from his berth and slam down the window with ferocious Muscovite oaths. He arose each day a little before noon, dressed without undue attention to his toilet, pulled on a pair of high boots and repaired to the *wagon-restaurant*. There he purchased a liter bottle of vodka of 90 proof, and would swig down a few small glasses of this before the second service of luncheon at one o'clock. He consumed more vodka with his lunch, and spent the afternoon at the table reading, drinking vodka and smoking cigarettes, varying his libations with an occasional glass of tea.

When the time came for the waiters to set the table for the first dinner service, he was forced to leave the restaurant car and come back to the compartment with his bottle of vodka, his book and cigarettes until the second service was ready. I would be sitting there reading, or looking out at the alternating stretches of gently rolling steppes and white birch forests as the express rocked over the single track at an average speed of fifteen miles an hour. The white birches of New England, of Burgundy and other temperate climes are lovely trees of great appeal, especially when set off against the evergreens. But the vast stands of birches in Russia, of moderate height and unrelieved by any contrast, produce rather a melancholy impression which is often reflected in Russian music.

The locomotives of the Trans-Siberian express—on the long up-grades across the Ural Mountains and east of Lake Baikal there would usually be two hitched in tandem—were fired with white birch billets. At night the sparks scattered to leeward over the steppe like expended fireworks on a Chinese New Year. The odor of the white birch smoke, coupled with that of Russian cigarettes from which I could never escape, endures in my memory as the olfactory symbol of the Trans-Siberian Railway in the days of the Tzar.

I was unfortunate in my Russian companion, most of the Russians I met in those days being genial and friendly. He was, perhaps, a forerunner of the Bolshevik ilk. In any event I found him a very great boor. He rarely troubled to return my salutation of courtesy when we encountered one another, and we sat glumly across the table of the restaurant car without exchanging a word, while he drank his vodka, smoked his cigarettes and read.

After dinner, at about ten in the evening, I would leave the restaurant car with a slight inclination of my head which my companion never once acknowledged. I would undress, raise the window a few inches, turn out the lights and go to bed. Around one o'clock he would come back from the restaurant car with his bottle and his cigarettes, turn on the lights and slam down the window to an accompaniment of spluttering Asiatic curses. With no other preliminaries than taking off his boots and outer clothing he would clamber into his berth and read until five in the morning, polishing off what was left of the liter of vodka, smoking without a moment's respite and throwing the cardboard tips on the floor. Then he went to sleep and snored resonantly, with the lights still on and the atmosphere of the room so thick that one felt one could walk on it, like crusted, dirty snow.

The second day out of Moscow, with another eight to go, I revolted. I sought the *chef de train*, who spoke French, and told him that I was not happy in my companionship. "I may have a mild appearance," I said, "but appearances are often deceptive. If this continues there will be, some morning, either a dead Russian or a dead American in this compartment, and I rather think it may be a dead Russian, or perhaps no Russian at all.

"If he must smoke all night and keep the lights on—I don't care how many bottles of vodka he drinks, nor do I object to his reading though I think he rather overdoes it—then he must allow me to have the window part way up because otherwise I cannot breathe. And if he does not agree, please tell him that one of these nights, not so far off, I will club him over the head with his own vodka bottle, open the window and throw him out."

The *chef de train* solemnly translated this, and I believe supported my proposal. "These foreigners are queer," he may have said, "but we have to make allowances for their peculiarities, and after all, half of the compartment is his." The Russian put up a stiff protest, spluttering like an over-fed samovar. But in the end he accepted, though with no good grace, the *modus vivendi* I proposed.

Thereafter, each night when he came into the compartment around one o'clock, he turned on the lights, regarded the partly opened window with a glowering antipathy, took off his boots and put on a fur coat. Thus garbed, he hoisted himself and the remnants of his bottle of vodka into his bunk, with a murderous glance in my direction. In the morning when I awoke he would be asleep, still in his fur coat, the bottle empty, the lights on, the floor carpeted an inch deep with the cardboard tips of Russian cigarettes.

The Trans-Siberian Railway avoided all the towns along most of the length of its route. I was told that the alignment had originally been laid out with a ruler on a small-scale map. There were fairly frequent stations, where peasant women garbed in a multiplicity of petticoats, with scarves over their heads, offered eggs and fruit, vegetables, cheese and milk for sale to the second- and third-class passengers who did not frequent the restaurant car.

These stations were located on the open steppe anywhere from two to twenty miles from the towns they were supposed to serve. Within their cheerless wooden structures, stretched out on verminous bedding spread upon the earthen floor, many lethargic travellers awaited the coming of a train that might arrive the next day, or perhaps in three or four days. They took this as a matter of course. Time-tables were of little concern to them as they could not read, and the Russian villagers were accustomed to trekking to the station and camping there until a train headed in the general direction of their destination came along in a day or a week. It really did not matter: one day was like another.

There was a time-table for the Trans-Siberian express. It showed the hours at which the train should arrive at certain halting points and when it should leave. As far as I could observe it had little relation to reality. At the places where the schedule indicated that the express would halt for five minutes, it often remained for three hours. Where an hour's stop was scheduled it would sometimes start off in four minutes.

This was the more disconcerting since the system of signalling the train's departure was highly erratic. In principle it consisted of ringing a brass bell with a leather strap attached to its tongue, suspended from a pole at each station. The conductor sounded it once as a general warning of the proposed take-off; twice, two minutes later, to bring those passengers who were milling around the earthen platform up to the steps of the cars; three times, two minutes after the second warning, just as the locomotive, belching a shower of birch-wood sparks, lunged forward to drag the train on its eastward course.

In practice it worked differently. Sometimes the resonant clang of the first bell had barely died out when it would be followed in rapid succession by the second and third, separated by no more than two or three seconds. The passengers who had been taking the air, stretching their legs and buying fruit and cheese would bolt for the train in a frantic stampede, swarming up the steep steps of the cars as they jolted off towards the Orient with the locomotive's absurd whistle squealing a falsetto: "Here we go!"

On nearly every trip someone was left behind at one or another of the stations, the *chef de train* informed me casually. "Usually there are several," he said. "They get careless and go too far from the train to catch it when it starts. Three weeks ago we lost eight passengers."

"And what happens to them?" I inquired.

"Oh," he said, "they wait a week for the next express and follow along by that. We hold their baggage for them at Harbin.

Of course, there are no accommodations for them on the next express, since everything is booked ahead for weeks, so they have to sleep on the floor of the baggage car. It isn't very comfortable, since they are without luggage."

As we proceeded eastward the rude wooden structures around the stations gradually took on an Eastern aspect, the corners of their roofs flaring slightly upwards; as did also the eyes of the people. Just before reaching Lake Baikal, which we crossed on an ice-breaker though there was no ice, the train stopped for a scheduled hour and forty minutes at a station three or four miles from the town it served. The hirsute co-sharer of my compartment engaged an ancient droshky that was standing at the station with two scraggly, dispirited horses and an apathetic driver in a padded blue coat, to take him into the town for some matter he wished to transact, and bring him back before the train renewed its leisurely progress towards Harbin.

One hour later the first, second and third bells rang in rapid sequence. The train started off with a jerk and a spatter of sparks from the locomotive. I stood on the step of my sleeping-car as we gradually gathered momentum. In the distance I could see a droshky bouncing over the steppe with two people standing upright in it: one the driver, lashing his underfed steeds; the other my room-mate, waving what looked from that distance to be a pistol at the back of the driver's neck. I do not know whether he shot the driver or not, as the express was by then up to its full fifteen miles an hour average and I never saw either of them again. I went to the dining car and drank three vodkas before dinner: one for each bell of the train's departure.

Some years later my father had an experience with vodka. It was during the Peace Conference at Versailles in the winter of 1919. He had a Packard car equipped with a pre-heater to carburet the war-time motor fuel which he had been making from coal. With Sir Thomas Barclay, the Paris correspondent of the London *Times*, and an American newspaper correspondent, he drove across Germany, drawing gasoline from American and captured German military depots, and eventually arrived in Warsaw. The then President of Poland, the pianist Paderewski, was an acquaintance of my father and a close friend of Sir Thomas Barclay.

They dined in Warsaw with the President, who asked if there was anything he could do for them. My father said that the thing he most needed was an authority to draw gasoline from Polish government supplies, since it was unobtainable anywhere else. Though the car was fitted with a large reserve tank, this was running low. President Paderewski had an official letter prepared which he sent to my father by hand the next day. The secretary who brought it, however, offered many apologies. He said the letter constituted an authority to draw gasoline, but that to everyone's deep regret there wasn't a liter in Warsaw and no one could predict when any was likely to arrive. Would it be possible for my father to use anything else in his car?

My father asked what else was available, and the secretary said they had a large supply of vodka from confiscated stores. My father thought that high-test vodka ought to work well enough with the pre-heater, if he could get the engine started. There was a small, separate tank back of the engine, which he had installed during the war for starting on gasoline when the main tank was filled with low-grade fuel cracked from coal. Learning that he could get chloroform in Warsaw, he filled the starting tank with three parts vodka to one part chloroform. On this mixture the engine kicked off with no effort.

Switching then to pure vodka, and using the pre-heater for the first half hour when the weather was very cold, he found that the engine reacted very favorably to its alcoholic potations. In such fashion he drove more than six hundred miles. The vodka was issued free on a military requisition by order of the President of Poland, which was an added advantage.

A description by Sir Thomas Barclay of my father mending a tire in the snow on a cold and wind-swept road, not long after they left Warsaw, harbors in my recollections. They suffered a good deal of tire trouble, the roads being spattered with horse-shoe nails, jagged bits of metal and other debris of war. New tires of the right size were unobtainable. In those days the outer covers were attached to the rims with metal lugs, a Satanic device to test the patience of the stoutest man when a change had to be made. I gathered that my father's two passengers were of no great help in effecting repairs.

"It was the last usable spare cover we had," said Sir Thomas, "and it was not in good condition. Your father cut up a raincoat to make sleeves for the inside of the cover and patch an inner tube. Then we took turns pumping up the tire with the hand pump, but he did most of it. The cold wind bit through our coats even when we were pumping.

"When he finished the job he threw the pump into the back of the car and produced an enameled cup from one of the pockets. 'I don't know about you,' he said, 'but I'm going to have a drink.' Raising the bonnet of the engine he held the cup under the carburettor drain-plug and opened the valve, filling the cup. He sampled the contents of the cup, smacked his lips, and passed it around. 'Damn good!' he said. 'I'm just as glad the Poles didn't have any gasoline!' We finished off the cup and had some more, and we all felt considerably better. That was the first time," said Sir Thomas with a twinkle, "I ever drank motor fuel."

There was a Russian friend of mine, since passed on to his forebears, whose first name was Nicolai. He lived in his youth in the Crimea where his father had a large estate. It was a pleasant place, with many servants and the amenities of gracious living. As he grew to young manhood he would occasionally throw a party for his friends of about the same age who lived within driving distance, when his father was away.

In the then Russian style he invited them to come on a Thursday, or whatever day it may have been. There was no time set either for arrival or departure. They drove in by dog-cart and troika, or rode horseback, over considerable distances; very few by motorcar, as these were rare then in the Crimea. They arrived at any time from three in the afternoon to nine in the evening, and took their departure from about three in the morning until perhaps noon the next day.

Nicolai toasted each new arrival individually with a glass of vodka, emptied in a single gulp with a quick toss of the wrist. Though the glass was small his over-all consumption was not inconsiderable when he had perhaps sixty guests, arriving in small groups spread over five hours or so. At dinner he drank Caucasian wines, champagne and cognac.

The dinner was served continously from nine o'clock on. It was preceded by masses of zakouskas, accompanied by more vodka—*hors-d'oeuvres* that were nowhere better turned out, in those days, than in the Crimea. Then, depending on the season, came swordfish and sterlet from the Black Sea, platters of quail lying on their backs on bits of toast, spitted wild boar, pilaffs of lamb with rice, turkeys and a multitude of other things. This went on as long as anyone had any appetite left, or any thirst.

After one of these parties, Nicolai said, he went to bed late in the morning, in broad daylight, having bade god-speed to his last guest. He woke up in the dark of evening sprawled on his large four-poster bed, feeling an urgent need for hot tea. With one hand he reached out and managed to grasp the embroidered bell-pull hanging beside the bed. This was attached to a wire that led through a hole in the wall, went down the staircase and eventually ended in the kitchen in a squiggle with a cow-bell dangling from it. That was the system of summoning the servants.

A few minutes after he yanked on the bell-pull, three servants came up the stairs into the room. He could not see them at first as he was unable to open his eyes wider than the merest slits. One of them handed him a steaming glass of tea, which he gulped down and thereupon felt better. He pried open one eye with his fingers, and saw that the second servant was holding a chandelier with several lighted candles screened under tulip-shaped glass shades.

He drank another glass of tea and decided that he was going to live. Prying open his other eye, he saw a third servant holding a large, cylindrical object done up in brown wrapping paper. He stared for a moment at this and then asked: "What in God's name is that?"

"Sir, I do not know," replied the servant, "but there is a writing with it," and produced a letter. Nicolai pried his eyes a little farther open and summoned the bearer of the candle lamp to approach closer to the bed. Nicolai perused the letter with some difficulty, as the writing was not much clearer than his eyesight.

"My dear Nicolai:" it read. "Thank you very much for a charming evening. I enjoyed myself thoroughly, as I always do at your house. I am taking advantage of this opportunity to return to you the parrot-cage you were good enough to lend me this morning as a lantern to light my way home by."

It is only when blended with the flavor of Russian cigarettes that white-birch smoke brings recollections of the Trans-Siberian Railway in the days of the wood-burning locomotives; coupled with tales of vodka tracing back to my initial experience on that then quaintly operated railway. White-birch smoke and broiling bacon, on the other hand, recall an incident that had to do with bears, and so might well be another Russian memory, but is not. It was at a camp in Maine.

The camp of my classmate Harry Cannon was located in the woods on the edge of Russell's Pond, north of Moosehead Lake. To reach it one drove by car when the snow was not too deep, or by sled when it was, up the Great Northern Paper Company's tote road to a small clearing in the forest along the edge of the road which Harry called his "landing." From here one hiked through the woods by an obscurely marked trail which led to the camp, some six and a half miles as I recall it, over two or three moderately steep ridges.

We set off for camp from the "landing" one autumn afternoon with two Indian guides, who had made a previous trip a week before, taking in supplies. Each of us carried a fairly heavy pack, and I, with muscles out of practice in carrying a pack, felt grateful for the two-minute rest every twenty minutes. Louis, the old guide, was leading, I a yard behind him, when we eventually came to the clearing where the camp was situated. Louis stopped short, and I saw him staring into the air.

"Jeez Christ!" he muttered. "Now what is te meaning of tat?" I, too, looked up, and caught myself repeating the same comment. The trees on our side of the camp were festooned with toilet paper in long ribbons drooping from the topmost branches. At first I thought this quaint display must have been meant as a gesture of welcome to us on the part of the two Indians who had been up there the week before, until I noticed that they were quite as surprised as Harry and myself. We proceeded to the camp and went to a door that led into a covered passage connecting the main camp building with the cook-house. The door was open, hanging on one hinge. There were heavy claw marks on it and all over the jamb.

"Bears!" grunted Louis. This was fairly obvious, but Louis' observations went beyond mine. "Two big ones and one little one," he said after studying the claw marks and tracks for a moment. Inside the covered passage there were shelves on which had been stored the supplies the Indians had brought up the week before. The shelves were empty. The bears had pulled everything down from them and had dragged their loot outside.

Around the door the ground was littered with the remnants of their take. From this it was simple to figure out their procedure. They had carried off for future use two sides of bacon and a ham. They had opened eighteen tins of condensed milk, holding them in their paws and biting off the lids, and had drunk the contents on the spot. We could see blood around the edges of the tins where the bears had cut their tongues on the jagged metal. They had done the same with tinned butter, guava jelly and orange marmalade.

When they sampled the pepper, salt and spices, they were infuriated by the taste and flung the containers heavily to the ground, which was spattered with the contents. Some things that neither pleased nor particularly annoyed them they had heaved casually away. Among these was the toilet paper.

It appeared that they had bitten into each of two dozen rolls, and had flung one after the other into space with a broad sweep of stout paws. The paper had unwound as the rolls sailed up into the trees and caught there, leaving long white trails of tissue dangling from the branches. The effect was as if a bunch of junior high school boys had gone on a spree after winning the last football game of the season.

"T'em goddam bears," Louis grunted, "t'ey sure play hell. Jus' about clean us out of grub!"

"You find me those bears," said Harry, "and I'll teach 'em not to do *that* to us again!" But the bears were wily and we never caught them.

The next day Louis and Albert went down to Greenwood to restock. They returned late in the afternoon with more bacon, among other things—a basic supply in camp. Albert broiled some slices for supper over a fire of white-birch billets. The blend of the two odors—the crackling bacon flavored with the smoke of the white birch—remains the symbol of that camp in the Maine woods, with the trees to one side all festooned with toilet paper flung into the branches by dispassionate bears who found the taste of this commodity insipid.

There are very many odors unconnected with wood smoke, or any blend of wood smoke, that persist in memory together with the places they invoke. Among these are the aromatic smells of freshly plucked balsam tops used as camp bedding on canoe trips in northern New England; the dung-fed fires in India—one of the most haunting of all aromas; the lavender-scented uplands in Persia, and the saffron and spices and pungent condiments in a Persian bazaar; the well-flavored piles of rotting cow manure neatly stacked alongside Swiss farmhouses.

There is the smell of the Irrawaddy River in Burma—all rivers have their own particular odors—with drying fish floating down on funny, high-sterned river boats with painted eyes afore so that they may see where they are heading; of crackling pig skin over a charcoal fire in Canton, where some of the most improbable and delicious dishes were prepared by a solemn, half-naked Cantonese cook; of incense burning in the Russian church at Tallin in Estonia during Easter, while elaborately garbed Orthodox priests intoned in voices ranging from the bellow of a wounded bull to the tremulous call of a lost ewe lamb.

There is an odor that dwells in my thoughts with a dual association, though the two parts were not far separated either in time or locality. It is the scent of sandalwood perfume. The earlier of the incidents that this particular odor recalls occurred in Holland. I was representing the United States Army at the ELTA —the first post-World-War-I international aviation exposition, held in Amsterdam in 1919. I had made the acquaintance, which developed into an enduring friendship, of Lieutenant Albert Plesman of the Netherlands Air Force, who was in charge of the ELTA.

Plesman told me one evening over several Holland gins: "In a few weeks, I start a little airline." He did. It was the K.L.M., the world's oldest air transport service and very far from a "little" airline now.

Before this happened, a banquet was given by the Dutch for the foreign participants, in the ELTA grounds on an island in the river. Early in the dinner I noticed the waiters going off with bottles of wine still a third or half full, returning with fresh ones. Later the champagne was taken away half-emptied, and as there appeared to be an inexhaustible quantity the returning waiters began to follow a more and more zigzag course. Before we had finished dessert the whole serving staff was a good deal the worse for wear. Madame Roget on my left, wife of one of the French star pilots, expressed her concern. Madame Roget exuded an aroma of sandalwood perfume, which I had remarked when I first came into the banquet hall with her.

"They're as tight as monkeys," I agreed. "They might well be, having drunk nearly as much wine and champagne as the entire dinner-party together—and we certainly have not been skimped."

"I hope they won't make trouble," she continued. "One says they are very communistic, these waiters." She had barely uttered the last words when, with a sharp *whrrr—c-r-rash!* a plate sailed between our heads and smashed to fragments against the wall behind. We jumped up, to see one of our party catch another dish squarely on the forehead and go down like a slaughtered ox.

A phalanx of waiters, cooks and kitchen-boys was making towards us from the service doors at the far end of the banqueting hall. They carried stacks of plates, bottles, candle-sticks; several brandished carving knives. Behind a heavy barrage of crockery and table-ware they advanced, shouting guttural scurrilities. They were ugly and inflamed with drink, but not so drunk that their aim was bad.

Covering the hasty retreat of the ladies—in a swirl of sandal-wood perfume from the one I was partnering—we hurled everything there was on the table at the oncoming crowd. Then, armed with folding chairs, we counter-attacked on both flanks, cheering lustily. It was quite a good brawl while it lasted. We outnumbered them, but they had heavier ammunition. Major Christopher Draper—an English pilot of outstanding precision— two Dutch officers and I drove a charge with chairs in lieu of bayonets clear through the enemy's ranks. We engaged then in a grand dog-fight.

I was swinging on a kitchen-mechanic whose unamiable appearance was heightened by the long cleaver he wielded, when a reinforcement arrived at my side. The coat-room porter plunged into the fray, a gigantic Dutchman with a hand like a ham in which he grasped a knob-stick I had checked with my cap and British Warm. I saw him make a swipe: the cleaver-wielder crumpled as though hit by an electric hammer. It was a real stout swipe, for it shattered my knob-stick across the fellow's pate. The knob-stick was one of Messrs. Swaine & Adeny's best, of split whalebone with a lump of lead the size of an egg for its head, all covered over in plaited kangaroo-hide. I felt sorry to see it break up, but it served its purpose.

A moment later Plesman charged in with a force of Exposition guards he had gone outside to fetch. That was the end of the fight. Eight of the enemy were taken to hospital. The police put the rest in jail, nor were these all intact. I believe we would have sent the lot to hospital had Plesman's forces not spoiled the show, with such vigor and enthusiasm were we mopping up. But the banqueting hall was left a scene of melancholy ruin. I was still panting, considerably dishevelled and grasping the remnants of a battered folding chair when I again sensed the odor of sandalwood. Someone put a slim arm through one of mine. It was Madame Roget, who had returned to the scene of the fray.

"You have make very good fight against those *brutes*, I think!" she said.

"It was a very good fight while it lasted, Madame," I replied. "But our attackers were bound to lose. You see, they did not have any charming ladies to defend!" She mopped my brow with her small handkerchief, which had been well dabbled in her perfume.

Plesman took a look around. "*God verdommte* communists!" he swore. "Now we will have to go elsewhere for our coffee and liqueurs!" Arm in arm with Madame Roget, in a fragrance of sandalwood that we then both exuded, I followed him down the stairs.

The second association of sandalwood perfume is with an incident that occurred a year later in London, where I was Assistant Military Attaché for Air to the American Embassy. Major Hamilton Maguire and I went together one evening from a large dinner at Lord and Lady Reading's to a dance given by Sir Alfred and Lady Mond in honor of the King of Spain. As we came into the Monds' entrance hall I remarked a goodly number of liveried footmen in white satin knee-breeches and silk stockings, flanking the marble staircase up to the intermediate landing where Sir Alfred and his lady stood to receive their guests. The King had not yet appeared on the staircase.

The footmen at the door—there were four, as I remember—advised us on entering the hall that the gentlemen's cloak-room was to the right, so we turned in that direction, to find the way blocked by a long line of newly arrived guests interspersed with numerous breeched and stockinged men in velvet swallow-tailed coats, like the flunkeys on the stairs. After the Readings' excellent dinner we did not somehow feel in the mood for standing in line to park our outer garments, especially as there were so many flunkeys about.

"Probably one of these men will take our things," I suggested to Ham Maguire. "The cloak-room seems to be over-crowded." We doffed our overcoats where we stood, put our scarves and gloves in the pockets, and offered them with our silk hats and sticks to one of the elaborately garbed attendants standing in the line.

"Perhaps you would take these for us?" I asked. "We would like them to be kept together, if that might be possible. And we will wait out here for the checks." The numerous knee-breeched attendants were facing half away from us towards the cloak-room door. I had not regarded them carefully, until the one I addressed turned around. I then remarked that his coat was emblazoned with decorations, and my nostrils caught the distinct scent of sandalwood perfume. It suddenly struck me that I had made a mistake.

"With pleasure, sir," he said affably, "but preferably at some other time. At the moment I am in attendance on my King." The King was in the cloak-room. He emerged a moment later, dapper as he always was. The line of waiting males bowed as he passed to mount the marble stairs and greet his host and hostess. Those men in breeches and silk stockings, to one of whom I had offered Ham Maguire's and my coats, top hats and sticks to park in the cloak-room, were not flunkeys. They were Grandees of Spain.

There clings in remembrance the acrid stench of an earthquake and fire at Sienna in Italy, when my first sensation was of utter bewilderment as an Anglo-Indian named Stuart Murray and I watched in fascinated incredulity while our glasses of beer hopped across the marble-topped café table where we were having a drink together, and jumped off without our attempting to stay them, to shatter on the sidewalk below.

The crash was realistic enough, and was followed by two fear-maddened horses galloping down the steep cobbled street spattering a shower of sparks from their shoes and from the hubs of the empty carriage careening crazily behind them, swiping against both sides in the frantic descent. We dived for our lives through an open doorway, just missing a side-swipe of the carriage's rear end. When we emerged, our table, along with all the others, was gone and we were bouncing as our beer glasses had done a moment before. There was no doubt then as to what was happening.

We staggered down the street like two very drunken men, for it was difficult to keep one's footing. Hysterical people kept pouring out of doorways, and out of windows where the doors were jammed. Some carried unbreakable items like bedding down the stairways from upper rooms, and dropped breakable objects out of the windows. It was evening and all the lights had gone out. Fires were catching here and there. Above the general din rose the high-pitched wails of people calling on the Virgin Mary.

The main piazza filled rapidly with a terror-stricken crowd. The shocks gradually became stronger, though less rapid in sequence, as the seismic center moved away from Sienna. Intermittently they continued for hours and the people remained packed in the square, praying volubly and raising their hands to heaven while the great reddish campanile rocked above them, losing some of its stones and tiles, but did not collapse.

A good many less well-built structures did collapse; the air was full of dust, and there were red glows of buildings burning round about. The smell was most peculiar. It was an acrid mixture of brick dust and plaster, of bitter smoke from burning domiciles, of garlic on the breaths of the people praying in the piazza, and of sulphur that had to do with the earthquake and came from some opened fissure, I know not where. I have never smelt anything quite like it.

There are many aromas that have long since disappeared from the places with which they were associated, yet whose associations endure in memory as clearly as though they were characteristic today. One of these is the odor of benzole on the avenues and streets of Paris in my student days before the outbreak of the war in 1914. It was exuded by the dumpy two-cylinder taxis operating on that pungent fuel, their drivers squawking two-toned bulb horns like the braying of donkeys. Even now I am often vaguely conscious of something missing from the *bouquet* of Paris air. It is the smell of benzole that was so prevalent in the streets a third of a century ago.

Another redolence that has gone forever from its original locale, I have around me on my hillside today. This is the smell of old leather, wood shavings and sawdust, horse and horse manure and the ammoniac sharpness of urine, of Vermont livery stables. The livery stable has disappeared these many years, but not its odor, though I do not mean to imply that the odor of a livery stable in Vermont differed notably from that of one in some other state.

I used to be fascinated as a youngster watching the disillusioned livery horses and buggies coming in and out of the stables, the harnessing and unharnessing, the loudly dressed drummers about to take their local girls out buggy-riding, swapping vulgarities with the ostlers. My father had horses and carriages, but his stable did not smell like the livery stables. It smelt of clean straw, and disinfectant and saddle soap, and consequently was far less interesting to a boy.

The horse barns of many Burgundian farms smell like the long-defunct livery stables of Vermont, and so ring nostalgic echoes of a day gone by and something that was a part of the American scene.

L'ENVOI

HAVING JOURNEYED over this disunited sphere during most of my life, I admit to being considerably depressed by the impact of the technical, social and physical changes that have altered its aspect so incredibly from what it was when I first began to take notice of our way of existence.

Certainly much of the world is a far less pleasant place to live in, at least for the majority of its more cultured inhabitants, than it was thirty-five or forty years ago. In very many respects it is a poorer place, both physically and spiritually, despite all our vaunted progress of a material sort. The technological advances, amazing as these have been, even the unquestioned betterment in the situation of manual workers in many parts, do not appear to have rendered humanity as a whole the happier. Nor has the process of levelling downwards achieved a very gratifying result.

Humanity, as things stand today, has lost much more than it has gained since the ending of an epoch by a pistol shot at Sarajevo in 1914. Perhaps I am not a very good judge of all that we have gained—many of our technical achievements I would gladly sacrifice for a return to the graciousness and ease of living of that day—except in surgery: for the wound I received from a German bullet in Normandy in 1944 would have left me considerably more crippled in 1914.

The destruction of so much that was beautiful, so many monuments and treasures from the patient efforts of skilled and loving hands in ages past, has impoverished the aesthetic world immeasurably. I have few racial prejudices, and I have had some good German friends. But I cannot forgive the Germanic people, who earlier destroyed the civilization of Greece and Rome, for the destruction they have brought upon the world of my day, not only in human life but in the age-mellowed inheritances of architectural beauty and charm, through their readiness, even enthusiasm, to follow leaders lusting for conquest and power. I feel as personally affected by this as by the German chlorine gas in 1915 that left my nasal tissues partly burned out, the German bullet graze in 1916 that damaged the sight of one eye, the German bomb-splinter in a leg in 1918, and the German bullet through my knee in 1944—four mementos of their geniality over twenty-nine years.

And if all the unhappy aftermath is not solely traceable to the Germans' door, theirs is the primary responsibility for having brought about the conditions, the misery and want and discontent, that foster social conflict; that lead to the fomenting of hatreds and distrust between the people on one side of a frontier and those across the border, whether it be a physical or an ideological line of demarkation.

Social evolution, perhaps also the most rapid material progress, take place in times of struggle rather than when things are peaceful and static. Such periods of transition as the one through which we are now passing are usually unpleasant. Death and change are normal processes of nature: something new evolves from the refuse of the old forms of life, as from rotting vegetation, though not necessarily in a higher form. But to speed up the process by insensate destruction of the beautiful seems an unhappy way to attain progress, even if there is ample precedent through the past ages.

Not only is it war's destruction that has impoverished the world. In the inexorable march of modernity, which has produced such unlovely appliances as the juke-box and the neon and other fluttering lights that render our streets and highways hideous in nauseous combinations of color, so much of the picturesqueness, the individuality of ways of life, of types and costumes and manners, has disappeared, given way to uniformity of ugliness or ersatz imitation, in the name of progress. In similar manner, professional idealism has waned under the impact of mass production and accelerated tempo. The pride of the artisan in a beautiful piece of hand work—were this a pair of shoes, a shotgun, a delicate bit of laundering pressed with multiple pleats, or a dinner prepared by a chef whom the mere thought of employing a synthetic product in his sauces would have left apoplectic—has yielded to indifference because hand work no longer pays and so many people have become accustomed to substitutes and machine-made standardization.

There are some exceptions to this, of course, such, for instance, as Steuben glass. But we are not apt to find today another Fréderic of the Tour d'Argent in Paris, who not long before the outbreak of war in 1914 refused flatly to serve two well-financed would-be customers of his restaurant because they ordered champagne with *caneton pressé*, the particular masterpiece of culinary perfection on which the reputation of the Tour d'Argent had been built, and which Fréderic always pressed himself. One should drink burgundy, not champagne, with *caneton pressé*, and it was his art, far more than his guests' ability to foot a tidy bill, that was Fréderic's primary concern.

We are indebted to the Germans for the word "ersatz"—a substitute, an imitation—and to a large extent to the German-engendered wars for the fact that so many of the good, natural products of this earth are now scarcely obtainable in many parts of the world save in some synthetic reproduction.

When I first started travelling one could proceed without other thought than one's destination and schedules of transportation, without passport save for Russia and Turkey, to almost any part of the globe. One was received genially, served with deference and with no feeling on the part of those who served that they demeaned themselves in doing so, and was speeded on one's way. Money, whatever currency it might be, had a fixed value and could be changed practically anywhere without fuss at a small discount. Commodity values were moderate and stable; food ample and, at least throughout the whole of continental Europe and the Near and Middle East, marvelously prepared. Well, try all that out today.

Gustave Flaubert wrote that even as a boy he had contracted a profound aversion to the human race. I do not hold the same view. I have encountered too many good and kindly people of many different walks of life in too many countries to concur in quite so low an appraisal of humanity. From my own observation I suspect that the percentage of people of good will, of those who are potentially good if given a reasonable chance and an under-standing approach, of those of a mentality to rise to the lure of the blatant propaganda of rabble-rousers and the art of singing commercials but not much above this, and of those who are definitely evil and avaricious, violent and aggressive, is pretty much the same among most races, even though standards may vary considerably with environment.

But I must confess that humanity in its mass manifestations presents a melancholy and depressing spectacle. The old order changes, giving place to new disorder. The barbarization of the white race, as of the yellow and brown, proceeds apace under the orders of the Kremlin, supported by the sheer weight of a horde like the second coming of Genghiz Khan and furthered by a com-paratively small minority of persons strategically placed in many areas who seek to enslave the world, not uplift it. The progressive disappearance of individual liberty, of paternalism, of the free expression of the will of *all* the people, is the most profoundly distressing aftermath of the war.

While the will of most of the people in America may be openly expressed, it does not follow that we hold any monopoly on freedom. For freedom is a relative matter, and we have gone no little way in the past four decades or so in bartering at least some part of individual liberty for material gain, in allowing the mass-production tools of our creation to enchain, physically and spiritually, the very people who should control them.

The Burgundian peasant-farmer, the mountain folk of the Swiss Alps, the nomadic tribesmen of the Arabian deserts, have perhaps much less to point to materially, but they have more liberty in themselves, are far freer in spirit, and by and large I think a good deal more contented than those who have chained themselves to the machines of a materialistic age, yet consider themselves free. The basic values of life are not all a matter of numerics: of money, quantity and size.

People bound to agriculture are perhaps more profound and more genuine than most others. One can see the loving care that has been devoted to the land of Europe. There is a quality of natural pride which ennobles the farmer who cultivates the inherited soil that his ancestors have worked on for generations in countries of ancient culture. Collective farming, should it come to such areas, will soon knock this out. And though the older farmers feel bound in sentiment to their farms, many of the younger generation are leaving them for the precarious and deceptively alluring benefits of the towns.

The preservation of what is left of human freedom, at least in that part of Europe which has not yet succumbed to the Soviet-induced destruction of all individual liberty, would seem to be some form of federation towards which a cautious and hesitant start has already been made. Rabid nationalism is not the answer; and I, among many, am profoundly convinced that the Russian form of internationalism is not.

World citizenship, or, in its earlier stages, federal citizenship, does not necessarily preclude national feeling. The potential mutual benefits of union are apparent. So are many of the difficulties in the way of achieving this. But if these difficulties are not overcome, I feel that the change in the aspect of this globe since I first took an interest in it will in the measurably near future be far greater even than it is today.

The first time that I saw my Burgundian hillside after the war, I flew over it in a C-47 on my way from Rome to Paris. I had two American Red Cross girls aboard who were hitch-hiking their way to Paris and London on a fortnight's leave, whom I picked up in Istres. It was on a Sunday afternoon in late Decem-

ber, and when I flew low over my walled garden the grey rain
of winter was falling. There was no one in the garden. I had not
expected that Père Olart would be working there on a Sunday
afternoon in the winter rain.

Beyond the garden I pulled the plane steeply up over the
hillside and circled the towers of the Basilique de la Madeleine.
There were very few people in the streets. Then I flew over the
Hôtel de la Poste et du Lion d'Or where Madame Danguy holds
forth, and circled the open *Place* in front of the hotel while my
co-pilot dropped a letter affixed to a long white streamer, addressed to Père Olart, who cannot read. The co-pilot dropped it
from the rear of the airplane on my signal to release parachutists.
It was a beautiful shot, for it landed right in the middle of the
Place.

I saw a youth run out from the hotel and retrieve the message; and I knew that it would reach Père Olart, would be duly
read to him, and increase his prestige locally, for I had addressed
it: "To Monsieur Jules Olart, dropped by Colonel Hall from the
air over Vézelay."

And then my co-pilot came forward to the pilot's cabin.
"Sir," he said, "you have two very sick ladies aboard!" I had completely forgotten about them. I straightened out the plane and
flew through the rain to Villacoublay, on the outskirts of Paris.
The two Red Cross girls were still feeling a bit shaken when we
landed.

On the way up from Rome I had flown for some hours
above a thin but solid overcast of fairly even clouds whose tops
averaged around five thousand feet though there were columns
and hammer-heads piling considerably higher. The irregularity
of such formations, the fluffy white cloud-tops billowing, glisten-
ing, and unbroken, opalescent in the full rays of a sun unob-
structed by the dust and smoke of earth, have an ethereal, a
spiritual effect that fortifies and stimulates the soul.

This for a while, and then there comes a feeling of pervading loneliness. Not a vestige of life—not a bird, not another air-
craft save only one's own shadow on the clouds, breaks the vast,

inverted blue bowl of the skies over the tumbled white billows.

And then at length I saw Mont Blanc and the high Alpine range rising above the clouds, snow-covered save for the dark streaks of sheer rock showing through, and there was no more loneliness. For in those mountains there was substance: not what a casual flier wishes to collide with in a cloud, but something of permanence, of dignity and immutability in a world that so many people appear bent on tearing apart.

INDEX